The GIANT BOOK of CATHOLIC BIBLE ACTIVITIES

The GIANT BOOK of CATHOLIC BIBLE ACTIVITIES

TAN Books

Gastonia, North Carolina

Activities authored by Ashley Gallagher and Jen Klucinec.

Compiled by Jen Klucinec.

Cover design by Caroline Green

Cover image: Noah's Ark by Teguh Mujiono/Shutterstock

ISBN: 978-1-5051-1526-0

Published in the United States by
TAN Books
PO Box 269
Gastonia, NC 28053
www.TANBooks.com

Printed in the United States of America

For Parents

Make sure to read these helpful tips before embarking on all the fun!

What's in this book?

A lot!

Okay, we'll be more specific. There are over 200 activities crammed into these pages, each tied to a different Bible story. These include short summaries of the stories themselves, oral exercises, crafts, mazes, word searches, crossword puzzles, snack recipes, coloring pages, and more.

How to use this book

The short answer is: however you want. The benefit of this book is its flexibility. But let us give a little direction that may prove helpful.

There are 55 different chapters, each beginning with a short summary of a certain biblical account, moving chronologically through the Bible. Following this are three discussion questions that are meant to be done orally with your child. Then, finally, there are anywhere from 2–5 fun activities that relate to the given story.

It's ideal to read the summaries aloud and then discuss the oral questions before doing any of the activities. This way, you know they are learning the biblical lessons, both historical and spiritual, before moving on to the puzzles and crafts. Additionally, some of the activities won't make much sense without knowing the story or characters it relates to.

Once you do move on to the activities more geared toward fun, just follow the directions for each. Some may require outside materials, but most of these items are found in any average domestic setting.

How to approach the oral exercises

Feel free to let your children follow along as you read each story. Then, turn to the questions to help reiterate the major themes and lessons of the story. Answers to these questions are written in the answer key.

One thing to know is that not every child will get these perfectly correct. *And that's okay.* They don't need to absorb every detail or memorize certain facts; you just want to make sure they are getting the major themes. Often, they will struggle to get the answers, but walking them through it and prompting them with helpful queues is expected, and even encouraged. This is how children learn.

Do the activities require an answer key?

Some yes, some no.

As we already mentioned, the oral discussion questions have answers in the back of the book, but your child doesn't have to regurgitate these word-for-word.

With the other activities, it will depend. Things like crafts and coloring pages have no objective answer, while others, like mazes, word searches, and crossword puzzles, will. For these, please, again, see the answer key in the back.

How long do the activities take?

It obviously can vary, but generally speaking, it should take about 5–10 minutes to read through each story and go over the oral questions. After that, completing an activity or two can take anywhere from 10–30 minutes. So, each chapter should be less than an hour.

Should I do all the activities?

No! There is no way someone could complete all the activities in this book. The charm of it is its flexibility. It's ideal to move chronologically through it, but your child will show a greater interest in some of the content or activities. Feel free to skip things depending on your schedule or child's interest level, and most importantly, don't feel guilty about it! Individually, the various activities are of little importance, but collectively moving through this book over several months will lay an important foundation for scriptural literacy in the years to come.

Where do the Bible stories come from (i.e., who wrote them)?

In 2015, TAN Books released *The Story of the Bible*, an entire series of products that introduced young readers to the Bible. The text for the series was based on an earlier TAN title called *Bible History: A Textbook of the Old and New Testaments for Catholic Schools*, written by Rev. Fr. George Johnson, Ph.D., Rev. Fr. Jerome D. Hannan, Ph.D., J.C.D., and Sr. M. Dominica, O.S.U., Ph.D. TAN Books editor at that time and best-selling Catholic author, Dr. Paul Thigpen, updated the original work to create *The Story of the Bible*. The stories found in this book are condensed versions of that updated work.

While the narratives are relayed in storybook form, they are accented by actual Scripture, chiefly through dialogue. The Scripture is pulled from the Revised Standard Version of the Bible—Second Catholic Edition (Ignatius Edition).

Is there anything else I need to know?

Nope, just make sure to have fun with your children. That, and drawing them closer to Jesus, are the primary goals of this book. But if you should have any questions, feel free to email our customer support staff: customerservice@tanbooks.com.

THE OLD TESTAMENT

CHAPTER 1
Creation: Adam and Eve

Creation and every beautiful thing in the world tell us about God. Since he is the Creator, we might think of him as the author of a book, and the world as that book called *The Book of Nature*. Now, after he created the world, God wanted to make a creature in his own image out of the dust of the earth. He breathed into him the breath of life, and he called him Adam. Then he placed Adam in a beautiful garden called Eden where there were two trees: the Tree of Life and the Tree of Knowledge of Good and Evil.

Not wishing for man to be alone, he caused Adam to fall asleep and took out one of his ribs, which he made into a woman called Eve.

Adam and Eve were very happy in Eden. Everything was beautiful, and there was plenty of food of every kind. They loved to walk through the garden, talking to each other and to God.

God told them they would always be happy and never die, and they would live with him forever. He then gave them a test to see if they would love and obey him. He told them they could eat from any tree in the garden except from the Tree of the Knowledge of Good and Evil. While all this was happening, the powerful demon Satan was watching. He envied Adam and Eve for their relationship with God and tried to lead them away from him.

Satan appeared to Eve in the form of a serpent (a nasty, slimy snake!). He asked her whether God had commanded her not to eat from any trees in the garden. Eve explained that they could eat the fruit from many trees in the garden, but they were to stay away from just one tree: the Tree of the Knowledge of Good and Evil. If they didn't, they would die.

"You will not die," replied the serpent. "God knows that when you eat it your eyes will be opened, and you will be like God, knowing good and evil."

The serpent was trying to trick Eve into disobeying God. When she heard these words from the serpent, she forgot how happy she had been and how good God had been to her. She then considered how the fruit from the forbidden tree was beautiful to look at. Eve wondered how wise she could become if she ate the fruit. She took some, ate it, and brought some to Adam. She told him about the serpent, and then he too ate the fruit. They both soon realized what they had done. They were ashamed and afraid, so they tried to hide from God.

The Lord found them and asked Adam, "Have you eaten of the tree of which I commanded you not to eat?"

Adam answered by trying to blame Eve for what he had done, since she had brought him the fruit. Then Eve tried to pass the blame on to the serpent, insisting that it had tricked her. But they couldn't run away from what they had done. God knew exactly what had happened.

God said to the serpent, "Because you have done this, cursed are you above all wild animals; upon your belly you shall go, and dust you shall eat all the days of your life. The last warning that God delivered to the serpent was the first promise of the Redeemer who would one day come.

After turning from the serpent, God told Eve that he would multiply her pain in giving birth to children, and her husband would rule over her.

Since Adam had gone against what God commanded, God told him that from then on, his labors would be difficult as he tried to provide food for his family. In the end, they would both die, and their bodies would return to the soil from which they were made.

Then God clothed Adam and Eve with clothing made from animal skins and cast them out of the Garden of Eden. He stationed angels called cherubim, along with a flaming sword to guard the way to the Tree of Life. He

QUESTIONS FOR REVIEW

1. Of what tree did God forbid Adam and Eve to eat?

2. Why did Satan want to tempt Eve?

3. What was the last warning God delivered to the serpent?

ACTIVITIES

CRAFT PROJECT: BOOK OF NATURE

Remove and color pages 11–14. Cut the pages around the outside border and fold the pages together making a book. Staple in two places on the fold line to bind.

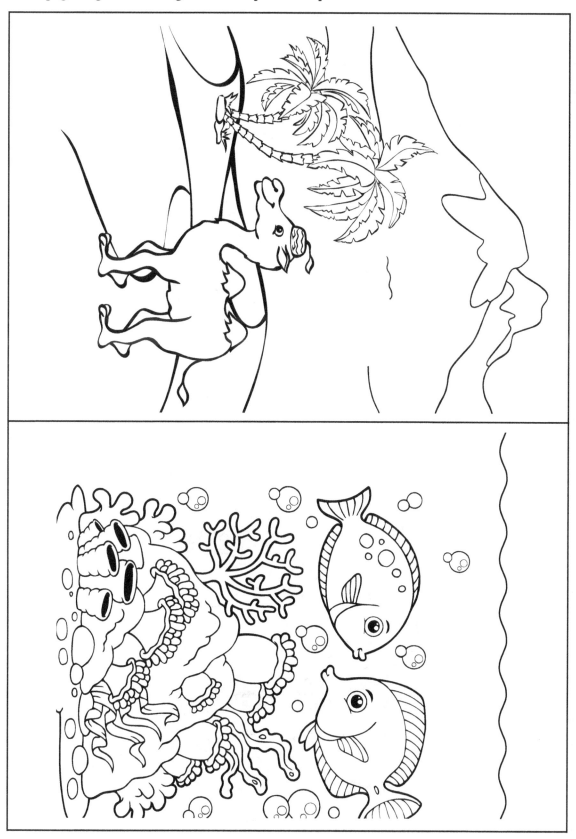

The Book of Nature

CRAFT PROJECT: PAPER PLATE SNAKE WIND TWIRLER

Materials:
- ☐ paper plate
- ☐ any color washable paint for your snake
- ☐ hot glue gun
- ☐ red yarn
- ☐ craft googly eyes
- ☐ scissors

Directions:

1. Paint both sides of your paper plate any color you want the body of your snake to be.
2. Use a pencil to draw a spiral beginning at the outside of the plate and circling your way inward (rings should be 1 to 1 1/2 in. thick).
3. Hot glue the googly eyes on the center circle of the paper plate.
4. Use scissors to cut along the circular lines being sure to leave a small circular area in the middle of your plate.
5. Use the hot glue gun to adhere the red yarn to your plate.
6. Holding the yarn, run with your snake behind you and watch as it twirls in the wind.

CRAFT PROJECT: MAKE THE TREE OF KNOWLEDGE

Materials:
- ☐ empty toilet paper roll
- ☐ 6 in. cardboard square
- ☐ brown pipe cleaner
- ☐ brown and green craft
- ☐ paint brush
- ☐ red craft beads
- ☐ hot glue gun
- ☐ hole punch

Directions:

1. Paint the toilet paper roll brown.
2. Paint the 6 in. cardboard square green.
3. Punch 6 holes, evenly spaced, at the top of the tree trunk.
4. Thread the brown pipe cleaner through the holes (use 2 pipe cleaners in each hole). They should cross the center of the toilet paper roll and go out the opposite hole. Bend and twist the pipe cleaner into branches.
5. Cut 24 small leaves (tear shaped) from the green construction paper and hole punch each one. Thread some of the leaves onto the pipe cleaner.
6. Now thread some of the red craft beads onto the pipe cleaner (these are apples).
7. Finish off by placing the remaining leaves on the pipe cleaner and securing the ends by twisting the pipe cleaner through and around the remaining red beads.
8. Enjoy!

SNACK PROJECT: GARDEN OF EDEN PIZZA PIE

Ingredients:

- ☐ 1 1/4 cup white sugar
- ☐ 1 cup butter
- ☐ 3 egg yolks
- ☐ 1 teaspoon vanilla extract
- ☐ 2 1/2 cups all-purpose flour
- ☐ 1 teaspoon baking soda
- ☐ 1/2 teaspoon cream of tartar
- ☐ 1 (8 ounce) package of cream cheese, softened
- ☐ 1 (8 ounce) container of frozen whipped topping (thaw)
- ☐ dash of salt
- ☐ 1 tablespoon cornstarch
- ☐ 1/2 cup of orange juice
- ☐ 2 tablespoons lemon juice
- ☐ 1/4 cup water
- ☐ 1/2 teaspoon orange zest
- ☐ strawberries
- ☐ kiwi
- ☐ bananas
- ☐ blueberries
- ☐ mandarin slices

Directions:

1. Preheat oven to 350 degrees F.

2. Grease a glass pie pan.

3. Cream together sugar and butter.

4. Beat in egg yolks and vanilla.

5. Add flour, baking soda, and cream of tarter and combine.

6. Press dough evenly into pie plate. You want the crust to be 1/4–1/2 in. thick. Refrigerate any left-over dough.

7. Bake in preheated oven for approximately 10–12 minutes. Keep an eye out as cooking times may vary.

8. In a large bowl, combine softened cream cheese and whipped topping (already thawed).

9. Spread cream cheese mixture over cooled pie crust.

10. Cut all fruit into flat pieces as a topping for the pie. If you use bananas, coat them with lemon juice to prevent browning.

11. Arrange strawberries, kiwi, bananas, blueberries, mandarins, and any other desired fruits over the topping. A circular pattern working from the outside in with a new fruit for each ring makes a pretty presentation.

12. Chill while you prepare the glaze.

13. In a medium saucepan, combine sugar, salt, cornstarch, orange juice, lemon juice, and water.

14. Place over medium heat and bring to a boil. Continue to cook 1–2 minutes or until it begins to thicken.

15. Remove from heat and add in orange zest.

16. Cool slightly, do not allow it to begin to set up.

17. Spoon over the fruit.

18. Chill pie for around 2 hours or until it has firmed enough to cut into slices.

19. Enjoy!

CHAPTER 2
Noah and His Ark

Adam and Eve had many descendants and soon the human family became quite large. Sadly, many of them were disobedient, selfish, and wicked (including one of their sons, Cain, who killed his own brother, Able). There were some good people, but in time, they, too, were drawn into sin. They no longer served God and soon forgot him.

Still, there were a few who believed in God and tried to serve him. Among these was a holy man called Noah. His sons were Shem, Ham, and Japheth. All three grew up to be good men like their father. They were obedient and did their best to love and serve God.

When God saw how sinful the people had become, he warned Noah that he planned to wipe out their wickedness with a great flood. He would send rain for days and days.

Because Noah and his family were faithful and pleasing to God, he intended to spare them. He told Noah to make a large ark. It would be 450 feet long, 75 feet wide, and 45 feet high, rising three levels.

When everything was finished, Noah began to fill the ark. He brought males and females of every kind of animal inside so they could form animal families. Finally, Noah took his family into the ark. Then it rained for forty days and forty nights.

Soon, the rivers and seas overflowed. The water rose higher and higher as the rain continued to pour down from the dark sky, until at last it stood twenty feet above even the highest mountain.

Every living thing left on the land was drowned in the flood. But the ark floated safely across the raging waters. So Noah, his family, and the animals in the ark were saved. After several weeks, the rain finally stopped and the skies opened up. In the five months following, the ark continued to float around on the water.

One day, it came to rest on a mountain. At first, Noah could see nothing from the window except water. But after a time, he saw the tops of some mountains. It was a sign that the water level was going down. He waited forty days longer and then sent out a raven and a dove. The dove returned because it could not find a place to rest.

A week later he sent forth a second dove. This time the dove returned, carrying an olive branch in its beak. This meant that plants had begun to grow again on the land. After another week, he sent the dove out a third time. This time, it did not return. Noah knew then that the flood was over.

Seven more weeks passed, and God spoke to Noah. He told him to come out of the ark, along with his family and all the animals. It was time for them all to make new homes. Then they could have new families so that the world could be filled again with creatures of every kind. Noah left the ark, grateful to God for having saved him and his family from the flood. He built an altar to God and offered on it several animals and birds. God was pleased with the sacrifice of

Noah, and promised he would never again destroy the earth by the waters of a flood. God set a rainbow in the sky as a sign of the promise he had made to reward the faithfulness of Noah.

QUESTIONS FOR REVIEW:

1. Why did God destroy the earth with a great flood?

2. How did Noah track when the waters had gone down?

3. Why did God set the rainbow in the sky?

ACTIVITIES

CRAFT PROJECT: NOAH'S ARK

Materials:
☐ Template from pages 21 and 23.
☐ scissors
☐ glue
☐ markers
☐ clear tape

Directions:

1. Remove pages 21 and 23 and cut out template pieces. Do not cut along the dotted lines.
2. Color the pieces in any way you want.
3. Fold the boat along the dotted line.
4. Bring up the bow of the ark and use clear tape to tape together. Repeat procedure with the stern.
5. Fold the "cabin" along the dotted lines and tape together at the bottom.
6. Use a glue stick to adhere the cabin to the center of the boat.
7. Enjoy!

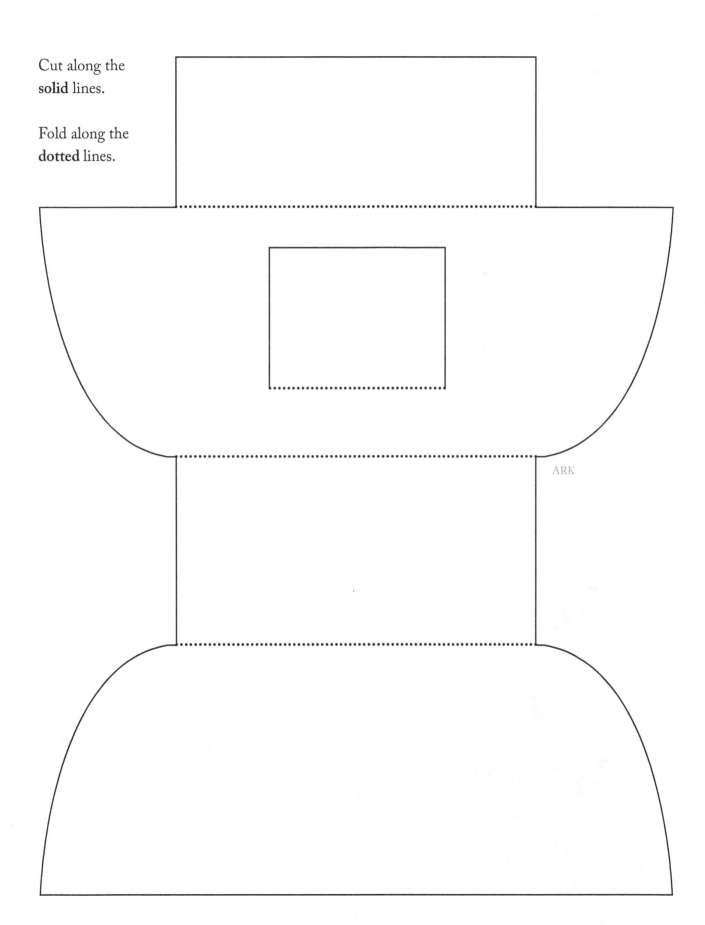

Cut along the **solid** lines.

Fold along the **dotted** lines.

ARK

For the rainbow: cut along the **outer edge only**.

RAINBOW

For the cabin and its roof: cut along the **solid** lines. Fold along the **dotted** lines.

CABIN

CABIN ROOF

Cut animals out with .25" border

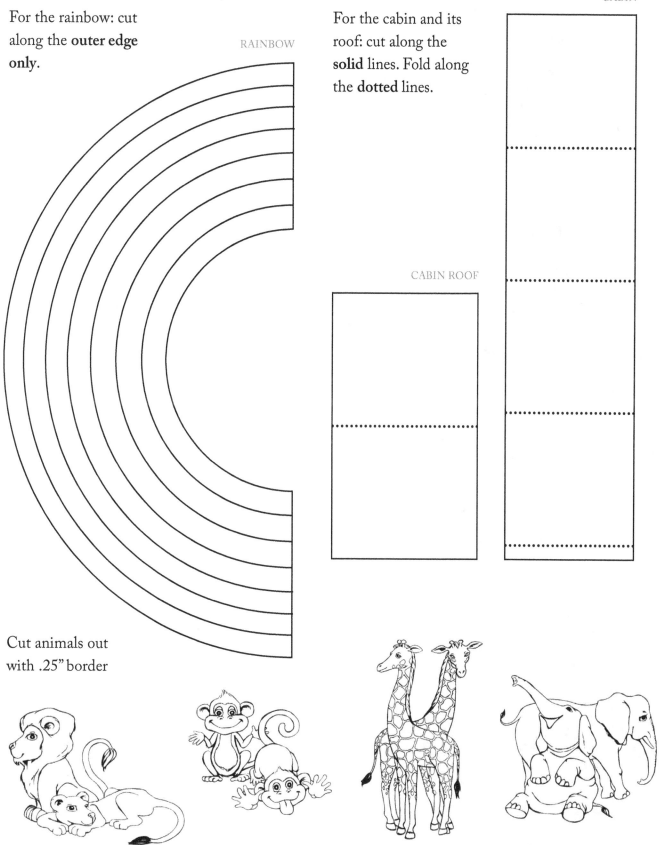

SNACK PROJECT: NOAH'S BANANA ARK

Ingredients:
☐ banana
☐ peanut butter
☐ animal crackers

Directions:
1. Place banana in a bowl and split in half lengthwise.
2. Add peanut butter to the center of the banana "ark."
3. Place animal crackers in the middle of the peanut butter.
4. Enjoy!

CROSSWORD PUZZLE: NOAH'S ARK

Across

2. God warned Noah about the great _____.
4. Noah left the ark, _____ to God for having saved him and his family from the flood.
6. The son Noah rebuked for disrespecting him.
7. The flood rose twenty feet above even the highest _____.
9. Houseboat.
10. The _____ branch meant plants had begun to grow again on the land.

Down

1. After the flood, Noah sent out this animal, and it returned.
2. Noah's family was chosen by God because they were _____.
3. Noah brought males and females of every kind of _____ inside his ark.
5. What God put in the sky as a sign of the promise he had made to reward the faithfulness of Noah.
8. Number of levels the massive ark had.

CHAPTER 3
The Tower of Babel

Noah went on to live many years after the flood, and his three sons had descendants spread throughout the lands. Yet sadly the sin of Adam and Eve continued to have miserable effects even on the new families that filled the earth.

As the human race grew larger and larger, the descendants of the sons of Noah were in need of richer fields and larger pastures. They moved to the fields of a land called Shinar to settle. There, they made plans to build a city with a tower so high it would reach past the clouds, all the way to the gates of heaven. If they created such an awesome tower, they thought they could become famous and well respected by the whole world.

So the people of Shinar began to build the city and the tower. They baked bricks, then hauled them higher and higher as the tower grew from day to day. From faraway lands, the tower could be seen piercing the sky.

But God could see more than their giant tower. He looked past the grand structure they were building to something much smaller: their hearts. Within them, he saw the truth. He knew that they were proud and worked only for their own selfish glory, so he knew he had to stop their project.

One day, while they were working on the tower, the people noticed something very strange. Even though they normally all spoke the same language, they suddenly couldn't understand one another as they spoke. The language of some became different from the language of others. They could no longer make sense of what everyone was saying. This kept them from being able to work together and they were forced to stop building the city and the tower.

The city and tower came to be called *Babel*, which means "confusion." When the one language everyone used became many languages, the people were left confused. The families separated, abandoning the tower of Babel. God had been behind this confusion of languages, scattering them into all the lands. By doing this, he showed that it is a grave sin to turn away from him and to try to do things for your own selfish glory.

QUESTIONS FOR REVIEW:

1. What were the people trying gain from building the tower into the heavens?

2. Why didn't they complete the tower?

3. What does the word "Babel" mean?

ACTIVITIES

COLORING PAGE: TOWER OF BABEL

WORD SEARCH: TOWER OF BABEL

Find the following words.

Babel, Glory, Selfish, Languages, Confusion, Shinar, Descendants, Scattered, Tower

```
O  B  N  Y  P  N  R  I  H  J  D  B  G  J  D
U  E  A  A  U  X  O  H  F  E  B  D  L  O  E
C  Z  C  B  S  R  S  I  S  H  F  P  O  U  R
W  X  P  W  E  I  U  C  S  Y  G  V  R  O  E
Z  M  J  K  F  L  E  H  F  U  J  A  Y  Y  T
B  Q  I  L  D  N  H  T  T  S  F  F  K  O  T
Z  Q  E  W  D  S  E  G  A  U  G  N  A  L  A
L  S  W  A  O  M  N  F  J  W  H  H  O  W  C
Y  H  N  V  B  M  N  S  R  U  L  U  I  C  S
Q  T  A  B  R  K  H  R  C  U  T  Z  G  C  M
S  X  I  P  E  M  B  M  N  T  P  K  L  X  G
J  E  F  S  R  C  I  R  O  C  F  Y  B  L  Z
L  G  C  M  T  E  Y  W  L  P  N  K  V  H  H
S  H  I  N  A  R  E  B  J  R  O  E  K  Q  N
U  F  Q  T  W  R  D  L  O  U  N  J  B  Y  I
```

Note: Some words may appear backwards.

CRAFT PROJECT: CLAY TOWER OF BABEL

Materials:
☐ Play dough or clay, any amount
☐ Plastic knife
☐ Paints, if desired

Directions:
1. Form the clay into any size spherical tower you desire.
2. Use the knife to carve in the "bricks" all around the tower.
3. Let dry. Paint if desired.
4. Your Tower of Babel is complete!

DRAMA ACTIVITY: TOWER OF BABEL SKIT

Characters:
Person 1
Person 2
King of Shinar
Narrator

Props:
Empty boxes or containers or couch
cushions to build the tower

Setting:
Land of Shinar

Person 1 and Person 2 standing and pretending to speak to one another.

Narrator: The people of Shinar were descendants of Shem, one of the sons of Moses. They were very talented people and built a great city. Everyone was happy and felt good about life.

King (enters from side): People of Shinar, we are doing pretty well here in this land of our ancestors of Shem. He would be proud of us. We have a fine city here. But we can do even more to improve it and make it the best so everyone will want to come and visit!

Person 1: Yes, we are very proud of it!

Person 2: Yes, very proud of everything!

Person 1: We can do almost anything we want because we are so talented.

Person 2: Take me for example. I built my own house out of the best stone there is and topped it with a roof of gold. I have a lot of money (beats his chest).

Person 1: Don't forget that I helped you with the design and construction of it. I did an amazing job helping you. Remember?

Person 2: Yes, you *are* really talented.

Persons 1 and 2: We *all* are.

King: Then we shall build a tower to reach the heavens! For we are good at so many things, nothing can stop us from making the biggest and best tower.

Person 1: And everyone will know we did it.

Person 2: Yes they will, and we will really make a name for ourselves!

King: Okay everyone, let's get the tower started.

Person 1 and Person 2 start to stack props to make tower.

Narrator: So the people began building the tower to reach the heavens, but God saw this and became displeased. It seemed that Shem's ancestors forgot that their talents came from God.

Person 1: This is going to be the best tower ever.

Person 2: We will certainly reach the heavens with it!

King: Keep going you two. I am not standing here for my looks. I was made king to keep this city going, and I'm pretty good at that job.

Person 1 and 2: Yes, your majesty.

Narrator: Then suddenly there was a problem.

Person 1 speaks gibberish to Person 2. They both seem confused.

Person 2: What did you say? I can't understand a word you are saying.

Person 2 then speaks gibberish to Person 1.

Person 1: What did you say? I can't understand a word you are saying.

Both Person 1 and Person 2 speak gibberish at the same time for several seconds, as if screaming at one another and waving fists in the air!

King: What in the world are you two saying?

The king begins to speak gibberish to the two of them. Everyone talks at the same time for several seconds until…

Narrator: The people became aware that they were not able to understand each other's language. There was such a babble among them that the tower later became known as the Tower of Babel.

Person 2: This is crazy. Suddenly none of us can understand each other. I guess that's the end of this idea.

Person 1 and 2 exit.

Narrator: God showed that he was displeased with the people of Shinar, so he confused their language. They were not able to complete the tower. Eventually they drifted away to other parts of the world. In this way, God showed that it offends him when we turn away from him. We should always remember to thank him for the talents he gives to us.

CHAPTER 4
Abraham and Isaac

Many, many years after the human race had been scattered from Babel, there lived a holy man named Abram who married a woman named Sarai. Even though they had no children, God promised to make him the father of a great nation. He changed his name from Abram to Abraham and then promised he and his wife would have a son one day. Abraham lived a long and holy life, and when he was one hundred years old, and Sarah was ninety, God's promise to them was at last fulfilled: they had a son, whom they named Isaac. Through Isaac, Abraham's faith in God was rewarded. Under the watchful eyes of his parents, the boy grew strong and holy. He was the joy of his father's heart. Because the boy was Abraham's son, he too would grow up to become the father of a great nation.

One night, Abraham heard the voice of the Lord calling him. He answered, "Here am I." The Lord replied, "Take your son . . . whom you love, and go to the land of Moriah, and offer him there as a burnt offering upon one of the mountains of which I shall tell you."

Abraham rose and saddled his donkey. He awakened two of his servants and Isaac. He cut wood for the sacrifice and, loading it on the donkey, set out on their journey.

They had traveled three days when Abraham saw in the distance the mountain God had chosen. He commanded his servants to stay behind with the donkey, while he and Isaac went up the mountain to make the sacrifice. He took the wood for the sacrifice and gave it to Isaac to carry, while Abraham himself carried fire and a knife. Together they started out for the mountain.

After a while, Isaac noticed that they had everything they needed for a sacrifice—except for a lamb. Where, he wondered, was the animal to be sacrificed? Abraham assured his son that God would provide the lamb when the time came.

When they reached the place that God had shown him, Abraham built an altar and laid the wood on it. He then tied Isaac up and placed him on the pile of wood. As he was raising his knife to sacrifice his son, an angel of the Lord called to him from heaven: "Abraham! Abraham!"

He answered, "Here am I."

The angel said, "Do not lay your hand on the lad or do anything to him; for now I know that you fear God, seeing you have not withheld your son."

Abraham paused and looked up. There in a nearby thorn bush, he saw a ram caught by the horns. So he took Isaac off the altar and offered the ram as a sacrifice to God instead of his son.

Then the angel repeated God's promise to Abraham: "Because you have done this, and have not withheld your son . . . I will indeed bless you, and I will multiply your descendants as the stars of heaven and as the sand which is on the seashore. And your descendants shall possess the gate of their enemies, and by your descendants shall all the nations of the earth bless themselves, because you have obeyed my voice."

This is a difficult story to understand. We might wonder why God would ask Abraham to sacrifice his son. One way to see this story is a test of Abraham's faith. We must love God above everything else and trust in him. Though Abraham loved Isaac, he knew he had to obey God. Unlike Adam and Eve, Abraham passed this test of obedience and faith. The second way to view this story is through the story of Jesus, who was God's son and who was sacrificed on the cross. This story is a foreshadowing of the story of Jesus. Just as Jesus would climb a hill while carrying the wood used to sacrifice him (the cross), so, too, did Isaac, though God provided a ram for the sacrifice at the last minute. God ultimately did not make Abraham sacrifice his son, but God himself would allow his own Son to be sacrificed many years later for our salvation.

We don't always understand everything God asks of us, but even when we are confused, we must trust in his love and care.

QUESTIONS FOR REVIEW:

1. Besides the promise of becoming the father of a great nation, what else did God promise to Abraham?

2. As he was raising his knife to sacrifice his son, who appeared and prevented Abraham from sacrificing his son?

3. Because Abraham did not withhold his son, what was again promised?

ACTIVITIES

CRAFT PROJECT: STARS IN THE SKY

Materials:
- ☐ 24 oz. or larger glass jar (pickle jar works great)
- ☐ piece of aluminum foil
- ☐ nail
- ☐ battery-operated tea light candle

Directions:
1. Thoroughly clean and dry out the jar.
2. Cut a piece of aluminum foil to line the interior of your jar.
3. Use the nail to punch holes of various sizes all over the piece of aluminum foil. You want TONS of holes.
4. Line the inside of your jar with the foil.
5. Place the battery-operated tea light in the middle of your jar.
6. Go into a dark closet and enjoy your stars in the sky. This craft works well as a night-light too.
7. Enjoy!

CRAFT PROJECT: A RAM FOR THE SACRIFICE

Materials:
- ☐ Template from the page 39
- ☐ cotton balls
- ☐ craft glue
- ☐ coloring pencils
- ☐ scissors

Directions:

1. Color the horns, face, and legs of the ram.

2. Cut the ram out.

3. Glue the cotton balls all over the body of the ram.

4. Enjoy!

CHAPTER 5
Isaac, Esau, and Jacob: The Birthright

When Isaac became a man, he married Rebecca. They had twins named Esau and Jacob. Esau, who was born first, grew up to be hunter, rough and hairy. Jacob, who was more gentile, became a herdsman. God told Rebecca that the younger son would be greater than the older, and that the older son would serve the younger.

This was strange to Rebecca because usually the oldest son received what was called the *birthright*. He was given a larger portion of his father's wealth and obtained a special blessing from his father before he died.

Esau, though older, didn't care much about the birthright. One day, Esau came home hungry while Jacob was cooking a stew. He said he would give him some food if Esau would give up his birthright.

Esau, more concerned about his hunger than his birthright, swore an oath to sell it to Jacob for some stew. Then he ate and went on his way.

As the years went by, Isaac grew old and blind. One day, he called for Esau.

"Go and hunt game for me, and prepare for me savory food, and bring it to me that I may eat; that I may bless you before I die."

Rebecca, who favored Jacob, overheard this and told Jacob that she would prepare food for him to bring to his father instead of Esau. That way Isaac would mistake Jacob for his brother, and Jacob would be the one to receive the blessing.

Jacob objected, "Esau is a hairy man and I am smooth." Rebecca assured him that everything would work out.

So Rebecca cooked the food. She covered his smooth neck and hands with the animal skins of Esau. Then she told him to take the food in to his father.

When Jacob entered, Isaac asked who was there. Jacob lied. "I am Esau, your firstborn. I have done as you told me; now eat that you may bless me."

Isaac questioned how he had found the food so quickly. Jacob claimed that God had helped him.

Isaac said, "Come near, that I may feel you, to know whether you are really Esau." Jacob approached him. Isaac felt his arms covered with the animal skin.

Isaac was confused, hearing a voice that sounded like Jacob, but feeling what seemed to be the hairy hands and arms of Esau. He questioned Jacob again, and Jacob lied again, saying he was Esau. After Isaac had eaten, he asked Jacob to come closer, so that he could receive a kiss from his son. Jacob came near and kissed him A moment later, Isaac blessed him.

Jacob left quickly after receiving the blessing. Then Esau returned, bringing with him the meat from the animal he had hunted and killed. He asked his father to stand and take the food he had brought in, so that his father could bless him.

Isaac shook with anger, wondering aloud who had brought him food earlier. It became clear to both of them that Jacob had tricked Isaac into getting the blessing that Esau was entitled to have.

Esau broke down and wept. He asked again for his father to bless him. Isaac's heart was touched with pity for Esau, but the blessing had already been given.

Esau hated Jacob for having taken away his father's blessing. He swore that after his father's death, he would kill his brother.

When Rebecca heard that Esau had threatened to kill Jacob, she sent for her son and told him to flee and to live with her brother, Laban. She instructed him to stay there until the fury of his brother had died down.

QUESTIONS FOR REVIEW:

1. What did it mean to receive the birthright?

2. How did Jacob and Rebecca deceive Isaac?

3. How did Esau respond to Jacob receiving the birthright?

ACTIVITIES

COLORING PAGE: ESSAU

SNACK PROJECT: JACOB AND ESAU HAM AND POTATO SOUP

(8 servings)

Ingredients:
- ☐ 4 cups diced potatoes
- ☐ 1/2 cup chopped celery
- ☐ 1 cup diced cooked ham
- ☐ 3 1/4 cups water
- ☐ 2 tablespoons chicken bouillon
- ☐ 6 tablespoons butter or margarine
- ☐ salt to taste
- ☐ pepper to taste
- ☐ 6 tablespoons all purpose flour
- ☐ 2 1/3 cups of milk
- ☐ green onions to garnish

Directions:

1. Combine potatoes, celery, ham, and water in a large stockpot.

2. Bring to a boil and cook over medium heat for about 15 minutes until the potatoes are tender and a fork easily slips in and out of the potato.

3. Stir in the chicken bouillon, salt, and pepper.

4. In a second saucepan, melt butter over medium-low heat and then whisk in flour with a fork. Stir continuously until thick. Slowly add in milk watching that lumps do not form until all the milk is added. Continue to stir over medium-low heat for about 5 minutes or until thick.

5. Stir milk mixture into the stockpot with potato mixture and heat thoroughly.

6. Serve in bowl garnished with green onion.

7. Enjoy!

CRAFT PROJECT: JACOB AND ESAU SPOON PEOPLE

Materials:
- ☐ 2, 10 in. wooden craft spoons
- ☐ Templates from page 47
- ☐ hot glue gun
- ☐ craft glue
- ☐ brown yarn
- ☐ markers

Directions:

1. Cut out and color Jacob and Esau's bodies from the Activity Book and hot glue them onto the spoons.

2. Cut 2, 12 in. pieces of brown yarn. Loop one piece at a time into several loops and then hot glue onto spoons as beards for Jacob and Esau.

3. Cut 8, 2 in. pieces of brown yarn. Glue 4 onto each side of Jacob's body (where arms would be, this is his furry covering for tricking Isaac).

4. Cut a small soup bowl for Esau and use craft glue to attach it to Esau's body (this is the soup for which he sold his birthright).

5. Cut a small piece of paper and label "birthright." Use craft glue to attach it to Jacob.

6. Use markers to draw on hair, eyes, a nose, and a mouth for both spoon figures.

7. Enjoy!

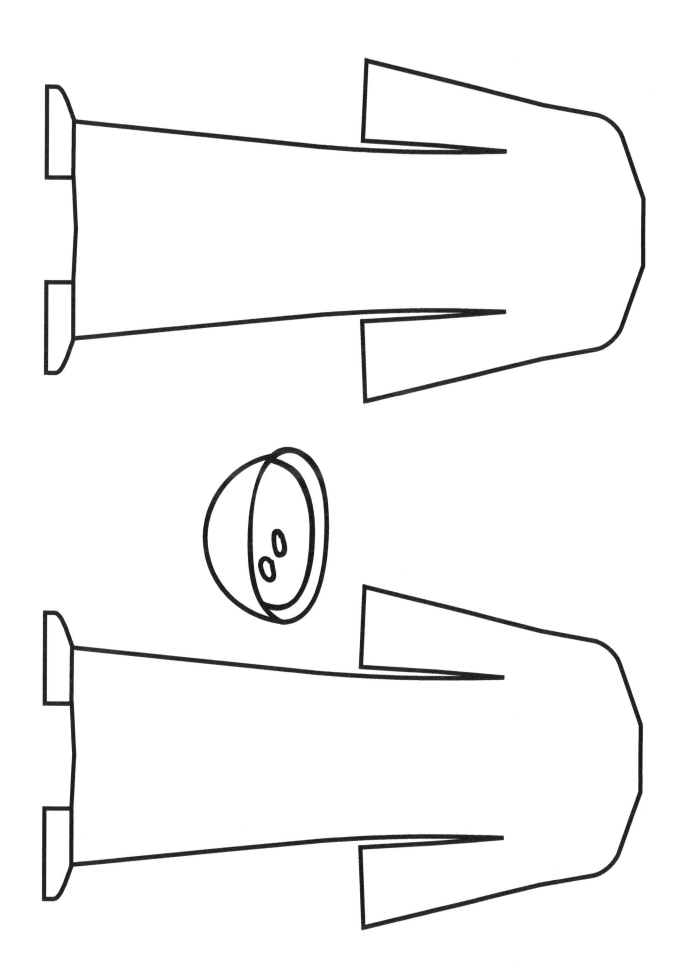

WORD SEARCH: ISAAC, JACOB AND ESAU

Find the following words.
Esau, Jacob, Isaac, Rebecca, Birthright, Stew, Blessing, Hunter, Herdsman, Laban

```
T  H  Q  Y  T  K  Q  N  H  A  K  U  Q  Z  B
S  H  M  N  A  B  A  L  U  U  Y  L  F  X  A
I  U  G  Y  X  M  E  Q  G  S  N  P  Z  W  D
X  T  O  I  S  F  O  F  X  G  G  T  P  A  F
G  S  L  D  R  B  W  Z  U  R  N  F  E  O  F
A  O  R  S  O  H  W  P  A  P  I  F  M  R  Y
M  E  W  T  O  M  T  L  T  W  S  W  J  I  F
H  Z  D  H  B  N  O  R  Z  K  S  E  A  R  U
T  R  E  B  E  C  C  A  I  B  E  T  C  X  T
B  Y  U  H  Z  I  O  Y  U  B  L  S  O  B  Z
D  E  E  A  S  V  Y  Z  I  R  B  S  B  W  H
M  T  X  A  S  D  E  C  Q  A  T  C  V  A  D
X  X  A  M  T  E  G  L  I  D  P  W  U  W  M
N  C  K  N  Y  W  H  I  O  E  J  Q  J  Z  H
T  H  M  J  I  Q  L  O  N  Z  A  G  R  G  G
```

Note: Some words may appear backwards.

CHAPTER 6
Joseph's Humble Beginnings

While Jacob had lived afar in fear of his brother Esau, he eventually married a woman named Rachel. Later, at God's request, he then returned to Canaan where he reconciled with his brother.

Jacob had many sons who were herdsmen, spending their lives tending their sheep and goats. Their work often took them far away from home, where their father couldn't keep an eye on what they were doing. One day his son Joseph saw his brothers doing wrong. He went home and reported it to his father, and from that time on they resented him.

But there were other reasons why Joseph's brothers didn't like him. They knew that their father loved Joseph very dearly, and when he gave the boy a fine coat of many colors, they became very jealous. Joseph also had strange dreams that foretold his future greatness and the power he would one day have over his brothers, and he was not shy about telling his brothers this. Not surprisingly, these dreams angered them.

Joseph told about his first strange dream, in which he and his brothers stood in a field bundling up grain. Joseph claimed that his bundle was the largest and stood upright, while his brothers' bundles of grain all bowed before it. Joseph interpreted this to mean he would one day rule over his brothers. They resented his dream and his words about it.

Then Joseph reported another dream to his brothers. He claimed that he saw the sun, moon, and eleven stars bowing before him. This implied that not only his brothers, but even his father and mother would bow down to him. Once again, his brothers wanted to hear nothing of it. Joseph seemed to be saying that he would one day become their king.

Some time later, the brothers were forced to travel great distances from home to find grass for their flocks. While they were at Shechem, a place fifty miles from their home, Jacob sent Joseph out in search of them, to find out if all was well. When Joseph reached Shechem, he learned that his brothers had driven their flocks ten miles farther north, so he kept going.

When the brothers saw Joseph coming, they hatched an evil plan to kill him. But Reuben, the oldest brother, wanted to save Joseph from death. He persuaded the others to throw him into a pit, hoping to have an opportunity later to help Joseph escape.

It happened that some merchants, who were on their way to Egypt, were passing through the fields. The brothers stopped the merchants and offered to sell Joseph to them as a slave. The merchants offered twenty pieces of silver in exchange for Joseph. This sum satisfied the brothers, and Joseph was led away to Egypt.

While this was going on, Reuben was far away in another part of the field. When he learned what had happened, he was terribly upset. He knew that his father would place all the blame for the evil deed on him, since he was the oldest. In order to save Reuben from their father's anger, the brothers decided to deceive

Jacob. They dipped Joseph's brightly colored coat, the one their father had given him, into the blood of a goat. They sent it to their father and told him they had found it by the roadside.

Jacob believed that Joseph had been killed by a wild beast. He was filled with grief, and could not be comforted by his other sons.

This isn't the end of Joseph's story—far from it! But we will have to continue it in the next chapter.

QUESTIONS FOR REVIEW:

1. Give three reasons why Joseph's brothers did not like him.

2. What ended up happening to Joseph instead of being killed by his brothers?

3. How did Joseph's brothers deceive their father?

ACTIVITIES

COLORING PAGE: JOSEPH'S TORN COAT

CRAFT PROJECT: JOSEPH'S COAT OF MANY COLORS

Materials:
- ☐ several colors of construction paper
- ☐ paper grocery bag
- ☐ scissors
- ☐ craft glue
- ☐ clear tape (for reinforcement if desired)

Directions:

1. Cut armholes and a head hole in your brown paper grocery bag.

2. Cut open the front of your vest beginning at the bottom and working your way toward the head hole.

3. Cut 1 in. thick strips of construction paper (strips should be 1"x 11").

4. Glue strips in alternating colors onto the paper bag.

5. Use tape to reinforce tops and bottoms of strips if desired.

6. Enjoy!

PROJECT ACTIVITY: FAMILY TREE

Abraham was Isaac's father. Isaac was Jacob's father, and Joseph was Jacob's son. It is from this lineage that the Savior, Jesus Christ, would eventually come. Research your heritage by finding the names of your ancestors, grandparents, and great grandparents. Then draw a family tree to show your lineage.

CHAPTER 7
Joseph in Egypt: The Butler and the Baker

When the merchants brought Joseph to Egypt, they sold him to a man named Potiphar. Before long, Potiphar placed Joseph in charge of his house. Eventually Potiphar's fortune grew, and he became a wealthy man.

But Potiphar's wife was a wicked woman. She falsely accused Joseph of sin. Potiphar was furious. He believed his wife, and he cast Joseph into prison. There, the keeper of the prison was moved by God to look with favor on Joseph and placed him in charge of the other prisoners.

After some time, Pharaoh's butler and baker aroused his anger. They were cast into the prison where Joseph was in charge. Joseph saw that they were troubled one day and asked why they were sad.

"We need someone to interpret our dreams," they answered.

Joseph knew that God could grant him the proper interpretation, so he said, "Tell me your dreams."

The chief butler spoke first. "In my dream there was a vine before me, and on the vine there were three branches. As soon as it budded, its blossoms shot forth, and the clusters ripened into grapes. Pharaoh's cup was in my hand; and I took the grapes and pressed them into Pharaoh's cup, and placed the cup in Pharaoh's hands."

Joseph interpreted the butler's dream:

"The three branches are three days; within three days Pharaoh will lift up your head and restore you to your office; and you shall place Pharaoh's cup in his hand as formerly, when you were his butler."

Joseph then asked the butler to remember him when he was back at the Pharaoh's side, explaining that he had been wrongly thrown into the prison.

Next, the baker relayed his dream: "In my dream, there were three cake baskets on my head, and in the uppermost basket there were baked foods for Pharaoh, but the birds were eating it out of the basket on my head."

Joseph interpreted the baker's dream:

"The three baskets are three days; within three days Pharaoh will lift up your head and hang you on a tree; and the birds will eat the flesh from you."

Pharaoh's birthday was three days after Joseph had explained these dreams, and a banquet was being prepared. At the banquet, he remembered the chief butler and restored him to his office. But the baker he hung on a scaffold. In this way, both of Joseph's interpretations had come true.

When the butler was leaving the prison to return to Pharaoh, Joseph said, "Remember me and do me the kindness to make mention of me to Pharaoh, so I may leave here. For I was stolen out of the land of the Hebrews; and here also I have done nothing that they should put me into the dungeon."

But after the butler was released from prison, he forgot all about Joseph.

Now Joseph must have been wondering what God had in store for him. He believed, because of the special dreams, that he was destined for greatness. But here he was, confined in an Egyptian prison, betrayed by his brothers and falsely accused of wrongdoing.

When Joseph successfully interpreted the dreams of the butler, he must have hoped he could leave this prison at last. Surely, this man would return to Pharaoh and tell him about the young man who could read dreams. But that was not to be— at least, not yet. The butler forgot about Joseph and he remained in prison.

Joseph must have come close to despair in that prison. But eventually, it was again a dream—this time, dreamed by the Pharaoh himself—that would turn Joseph's life upside down. We'll learn about that dream in the next chapter!

QUESTIONS FOR REVIEW:

1. Why was Joseph thrown into prison?

2. Whose dreams did Joseph interpret while they were in prison?

3. What did Joseph hope for after successfully interpreting their dreams?

ACTIVITIES

CRAFT PROJECT: THE BUTLER AND THE BAKER SPOON PEOPLE

Note: These spoon people are clearly not what a butler and baker would have looked like in the time of Joseph; they are, however, a fun representation for the kids.

Materials:
- ☐ 2, 10 in. wooden craft spoons
- ☐ Templates from page 61
- ☐ coloring pencils
- ☐ hot glue gun
- ☐ scissors

Directions:
1. Cut out and color the bodies of the butler and the baker from the Activity Book. The butler should have black suit and tie, and a white rectangle in the middle of his body. The baker can be any color.
2. Hot glue the bodies of the butler and baker to the wooden spoons.
3. Cut out the baker's hat and glue it to the top of the spoon.
4. Draw eyes, a mouth, and a nose on both spoons.
5. Cut and color a couple small pastries from the template in the Activity Book, or draw and cut out your own! Glue them onto the baker.
6. Enjoy!

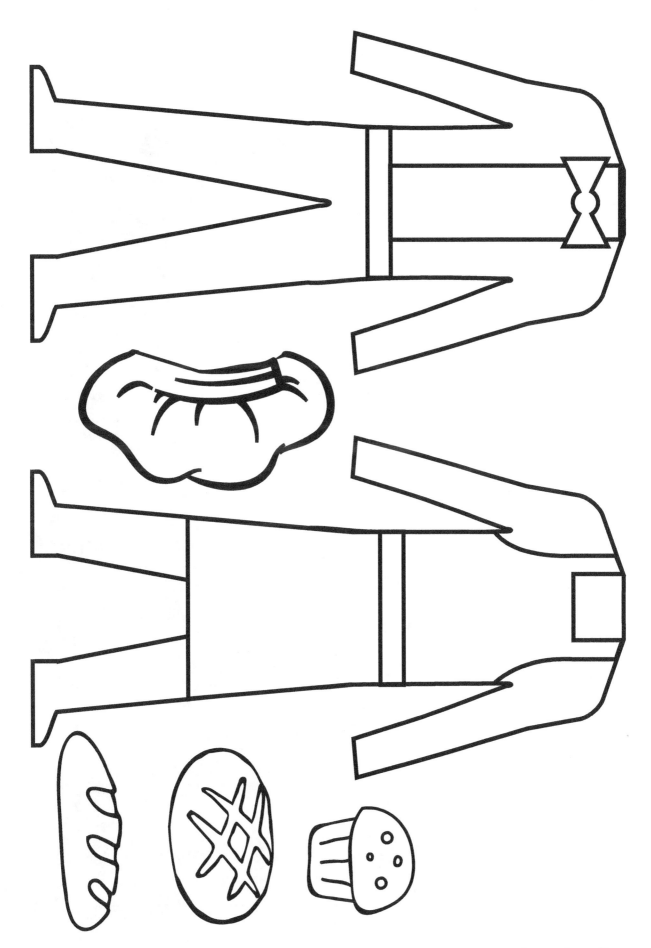

DOUBLE PUZZLE: JOSEPH IN CHARGE

Unscramble the words. Copy the letters in the numbered blocks with the corresponding numbers at the bottom to help answer the question.

BEARK

⬜⬜⬜⬜⬜
        8

TERLUB

⬜⬜⬜⬜⬜⬜

POJSEH

⬜⬜⬜⬜⬜⬜
    1   6

RINPOS

⬜⬜⬜⬜⬜⬜
   4

HAAROHP

⬜⬜⬜⬜⬜⬜⬜
5

MDERSA

⬜⬜⬜⬜⬜⬜
    7

TAQUNBE

⬜⬜⬜⬜⬜⬜⬜
     3

RIOTEEPISRATNTN

⬜⬜⬜⬜⬜⬜⬜⬜⬜⬜⬜⬜⬜⬜⬜
   2

Who placed Joseph in charge of his house?

1 2 3 4 5 6 7 8

CHAPTER 8
Joseph Meets His Brothers Again

About two years later, Pharaoh had a dream in which he stood by the Nile River. Seven cows came out of the water, beautiful and fat. But seven other cows, thin and sickly, followed. The lean cows then ate the fat cows, but still remained thin. Pharaoh then had a similar dream with thick and thin ears of grain.

Pharaoh could find no one in his kingdom to interpret these strange dreams. It was then that the butler remembered Joseph and told Pharaoh about him. Pharaoh sent for Joseph, who interpreted the dreams by saying seven good years of crops would come to Egypt, followed by seven years of famine. He advised Pharaoh to store up some of the grain during the good years so the people would have food during the famine. Pharaoh found Joseph very wise and, instead of sending him back to prison, appointed him governor.

Famine did eventually come, and Jacob and his family were among those who suffered. He sent ten of his sons to Egypt to buy grain. Benjamin, the youngest, he kept at home.

When they came to Egypt, they were sent to Joseph the governor. Joseph had changed a great deal since his brothers had sold him to the merchants of Egypt, so they didn't recognize him—but Joseph recognized his brothers.

In order to test them, Joseph accused them of being spies. They tried to convince him of their innocence. They also told him about Joseph, another brother, who was dead. They had no idea it was Joseph they were talking to at that very moment!

They explained that they had come to Egypt to buy grain. But Joseph pretended not to believe them. He cast them all into prison for three days. Then he released all but one: Simeon. This brother would have to remain in prison until the others brought to him, as a proof of their good intentions, the brother they had left at home.

The brothers spoke among themselves in their own language, right in front of Joseph. He had been speaking to them in the language of the Egyptians, through an interpreter, so they didn't know he could understand them. They admitted among themselves that they deserved to be treated in this way for their sin against their brother so many years ago.

Secretly, Joseph wept for joy to see his brothers repent of their sin, though they didn't know he was aware of the whole story. Even so, Joseph still insisted that Simeon remain in prison. Then Joseph commanded his servants to fill the sacks of the others with the grain they had purchased.

Without his brothers' knowledge, however, Joseph told the servants to place in their sacks the money his brothers had paid for the grain. In addition to the supplies of grain, he also gave them provisions for their journey. But they didn't discover what had been done until they stopped along the way home to spend the night.

When the brothers arrived in Canaan, they told their father, Jacob, all that had happened.

At their father's instruction, they took back with them the money they had found in their sacks. They were ready as well to give Joseph gifts and double the amount they needed to buy more grain. They wanted to make certain Benjamin and Simeon would return.

When Joseph saw his brothers returning with Benjamin, he ordered his servants to prepare a feast. Then Simeon was released from prison. Joseph spoke with his brothers, asking if their father was in good health. At one point, as he laid eyes on his youngest brother, Benjamin, he was so overcome with joy that he went into his room and wept. Still Joseph's brothers didn't recognize him.

After the feast, Joseph told his servants to fill his brothers' sacks with grain. Again he commanded them to place in their sacks the money they had paid. But he also had another plan.

"Put my cup," he told his servant, "the silver cup, in the mouth of the sack of the youngest, with his money for the grain."

The next morning, the brothers departed for Canaan with their sacks, not knowing all that Joseph had done. After his brothers had gone some distance, Joseph sent his chief servant after them. When the servant caught up to them, he accused them of stealing his master's silver cup.

They knew nothing about the cup. They were so certain they didn't have the cup that they made a proposal: If any one of them had it, he should be put to death. They added that they were ready to become Joseph's slaves if the servant found the cup in any of their sacks.

They took down their sacks from the animals that carried them and opened them without hesitation or fear. But they all recoiled in shock when the silver cup fell out of Benjamin's sack!

The servant ordered them to return to Joseph. When they entered the house, Joseph asked them why they had tried to steal his silver cup. But they didn't know how to answer. All fell to their knees and offered themselves as his slaves. This act was in fact a fulfillment of the dreams Joseph once had as a boy.

Joseph said that he wanted only the man who had stolen his cup as his slave—that is, Benjamin. But Judah pleaded, telling him the story of the brother Joseph they had lost so many years ago. He said that the loss of Benjamin would be too great a sorrow for his father to bear, and would certainly cause his death. Judah offered himself as a slave to Joseph in Benjamin's place.

At this point Joseph could no longer hide his identity. He finally spoke to them in their own language, amidst tears of joy.

"I am your brother, Joseph, whom you sold into Egypt. And now do not be distressed, or angry, because you sold me here; for God sent me before you to preserve life."

Joseph went on to explain how it was God's will that he had been sent to Egypt to save his father and brothers from the famine. Then he sent his brothers back to their father to tell him of his success in Egypt, and to invite his father to come with all his family to live in Egypt.

Pharaoh was pleased with Joseph's invitation to his father and his brothers. So he sent wagons to move their possessions to Egypt. He gave presents to all the brothers, but he was especially generous to Benjamin. To Jacob, he sent clothing made of the finest material, along with three hundred pieces of silver.

QUESTIONS FOR REVIEW:

1. How did Joseph first test his brothers?

2. After the feast, how did Joseph again test his brothers?

3. What was the fulfillment of one of Joseph's dreams as a boy?

ACTIVITIES

COLORING PAGE: JOSEPH AND HIS BROTHERS

SNACK PROJECT: SACK OF GRAIN-OLA

Ingredients:
- ☐ 4 cups rolled oats
- ☐ 3/4 cup oat bran
- ☐ 3/4 cup ground flax seed
- ☐ 1/2 cup sunflower or pumpkin seeds
- ☐ 3/4 cup finely chopped pecans
- ☐ 3/4 cup finely chopped walnuts
- ☐ 1/4 cup brown sugar
- ☐ 1/4 cup and 2 tablespoons honey
- ☐ 3/4 teaspoon salt
- ☐ 1/2 cup oil (you can use vegetable, canola, coconut, whatever your preferred baking oil is)
- ☐ 1 1/2 teaspoons cinnamon
- ☐ 1 1/2 teaspoon vanilla extract
- ☐ chocolate covered coins OR colored chocolate candies
- ☐ paper lunch bags

Directions:
1. Preheat oven to 325 degrees F.
2. Line a large baking sheet with parchment paper.
3. Combine oats, oat bran, flax seed, seeds, pecans, and walnuts in a large bowl.
4. Combine brown sugar, honey, maple syrup, salt, oil, cinnamon, and vanilla in a medium saucepan and bring to a boil over medium heat.
5. Pour mixture over the dry ingredients. Thoroughly coat.
6. Spread out mixture onto parchment paper lined baking pan and bake at 325 degrees F for 15–20 minutes.
7. Toss the mixture once during the baking process.
8. Cool completely.
9. Separate the mixture into paper lunch bags and hide either the chocolate coins or the colored chocolate candies inside. This will represent that without his brothers' knowledge Joseph told his servants to place in their sacks the money his brothers had paid for the grain. They did not discover that this had been done until they stopped along the way home to spend the night.
10. Enjoy!

CROSSWORD PUZZLE: JOSEPH AND HIS BROTHERS IN EGYPT

Across

2. Joseph accused his brothers of being _____.
5. The color of Joseph's cup
6. Youngest brother

Down

1. The brothers came to Egypt to buy _____.
3. The brother left in prison
4. Placed the cup in Benjamin's sack
7. Joseph wept for _____ when he saw his brothers

CHAPTER 9
The Origins of Moses:
From Birth to Prince of Egypt

The descendants of Jacob and Joseph came to live in Egypt for many years. They were called the Israelites, but they were also known as Hebrews, or Jews, especially in the story of Moses.

The new Pharaoh was jealous of the strength and wealth of the Hebrews living in his lands and feared that they might have ties with rivals of Egypt. They also needed slaves to build their temples, canals, and cities, so he enslaved the Hebrews.

Unfortunately, in their previous time of freedom and happiness, many of the Hebrews had also fallen into imitating the evil ways of the Egyptians. They often worshipped the false gods of Egypt instead of the true God of Abraham, Isaac, and Jacob.

In spite of all they had to undergo, the Hebrews in Egypt constantly increased in number. Pharaoh feared that they might rise up in revolt against him. To keep down the number of those who could bear arms in battle, Pharaoh ordered that every Hebrew boy should be killed as soon as he was born.

The Hebrew families, however, found ways to protect their babies. Many little boys were saved, and among them was one called Moses.

For three months the mother of Moses concealed him at home. But as he grew, she feared that he might be discovered. So she made him a wicker basket and covered it with tar so it would be waterproof. She placed the baby in the basket and set it down among the reeds that grew close to the banks of the Nile River. Then she pushed it away, downriver, praying to God to take care of her little boy.

Miriam, the older sister of Moses, stood at a distance, watching to see what would happen. Now, just as the basket passed by, the daughter of the cruel Pharaoh approached the river to bathe in it. Pharaoh's daughter saw the basket and ordered one of her maids to bring it to her. When she uncovered it, she found the poor, crying baby.

The princess knew it was a Hebrew child. Miriam, at a distance, trembled for the safety of her brother. But when she saw that the princess looked lovingly at the babe, she asked whether or not she would like a Hebrew woman to nurse the child. The princess agreed. So Miriam went and got her mother to nurse the child.

When Moses was older, he lived in the palace. There he was educated as a prince. He ate the best kind of food and wore the finest clothing. Under private teachers, he learned to read and write the picture language of the Egyptians.

It was God's strategy to train Moses there for leadership: not as the ruler of Egypt, but as the champion of God's chosen people, who would lead them out of slavery back home to the land of their ancestors.

Though Moses lived like a prince, he never forgot his mother and other relatives. He loved his own people, the Hebrews, and it pained him to see how harshly they were treated.

One day when Moses had grown to manhood, he was walking in the neighborhood of the palace. The Hebrews were hard at work under an Egyptian boss. The boss became angry at one of the Hebrews and began to mistreat him cruelly. When Moses saw this mistreatment, he was filled with rage and killed the Egyptian.

The news of the killing soon reached Pharaoh. He ordered that Moses should be put to death. But Moses escaped and fled to a place called Midian, in the region of Mount Sinai.

On his way, he sat down by a well to rest. While he was there recovering his strength, seven daughters of a priest named Jethro came to water their flocks, but some shepherds drove them away. Moses defended the girls, and when they told their father what had happened, he invited Moses to his house.

During that time, he married one of Jethro's daughters, Zipporah, who bore him several sons. During these forty years, God prepared Moses for the great position of leading his chosen people, which we will read about in the next chapter.

QUESTIONS FOR REVIEW:

1. Name the terms used to identify God's chosen people.

2. Why did Pharaoh enslave the Hebrews?

3. How did Moses's mother protect him when Pharaoh decreed that every Hebrew boy should be killed? Did the plan work?

CRAFT PROJECT: MOSES BASKET ON THE NILE

Materials:
- ☐ paper plate
- ☐ white muffin liner
- ☐ green construction paper

Directions:

1. Color the paper plate blue (this will be our Nile River). You can add fish to the water if desired.

2. Color the muffin liner brown (this will be our basket for Moses) and glue in the center of the plate.

3. Cut an 8" x 3" section of green construction paper and staple along the edge of the plate (positioning does not matter).

4. Cut vertical slits in the green construction paper (these are our reeds along the banks of the Nile).

5. Mold a baby from the clay and allow to dry and harden. Use markers to create a face and blanket for baby Moses.

6. Place Moses in the middle of his basket.

7. Enjoy!

MAZE: MOSES FLOATS DOWN THE RIVER

Complete the maze by helping little Moses in the basket float down the river where he can be discovered by Pharaoh's daughter.

START

FINISH

CHAPTER 10
The Plagues

During his stay in Midian, one day God spoke to Moses through a burning bush, telling him he was to go back to Egypt to free the slaves. His brother, Aaron, went with him to see Pharaoh and to carry out God's instructions. But Pharaoh would not listen. God told Moses to raise his staff over the water so it would turn the river to blood. Immediately, the water was turned to blood. The river was polluted, the fish died, and the Egyptians couldn't drink the water. This was the first of the plagues.

But Pharaoh's magicians also turned the water into blood. So Pharaoh refused to believe the sign, and his heart was hardened.

When this plague had lasted seven days, Pharaoh still wouldn't allow it. So God warned that the entire land would be covered with frogs. But Pharaoh wouldn't listen. And frogs covered the land with the next plague.

When Pharaoh saw that the plague had ended, he refused to let the people of Israel leave Egypt. Then Aaron struck the dust of the earth with his staff, and God sent a plague of gnats that caused great discomfort. But Pharaoh was stubborn and still wouldn't budge.

So a fourth plague, one of flies, was sent on all the land of Egypt, except for Goshen, where the Hebrews lived.

Pharaoh finally agreed to let them leave, so Moses prayed that the plague of flies would be taken away. And it was so. But Pharaoh went back on his word, deceiving Moses yet again.

So Moses came to Pharaoh again. He told him that if he didn't let the Hebrews leave Egypt, all the camels, oxen, horses, and sheep in the whole land, except those in Goshen where the Hebrews lived, would be afflicted with disease and death. Pharaoh was filled with bitterness and refused again. Then all the animals of the Egyptians died, but those of the Hebrews were unharmed. Despite this, Pharaoh still wouldn't let the people of Israel leave.

For this reason, God brought even worse troubles on the Egyptians. This time, all the people, as well as the animals, were stricken with boils. The plague spread over all the land, and the suffering was very great. But Pharaoh refused to obey.

Moses went to Pharaoh and threatened another plague if he didn't yield to God's will. This time it would be damaging hail. Once more Pharaoh refused, and a great hailstorm swept over the land. It beat down the crops and destroyed the houses. Only Goshen was spared.

When Pharaoh saw all the destruction, he promised to let the Israelites go if the storm would stop. Moses went outside the city and stretched out his hands. The storm stopped. But Pharaoh was unfaithful to his promise, just as he had been before.

Moses and Aaron next threatened Pharaoh with a plague of locusts that would destroy whatever crops were left. The servants of Pharaoh came and begged him to let the Hebrews leave, so that no more harm would come to Egypt. Pharaoh said he would let the men leave, but he wouldn't let the women and children go.

Moses couldn't agree to Pharaoh's terms. So the eighth plague followed, and great swarms of locusts filled every field of crops, eating up every blade of grass.

Pharaoh sent for Moses and Aaron once more. He promised to grant them their wish if they would remove the plague. But after the plague was gone, Pharaoh's heart was hardened again, and he refused to let them leave.

Yet a new plague came, with darkness covering the land, even in the middle of the day. Pharaoh's servants and all the people were terrified. Pharaoh called for Moses and Aaron and told them to go. Not only the men, but also the women and children could go, but then changed his mind.

You may have noticed a pattern here! Pharaoh was obviously a man who did not keep his word. It would take one final and horrible plague to finally convince him to let the Israelites truly leave. We will learn about this final plague in the next chapter.

QUESTIONS FOR REVIEW:

1. What was the first of the ten plagues?

2. Who helped Moses carry out the plagues?

3. Why did Pharaoh change his mind so many times about letting the Hebrews go?

ACTIVITIES

SNACK PROJECT: FLIES PLAGUE DRINK

Ingredients/Materials:
- ☐ water
- ☐ ice cube tray
- ☐ mini plastic flies
- ☐ clear liquid drink such as apple juice, sprite, water, or lemonade
- ☐ clear drinking glass

Directions:
1. Place one plastic fly in each section of the ice cube tray.
2. Fill the ice cube tray with the flies with water.
3. Freeze over night.
4. Add the ice cubes with the "clear" liquid of choice to the clear glass.
5. Enjoy!

COLORING PAGE: MOSES AND THE BURNING BUSH

CRAFT PROJECT: BALANCE FROG FROM THE FROG PLAGUE

Materials
- ☐ Template
- ☐ green card stock paper (or white card stock colored green)
- ☐ scissors

Directions:

1. Using the template below, cut your frog shape from the card stock paper.
2. Color your frog if using white card stock.
3. Glue the googly eyes onto the frog.
4. Tape a penny to the underside of each front leg of the frog.
5. Balance your frog on one finger by placing the mouth of the frog on your finger and allow the weight of the pennies to balance each other.
6. Enjoy!

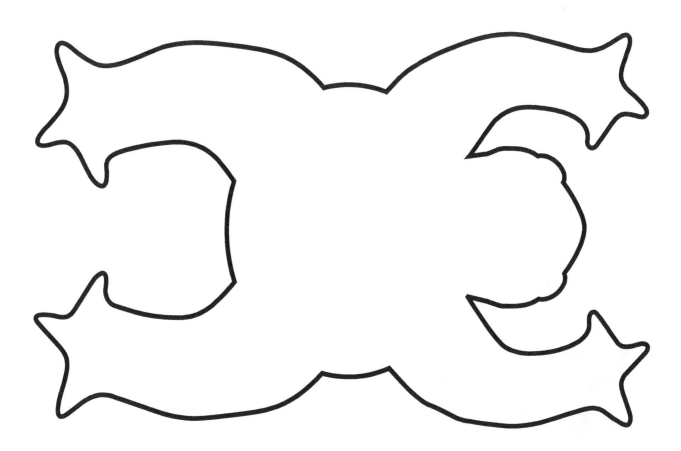

WORD SEARCH: THE PLAGUES

Find the following words.

Plagues, Locusts, Frogs, Boils, Gnats, Blood, Hail, Cattle, Flies, Darkness

```
I  E  F  B  S  M  K  E  N  K  A  N  D  I  S
B  Q  L  L  K  G  J  C  Z  U  X  F  A  Z  J
A  W  I  T  I  N  D  T  X  G  U  O  R  M  U
O  O  E  O  T  B  V  N  L  E  D  Y  K  O  Y
B  Y  S  F  W  A  P  Y  G  U  Z  K  N  S  T
U  Q  W  M  N  L  C  X  W  K  L  N  E  G  Y
I  G  N  Z  A  H  G  Y  Q  W  C  Y  S  O  E
W  P  F  G  N  A  T  S  K  J  V  L  S  R  A
W  R  U  G  B  T  G  D  T  Y  A  X  L  F  A
T  E  H  W  E  S  T  S  U  C  O  L  H  A  Q
S  V  W  U  B  P  B  L  I  U  K  A  C  J  U
I  C  M  K  Y  F  R  L  P  C  I  J  I  I  Z
T  J  Y  G  W  O  D  R  O  L  Z  G  Z  U  B
E  G  A  I  Q  C  W  V  Z  O  S  N  T  A  N
M  A  E  N  Q  L  J  S  Q  T  D  S  E  G  E
```

Note: Some words may appear backwards.

CHAPTER 11
The Tenth Plague and the Passover

God told Moses that he would bring one last plague on the Egyptians, a plague so terrible that Pharaoh would be forced to let the people of Israel go. To prepare for their departure, the Lord commanded the Hebrews to ask their Egyptian neighbors for gifts of gold and silver. These gifts were actually payment for the hard labor the people of Israel had performed for so many years.

The Egyptians had come to respect the Hebrews because of the astonishing things Moses had done. They were afraid to refuse their request, so they gave them all that they asked. In this way, before their departure from Egypt, the people of Israel were no longer poor slaves. They possessed gold, silver, and valuable clothing.

Even though the Hebrews received such wonderful gifts from the Egyptians, the Pharaoh still wouldn't allow them to leave. So the greatest plague, the tenth and final one, came on them.

The Lord said to Moses, "Yet one plague more I will bring upon Pharaoh and upon Egypt; afterwards he will let you go from here; when he lets you go, he will drive you away completely."

This last plague was to be the worst. God instructed Moses to tell Pharaoh that all the firstborn children of the Egyptians, even Pharaoh's son himself, would die. In addition, the firstborn of all the cattle would die as well. But the Hebrew children and cattle would not be touched. Such a drastic threat angered Pharaoh, but he still refused to let the people of Israel leave.

Seeing that Pharaoh still wasn't listening to the messages, Moses went back to the Israelites. He told them what God had said to do during this tenth and final plague.

Moses said to them, "Select lambs for yourselves according to your families, and kill the Passover lamb. Take a bunch of hyssop and dip it in the blood which is in the basin, and touch the lintel and the two doorposts with the blood which is in the basin; and none of you shall go out of the door of his house until the morning." That was the night the Hebrews were eating the Passover meal of bitters herbs, flat bread and lamb. So they used the blood from the lamb to carry out the instructions from God.

"For the Lord will pass through to slay the Egyptians; and when he sees the blood on the lintel and on the two doorposts, the Lord will pass over the door, and will not allow the destroyer to enter your houses to slay you."

About midnight, the destroying angel of the Lord entered every Egyptian home, from that of Pharaoh to that of the lowliest man. The firstborn of every Egyptian family lay dead. But seeing the blood of the lamb sprinkled on the doorposts of the Hebrews, the angel passed over their homes, and not a single Hebrew child was harmed.

This great sorrow finally softened Pharaoh's heart. He summoned Moses and Aaron and told them to lead the people of Israel out of the land of Egypt without delay. At the time of their departure, the Hebrews had lived in Egypt for 430 years.

QUESTIONS FOR REVIEW:

1. What was the tenth plague?

2. How were the Hebrews spared the plague?

3. When was Pharaoh's heart finally softened?

ACTIVITIES

SNACK PROJECT: PASSOVER BREAD AND DIP

Ingredients:
☐ Pita bread or any flat bread
☐ Olive oil
☐ Salt and pepper
☐ Fresh basil

Instructions:
1. Put 2 tablespoons of olive oil in a small bowl.
2. Tear up small pieces of the basil and place them in the oil.
3. Sprinkle with salt and pepper.
4. Tear small pieces of the bread and dip them into the oil mixture. Enjoy!

DOUBLE PUZZLE: THE PASSOVER

Unscramble the words. Copy the letters in the numbered blocks with the corresponding numbers at the bottom to help answer the question.

SARVSEPO

☐ ☐ ☐ ☐ ☐ ☐ ☐ ☐
   10   16

MLBA

☐ ☐ ☐ ☐
15

SORPOOTSD

☐ ☐ ☐ ☐ ☐ ☐ ☐ ☐ ☐
9   18   13 3

TIIMDGNH

☐ ☐ ☐ ☐ ☐ ☐ ☐ ☐
14 12   1

NAGLE

☐ ☐ ☐ ☐ ☐
6

SYHSOP

☐ ☐ ☐ ☐ ☐ ☐
4

GALPEU

☐ ☐ ☐ ☐ ☐ ☐
8

HOPHARA

☐ ☐ ☐ ☐ ☐ ☐ ☐
5

SSMEO

☐ ☐ ☐ ☐ ☐
7   17

LIENLT

☐ ☐ ☐ ☐ ☐ ☐
2 11

What did God command the Hebrews to ask of their Egyptian neighbors?

☐ ☐ F ☐ ☐   ☐ ☐   ☐ ☐ ☐ ☐   ☐ ☐ ☐
1 2   3 4   5   6 7 8 9   10 11 12

☐ ☐ ☐ ☐ ☐ ☐
13 14 15 16 17 18

CHAPTER 12
The Exodus and the Parting of the Red Sea

Six hundred thousand Hebrew men, plus their families, set out from Egypt that night with Moses and Aaron. They took with them all their possessions—their clothing, ornaments, vessels of gold and silver, weapons, and tents—as well as flocks of sheep and herds of cattle.

Before Joseph died, he had prophesied that the people of Israel would leave Egypt. He had made them promise to take his remains with them. Moses and the people remembered the promise their ancestors had made to Joseph, so when they left Egypt, they carried Joseph's body with them.

To show the way, the Lord appeared to them by day as a pillar of cloud, and by night as a pillar of fire. This was how he led them out of Egypt, choosing a route that would take them across the Red Sea.

Pharaoh soon regretted letting the Hebrews leave Egypt. He prepared his chariot and his entire army. With six hundred chosen chariots and all the captains of the army, he pursued the people of Israel.

He found them encamped by the shore of the Red Sea. Looking in the distance, the Hebrews saw the Egyptians coming after them. They were terrified, and they cried out to the Lord for help. They told Moses that it would have been better to be slaves in Egypt than to be killed in the wilderness.

Moses relieved their fears when he told them: "Fear not, stand firm, and see the salvation of the Lord, which he will work for you today; for the Egyptians whom you see today, you shall never see again. The Lord will fight for you, and you have only to be still."

The cloud of God's presence had led the Hebrews to this point. Now it moved behind them to shield them from the pursuing Egyptians. Moses prayed to God for more help. God replied, "Why do you cry to me? Tell the people of Israel to go forward."

This was a strange thing for God to suggest, for the Red Sea, a long and deep arm of the ocean, stood directly before them. But God spoke to Moses further.

"Lift up your rod, and stretch out your hand over the sea and divide it, that the sons of Israel may go on dry ground through the sea."

Moses did as he was commanded. The waters of the sea were divided, and a strong wind dried a path. The Hebrews were amazed. They crossed this path to the opposite shore between two walls of ocean water.

While they were crossing, the pillar of cloud was lifted. The Egyptian armies, with all their chariots and horses, hurried after the Hebrews through the path. But by the power of God, their chariots were bogged down, and their journey through the two walls of water was delayed. The Egyptians cried out, "Let us flee from before Israel; for the Lord fights for them against the Egyptians."

But it was too late. As soon as the last Hebrew had crossed over to the opposite shore, God said to Moses, "Stretch out your hand over the sea, that the water may come back upon the Egyptians, upon their chariots, and upon their horsemen."

Moses did as God commanded. The waters closed in and all the chariots and the Egyptian army were buried in the depths of the sea. The Hebrews were saved! In gratitude to God for their deliverance, Moses and the people of Israel sang a song of thanksgiving.

QUESTIONS FOR REVIEW:

1. To lead the way for them, what did the Lord appear to the Hebrew people as by day? And by night?

2. What did Pharaoh do as soon as he regretted letting the Hebrews leave Egypt?

3. What happened at the Red Sea that allowed the Hebrews to escape the Egyptian army?

ACTIVITIES

MAP ACTIVITY: THE ISRAELITES' EXODUS FROM EGYPT

1. Trace the portion of the already drawn route from the Land of Goshen to Mount Horeb.

2. Where the route crosses the Red Sea, draw Moses' staff to show that this is where God worked the miracle of the parting of the sea.

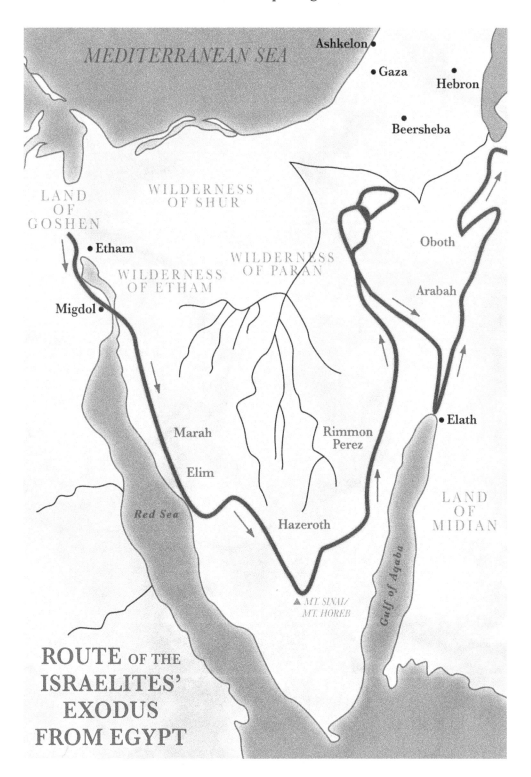

ROUTE OF THE **ISRAELITES' EXODUS FROM EGYPT**

COLORING PAGE: PARTING THE RED SEA

CRAFT PROJECT: PILLAR OF CLOUD AND PILLAR OF FIRE

To show them the way, the Lord appeared to them by day as a pillar of cloud, and by night as a pillar of fire.

Materials:
- ☐ 2 paper towel rolls
- ☐ craft glue
- ☐ cotton balls
- ☐ red, yellow, and orange tissue OR construction paper
- ☐ scissors

Directions:

1. Glue one side of each cotton ball and adhere it to the first paper towel roll. This is the pillar of cloud.
2. Cut the tissue or construction paper into small squares and slightly crumble.
3. Place glue on one side of each piece and adhere them to the second of paper towel roll. This is the pillar of fire.
4. Enjoy!

SNACK PROJECT: PARTING THE RED SEA CARROT MUFFIN

Ingredients:
- ☐ 1 1/3 cup all purpose flour
- ☐ 1 1/2 teaspoons baking soda
- ☐ 1 1/4 teaspoons baking powder
- ☐ 1 1/2 teaspoons cinnamon
- ☐ 1/2 teaspoon salt
- ☐ 3 eggs
- ☐ 1 cup white sugar
- ☐ 3/4 cup vegetable, canola, coconut, or other preferred baking oil
- ☐ 1 teaspoon vanilla
- ☐ 1 1/2 cups grated carrot
- ☐ 1/2 cup shredded apple
- ☐ 1/4 cup cream cheese
- ☐ 2 tablespoons softened butter
- ☐ 1 teaspoon vanilla extract
- ☐ 1 1/2 cups sifted confectioners sugar
- ☐ blue food coloring
- ☐ gummy bears

Directions:

1. Preheat oven to 325 degrees F.
2. Grease the bottoms of 12 muffin cups or line with 12 baking cups.
3. Sift flour, baking soda, baking powder, cinnamon, and salt together in a large bowl.
4. In a separate bowl, beat eggs and sugar until fluffy. Stir in the oil, vanilla, carrot, and apple.
5. Fold the flour mixture into the wet mixture.
6. Evenly separate the batter into the muffin cups.

7. Bake for 15–20 minutes. A toothpick inserted in the middle should come out clean.

8. Allow to cool completely.

9. Beat together the cream cheese, butter, vanilla, and confectioner's sugar until fluffy.

10. Tint with the blue food coloring until desired shade of blue.

11. Frost both sides of the cooled muffin leaving a centerline where the muffin itself is visible (this will be the track the Israelites took).

12. Use your gummy bears to march through the red sea.

13. Place several gummy bears in the middle of the muffin and then ice on top of these gummy bears (this is the sea covering the Egyptians).

14. Enjoy your snack!

CHAPTER 13
The Ten Commandments and the Golden Calf

After they passed through the Red Sea, the Israelites continued to travel in the wilderness. Then, God gave his law to the them from Mount Sinai. Lightning flashed across the sky, and loud thunder mixed with the shrill blast of a trumpet. Mount Sinai, which is nearly 8,000 feet high, was suddenly covered with a heavy cloud. Thick smoke rose from the mountain. The trumpet sound grew louder and louder, and an earthquake shook the mountain.

The people trembled with fear. As they waited, they heard God's voice proclaiming these Ten Commandments:

1. "I am the Lord your God, who brought you out of the land of Egypt. You shall have no other gods before me."
2. "You shall not take the name of the Lord your God in vain."
3. "Remember the Sabbath day, to keep it holy."
4. "Honor your father and your mother."
5. "You shall not kill."
6. "You shall not commit adultery."
7. "You shall not steal."
8. "You shall not bear false witness against your neighbor."
9. "You shall not covet your neighbor's wife."
10. "You shall not covet your neighbor's house or anything that is your neighbor's."

The people were struck with fear and moved back from the voice. From then on, God spoke to the people only through Moses.

Then Moses went up into the cloud on the mountaintop where God was, and God spoke to him. God promised Moses that his angel would lead the Israelites into the Promised Land.

Moses came down and told the people all the commands that the Lord had given him, and they promised to obey them.

A second time Moses was called by God up the mountain. This time, he took Joshua with him. Seven days after he climbed the mountain, God called him into the cloud, and there he remained for forty days and forty nights. It was then that God gave him, written on two tablets of stone, the commandments he had spoken to the people amid the thunder and lightning.

Moses stayed up on the mountain with God for so long that the Israelites feared he had abandoned them. They worried as well that God was no longer with them. So they decided to serve a different god.

The people collected their golden jewelry and brought it to Aaron. Then they forced him to make a golden calf. When the golden calf was ready, the Israelites worshipped it and made a great feast in its honor.

God knew what was happening with the people. He said to Moses, "Go down; for your people, whom you brought up out of the land of Egypt, have corrupted themselves."

Moses came down from the mountain with the two tablets of the commandments. When he saw the people worshipping the golden calf and dancing around it, he was enraged. He threw the tablets of stone on the ground, shattering them into many pieces. Then, he burnt the golden calf.

As judge of the people, Moses sentenced to death those who had led the others into worshipping the idol they had created. He cried out, "Who is on the Lord's side? Come to me." Immediately, the sons of Levi stood by his side. At the command of Moses, they drew their swords and slew the guilty and whoever came in their way. Twenty-three thousand men were killed. The rest of the people did penance, and God forgave them their sin.

God then commanded Moses to make two tablets like the first, replacing the ones he had shattered. These other tablets Moses took up to the mountain, and again God wrote on them the commandments. Moses remained on the mountain for forty days and forty nights. When he came down to the people, rays of light shone out from his face. The people were afraid to come near him, so he covered his face with a veil and told them all that he had learned while he was with God on the mountain.

QUESTIONS FOR REVIEW:

1. Name the Ten Commandments.

2. What did the people hear and see at Mount Sinai when God gave Moses the Ten Commandments?

3. What happened when Moses came down the mountain and saw the Israelites worshipping an idol?

ACTIVITIES

CRAFT PROJECT: THE TEN COMMANDMENTS

Materials:
- ☐ Templates from pages 99 and 101
- ☐ 4 sheets of gray or brown construction paper
- ☐ scissors
- ☐ craft glue
- ☐ clear tape

Directions

1. Using 4 full sheets of construction paper, copy the tablet template and cut it out. Each tablet gets 5 commandments. You will end up with 2 full sets of commandments.

2. Cut out the commandments and paste them to the tablets.

3. Cut one set of commandments into several pieces and then tape together (this is the first set of commandments that Moses broke).

4. The second set is from Moses' second trip up the mount.

5. Enjoy!

1. "I AM THE LORD YOUR GOD, WHO BROUGHT YOU OUT OF THE LAND OF EGYPT. . . . YOU SHALL HAVE NO OTHER GODS BEFORE ME."

2. "YOU SHALL NOT TAKE THE NAME OF THE LORD YOUR GOD IN VAIN."

3. "REMEMBER THE SABBATH DAY, TO KEEP IT HOLY."

4. "HONOR YOUR FATHER AND YOUR MOTHER."

5. "YOU SHALL NOT KILL."

6. "YOU SHALL NOT COMMIT ADULTERY."

7. "YOU SHALL NOT STEAL."

8. "YOU SHALL NOT BEAR FALSE WITNESS AGAINST YOUR NEIGHBOR."

9. "YOU SHALL NOT COVET YOUR NEIGHBOR'S WIFE."

10. "YOU SHALL NOT COVET YOUR NEIGHBOR'S HOUSE . . . OR ANYTHING THAT IS YOUR NEIGHBOR'S."

CRAFT PROJECT: TEN COMMANDMENTS DISCOVERY BAG

Materials:

1. A first place ribbon, trophy, medal, or a number 1 cut out by teacher. This symbolizes that God is to be first in our life.

2. Small tube of toothpaste or small container of mouthwash. This symbolizes that we are to keep our mouth clean by not using God's name in vain.

3. Photo of Mom and Dad. This symbolizes that you are to honor your father and mother.

4. A paper calendar with Sundays and Holy Days of Obligation circled in red. This symbolizes the commandment requiring you to keep holy the Sabbath and other Holy Days.

5. Plastic knife, pretend knife, or other weapon. This symbolizes that you should not kill.

6. A heart shape broken into 2 pieces (feel free to omit as this commandment may or may not be one you have covered with your children). This symbolizes the commandment forbidding adultery.

7. Cut a hand shape out of the construction paper and tape a piece of candy to the palm. This symbolizes that you are not to steal.

8. A strip of paper that says "lie, lie, lie" with each word increasing in size and in darkness (in other words, the lie grows as the further down the strip it gets). This symbolizes that you should not to bear false witness against your neighbor.

9. Two rings, plastic or real. This symbolizes the sacredness of marriage and the commitment. This will cover the ninth commandment. Here the emphasis will be on husband and wife appreciating and focusing on one another as they did the day they were married.

10. A piece of jewelry or other pretty object that the child might see as something special. This symbolizes that you should not to covet your neighbor's goods.

11. Pillowcase

Directions:

1. Place all items in the pillowcase and allow the child to draw out one item at a time and name the commandment that the object symbolizes. If the child guesses "wrong" they may have a reason for doing so. Talk it through and ask if another commandment might fit as well.

SNACK PROJECT: TEN COMMANDMENT COOKIES

Ingredients:
- ☐ 12 tablespoons softened butter
- ☐ 2 1/2 cups powdered sugar
- ☐ 6 egg whites
- ☐ 2 tablespoons vanilla extract
- ☐ 2 teaspoons almond extract
- ☐ 1 1/2 cup flour
- ☐ 16 oz. bittersweet chocolate, chopped
- ☐ 1 cup heavy cream
- ☐ 1/2 cup unsalted butter
- ☐ freezer bag with corner cut off OR piping bag with 1/4" plain tip

Directions:

1. Preheat oven to 350 degrees F.

2. Cream butter.

3. Incorporate powdered sugar and mix thoroughly.

4. Slowly beat in egg whites.

5. Add vanilla and mix.

6. Slowly add in flour, mixing just well enough to combine.

7. Fill piping bag or freezer bag with mix and pipe out 3 in. sections onto a baking sheet (keep in mind that these are going to be tablet shaped).

8. Bake for about 10 minutes or until a light golden brown.

9. In a small saucepan, heat cream and butter over medium-high stirring continuously until boiling.

10. Once this mixture begins to boil, pour it onto the chocolate chunks.

11. Wait a few seconds and once chocolate is melting, stir continuously until it is completely melted.

12. Allow mixture to cool and set up.

13. Completely coat one side of the cooled cookie with the cooled chocolate filling and then press another cookie to it, forming a sandwich.

14. Using a small tip piping bag or a freezer bag with a small corner cut, pipe on the roman numerals I, II, III, IV, and V.

15. Repeat the process with next two cookies and filling adding the roman numerals VI, VII, VIII, IX, and X.

16. Make as many sets of ten commandments as you like.

17. Enjoy!

CHAPTER 14
Joshua, Commander of the Israelites

Moses placed the new commandments in the Ark of the Covenant, and for years, the Israelites carried God's laws on their way to the Promised Land. After many years had passed, Moses passed on the leadership of the people to Joshua, who led the Israelites toward Canaan.

Canaan was to become the home of the Israelites after forty years of wandering in the desert. But first they had to conquer the land and drive out the inhabitants.

Before Joshua crossed the Jordan, he knew he needed to find out the strength of the cities they wanted to conquer. He sent two spies to Jericho and the surrounding neighborhoods. There, his spies lodged with a woman named Rahab. But before long, the spies were recognized and reported to the king.

When Rahab heard that the king was sending his soldiers after the men to arrest them, she hid them on the roof of her house. When the soldiers had gone, Rahab made the spies promise that when the city was taken, they would spare her and her relatives. In turn, she agreed to display a scarlet cord in her window as a sign to Joshua that the city was ready to fall.

When the spies agreed to this plan, she let them down from the roof by a rope, and they fled to the mountains. Here they stayed for three days before crossing the Jordan and rejoining Joshua. The spies told Joshua there would be no trouble in conquering the city because the people were overcome by fear even at the mere thought of the attack.

After three days, at God's command, Joshua ordered the priests to carry the Ark of the Covenant into the Jordan River. As soon as they had set foot in the water, the course of the river stopped, and a dry path appeared. The priests carried the Ark to the middle of the river and remained standing there until all the Israelites had passed over.

At the prompting of the Lord, Joshua then appointed the Israelites to build a monument in the middle of the river to honor their miraculous passage.

After the monument was completed, Joshua commanded the priests to carry the Ark out of the river bed. As soon as they had done so, the river began once more to take its natural course.

Soon, the Israelites would invade the powerful city of Jericho. One night an angel of the Lord with a drawn sword appeared to Joshua and gave him detailed instructions about how Jericho was to be taken.

As the Lord instructed, Joshua sent forty-thousand fighting men to march around the walls of the city every day for six days. On the seventh day, the soldiers, the priests carrying the Ark of the Covenant, and all the Israelites marched around the walls seven times.

At the end of the seventh time around the city, Joshua gave the command, "Shout, for the Lord has given you the city."

At that moment, seven trumpets sounded a continuous blast, the people gave a mighty shout, and the walls fell! The soldiers rushed into the city from wherever they stood and killed all the inhabitants except Rahab and her family, who had helped their spies.

Joshua had been God's faithful and obedient servant all his life. He was a great military commander, leading soldiers to victory in every battle. Now he divided the spoils among them and settled down to a peaceful life at Timnath-serah for the rest of his days.

QUESTIONS FOR REVIEW:

1. After wandering the desert for forty years, what did the Israelites have to do before making Canaan their home?

2. How did Joshua find out the strengths of the cities they needed to conquer?

3. What made the walls of Jericho fall?

ACTIVITIES

COLORING PAGE: JOSHUA

CRAFT PROJECT: BUILD THE WALL OF JERICHO

Materials:
☐ Lincoln logs OR wooden blocks OR Legos OR any other building block you have
☐ soldier figures OR Lego men OR stuffed animals OR any other figures you have to use as the army

Directions:

1. Build a fort out of whatever type of building blocks you have.
2. March your figures around the wall 1 time each day for 6 days and then 7 times on the 7th day.
3. Give a shout and use your trumpet from the craft project in this chapter.
4. It's time to wreck the wall! Knock the wall down and conquer the city.
5. Enjoy!

CRAFT PROJECT: TRUMPET AT JERICHO

Materials:
☐ paper towel roll
☐ markers
☐ scissors
☐ 4 buttons
☐ hot glue gun

Directions:

1. Color the paper towel roll any colors you would like your trumpet to be.
2. Cut 5, 3 in. slits along one end of the paper towel roll.
3. Glue the 4 buttons into place to be the trumpet keys.
4. Enjoy!

SNACK PROJECT: GRAHAM CRACKER JERICHO

Ingredients:
- ☐ sandwich bread
- ☐ graham crackers
- ☐ peanut butter or almond butter
- ☐ gummy bears

Directions:

1. Make a peanut butter or almond butter sandwich. Coat the outside crust with more peanut or almond butter.

2. Break your graham crackers along lines.

3. Line up each graham cracker piece vertically along the outside of the sandwich (this is our wall around Jericho so the graham cracker should be taller than the sandwich. The peanut or almond butter is our bonding agent to keep the graham crackers from falling).

4. March the gummy bears around the outside wall.

5. On the final lap every one gives a shout and you knock down the graham cracker wall.

6. Enjoy your snack!

WORD SEARCH: JOSHUA, COMMANDER OF THE ISRAELITES

Find the following words.

Canaan, Joshua, Jordan, Spies, Jericho, Ark, Trumpet, Inhabitants

```
I   E   A   H   Y   S   S   U   N   B   U   H   D   C   Q
X   N   T   W   E   O   S   G   A   H   E   P   M   B   P
M   P   H   I   N   B   P   T   D   U   O   H   A   R   V
R   K   P   A   X   D   R   D   R   I   S   F   T   K   D
P   S   D   W   B   U   A   C   O   X   S   M   B   J   L
R   W   F   N   M   I   R   U   J   K   S   G   I   S   T
L   G   X   P   U   S   T   O   H   W   L   G   O   H   Z
M   R   E   P   M   C   W   A   G   S   S   U   P   R   Y
Z   T   R   Y   J   A   C   M   N   G   O   W   M   U   E
A   P   D   L   E   O   D   C   X   T   I   J   U   N   R
A   R   K   E   R   Z   Y   R   S   Z   S   K   G   E   D
N   G   N   Q   I   S   Z   W   E   N   A   A   N   A   C
P   Y   D   C   C   A   K   W   T   U   I   N   X   F   P
Q   X   H   N   H   T   K   T   L   Z   V   B   U   M   C
M   F   N   F   O   S   B   J   L   S   D   D   R   R   M
```

Note: Some words may appear backwards.

CHAPTER 15
Mighty Samson

In the years following the time of Joshua, the Israelites again fell into idol worship and stopped worshipping God. As a result, God allowed a people called the Philistines to wage war against them. For many years, the Philistines harassed the Israelites.

At this time, an Israelite boy named Samson was born at Zorah. An angel had foretold his birth to his mother who, up until that time, had not been able to have children. The angel had commanded the parents to separate the boy from others for a special purpose. His hair was not to be cut, nor was he to drink wine or other strong drink.

Samson was dedicated by his parents to the service of God, who had destined him to be a curse to the Philistines. He had no army, but depended instead on his own tremendous strength. In fact, he was so strong that once, when he was a small boy and a young lion attacked him, he seized it in both hands and tore it apart!

After Samson grew up, he began his campaign against the Philistines in a strange way. He caught three hundred foxes and tied their tails together, then fastened lighted torches to them. He set the foxes loose in the fields of the Philistines so they would run rampant and set the crops ablaze.

All the corn in the fields, all the grapes in the vineyards, and all the olives on the trees were burned. In retaliation, the Philistines burned his father-in-law's house, and Samson's wife perished in the flames. Samson was furious and went into the city nearby. He slaughtered a large number of the inhabitants before fleeing into the territory of the tribe of Judah.

It seemed there was nothing the Philistines could do to capture and kill Samson—until Samson fell in love. The woman's name was Delilah, and she was a Philistine from the valley of Sorek. The Philistines, seeing that Samson was so taken by her, approached Delilah and said, "Entice him, and see wherein his great strength lies, and by what means we may overpower him, that we may bind him to subdue him; and we will each give you eleven hundred pieces of silver."

Delilah accepted the bribe. She went to Samson and asked what was the source of his great strength. At first, Samson resisted, telling her lies and tricking her into thinking the wrong thing about where his strength came from. But eventually he relented and confessed that the source of his strength lay in his long hair.

"A razor has never come upon my head. . . . If I be shaved, then my strength will leave me, and I shall become weak, and be like any other man."

So at night while he was asleep, Delilah cut his hair and called in the soldiers to capture him. The woman he loved had betrayed him. With his strength faded, the soldiers were able to control him. They blinded him and cast him into a prison in the city of Gaza. But in the darkness of the dungeon, Samson's hair began to grow back.

One day, a great feast was held in the city. Several thousand people were gathered in the banquet hall. Samson was brought from the prison so that the guests might amuse themselves by making fun of him, failing to realize that his hair had grown long once again.

A boy was leading the blind prisoner into the hall. Samson asked the boy to lead him toward the pillars so he could lean against them and rest. These were the same pillars that supported the roof of the great hall.

The boy led him to the pillars. Then, calling on the Lord to restore his strength, Samson took both pillars in his hands and shook them. The house fell and many were killed, including several princes of the Philistines. But Samson also perished.

QUESTIONS FOR REVIEW:

1. How were the Philistines finally able to capture Samson?

2. What began to happen to Samson while he was in the dungeon?

3. How did Samson conquer his captors? And what happened to him?

ACTIVITIES

COLORING PAGE: SAMSON

MAZE: HELP SAMSON ESCAPE GAZA

START

FINISH

CRAFT PROJECT: HAIR GROWING SAMSON SPOON

Materials:
- ☐ 1, 10 in. wooden craft spoon
- ☐ craft glue
- ☐ brown yarn
- ☐ hole punch
- ☐ scissors
- ☐ 2 hole punch reinforcements (colored brown)
- ☐ markers
- ☐ hot glue gun
- ☐ Template from page 121

Directions:

1. Cut out and color Samson's body from page 121. Hot glue the body onto the spoon.

2. Cut out the semi-circle template from page 121 and color it brown. Hole punch the semi-circle towards the top and add your reinforcements to both the front and back.

3. Hot glue this to the top of Samson's head. Make sure your hole is not covered by the spoon.

4. Cut 6 pieces of yarn to 10 in. in length.

5. Thread the yarn through the hole and tie a knot at the ends of each piece (to keep them from falling backwards through the hole), and tie them together on the backside of the spoon.

6. Draw a face for Samson.

7. Pull the hair back and forth through the hole to show how his hair was cut and then grew back while he was in prison.

8. Enjoy!

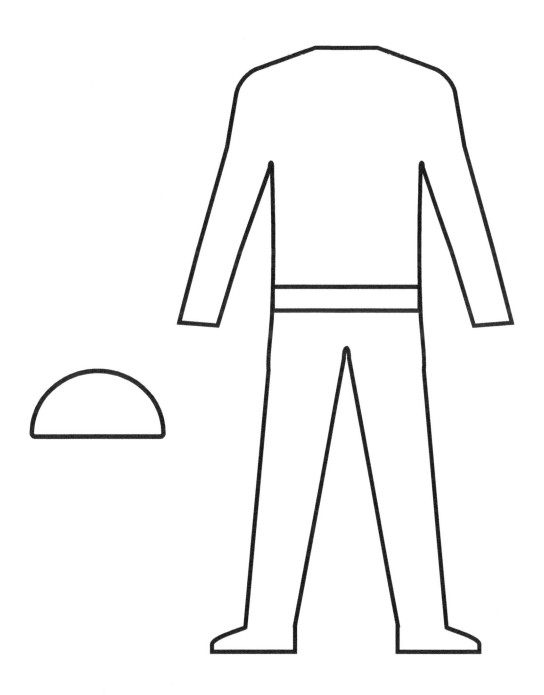

SCIENCE PROJECT: SAMSON'S GRASS HEAD

Materials:
- ☐ small plastic cup
- ☐ old pair of nylon stockings or knee-highs
- ☐ grass or alfalfa seeds
- ☐ potting soil
- ☐ googly eyes

Directions:

1. Cut a 10 in. section of the nylon stockings (make sure the toe is included).
2. Stretch the stocking over the opening to a glass or mug and spoon a teaspoon of the grass or alfalfa seeds into the stocking.
3. Fill the remainder with potting soil (to about a softball size).
4. Tie a knot to close the stocking.
5. This will be Samson's head. The excess fabric will go at the bottom and the top of his head will be where are seeds are located.
6. Make the nose and ears by pulling away small sections of the stocking/soil and twisting them into balls, two for the ears and one for the nose.
7. Cover the outside of the plastic cup with the brown material and hot glue into place.
8. Place the head, excess stocking side down, into the plastic cup container.
9. Use the hot glue gun to adhere googly eyes above Samson's nose.
10. Fashion eyebrows from the remaining brown fabric and hot glue into place.
11. Fashion lips from the red fabric and hot glue into place.
12. Dunk the head in a bowl of water and half fill the plastic cup with water. Make sure the excess stocking is sitting in the standing water in the plastic cup.
13. Place the Samson head in a window or somewhere where it will get plenty of light.
14. Check daily to make sure it stays moist.
15. It should begin to sprout in about a week. You will have enough hair for a haircut within 4 weeks.
16. Enjoy!

The science lesson here is on what plants need to grow. The student should be able to pinpoint water, sunlight, nutrients, and air as essential for the growth of the Samson head.

CHAPTER 16
The Prophet Samuel

At a time when the Philistines were at war with the Hebrews again, the Hebrews had been defeated in a battle. They decided to bring the Ark of the Covenant into the next battle, hoping this would prompt them to victory. But the plan failed and the enemy captured the Ark of the Covenant.

The Philistines, now in control of the Ark, placed it in front of a statue of their god, Dagon. The next day, Dagon lay face down on the ground. They put the statue back up, but the next day his head and hands had been cut off. Some of their people even became sick while the Ark was amongst them. So they sent it to another city, but people died there too. In fact, the Ark was moved from city to city with the same result until they finally decided to send it back to the Israelites, whom they had captured it from.

At that time, a prophet named Samuel told the Hebrews that the Ark of the Covenant was not a good luck charm and that God would indeed help them if only they just turned their hearts to him. So they repented and turned their hearts to God. The next time they were attacked by the Philistines, they were victorious. Eventually the Philistines stopped attacking altogether and peace came to the Hebrews.

When Samuel grew old, his sons took his place. However, they were not good men because they did not treat others fairly and took bribes. The elders asked Samuel to appoint someone new as king to govern Israel. Samuel prayed to God for guidance and God warned him that the Israelites were rejecting him as king by saying they wanted a human king. Samuel even told the people of God's warning, but they did not care. They still wanted a king. Eventually, God allowed it. That king would be a man named Saul.

QUESTIONS FOR REVIEW:

1. Why did the Hebrews think they needed to bring the Ark of the Covenant to battle?

2. What happened in the battle?

3. What did Saul warn the Hebrews about bringing the Ark into battle?

ACTIVITIES

CRAFT PROJECT: ARK OF THE COVENANT

Materials:
- ☐ Keurig coffee pod box
- ☐ Yellow or gold craft paint
- ☐ 4 Craft sticks
- ☐ Scissors
- ☐ Tape

Instructions:
1. With the box sitting oblong, put slits into the top four corners of the box. The slits need to be wide enough to insert the craft sticks.
2. Paint the box yellow or gold. Let dry.
3. Tape two of the craft sticks together to make one long one. Insert that into one side of the coffee box. Repeat with the other two craft sticks.
4. Enjoy the Ark of the Covenant!

WORD SEARCH: THE PROPHET SAMUEL

Find the following words.
Ark, Samuel, Prophet, Philistines, Hebrews, Dagon, Battle, Attack, Victorious

```
E X C K G C J H T P C P O Z Y
F V J J N M K S L H H R N W D
P H I L I S T I N E S O W E Y
A E F C H F I F B T G P Q A M
C N L Y T C H R Y A T H K R Y
G F K T P O E X D S T E C J P
A X V O T W R I X H A T A M T
Z J N Y S A W I U K B K T X D
U T I V F E B G O M B R T X L
A R K P U N U L Y U C F A Y P
G U J A E S V E B E S G V R T
I Z C Z L E U M A S H M Y Y I
V N K U O O Z D I Y W Q V W H
X K C W X N N N F W C I I B W
B O T F E U K O J U A D S R N
```

Note: Some words may appear backwards.

CHAPTER 17
King Saul and the Shepherd Boy David

Among the descendants of Jacob was a handsome man named Saul. He was out walking one day and met Samuel. The Lord had told Samuel that on this day he would meet the man who will become the king. And there he was! When Samuel saw Saul, he immediately knew this was the man who would rule the people. He invited Saul to his house, and the next day he anointed him with oil, kissed him, and told him he would be the king to rule over the Lord's people and save them from their enemies.

Saul was a good king and soldier. Since he had faith in God, the Israelites enjoyed many victories in battle. But soon Saul's heart turned from God. After one victorious battle, God had instructed him not to take any of the spoils of war, but Saul disobeyed, taking sheep and lamb, and whatever else he thought was valuable.

God told Samuel what Saul had done, but Saul denied doing anything wrong. Samuel said, "Why did you take the spoils of the battle when God had told you not to?"

Saul replied with a lie, saying, "I only took items with which to sacrifice to God and nothing else."

Samuel replied by telling Saul that the Lord cares more about obedience than sacrifice. "Because you rejected God, he now rejects you as king. The Lord has torn his kingdom from you this day and will give it to a more worthy king." Now Samuel had to find a new king who would rule the Israelites.

God told Samuel that the next king would come from the line of Jesse in Bethlehem. He arrived in the city and Jesse's seven sons lined up before him. But it wasn't until the youngest son, David, a shepherd boy, appeared that Samuel had found the next king. God told Samuel David would be the new king, so Samuel anointed him and from that day forward, God was with David.

During this time, Saul still thought of himself as king and acted as king. But he was starting to lose his mind. His servants had heard of a shepherd boy who also played the harp, and they thought the music might sooth him. David just so happened to be this boy who played the harp. So David came and played his harp for Saul, and Saul was happy. He grew to love David, but soon this love would become spoiled by envy and jealousy.

QUESTIONS FOR REVIEW:

1. How did Samuel know that he had met the man who was to become king?

2. What did Saul do to displease God?

3. How did the shepherd boy, David, help Saul?

ACTIVITIES

CRAFT PROJECT: DAVID'S HARP

Materials:
- ☐ Small rectangular piece of plywood (approximately 5 x 6 inches)
- ☐ Rubber bands or thread
- ☐ Scissors
- ☐ Nails
- ☐ Hammer

Instructions:
1. Hammer 4 nails into the board about ½ inch from the top, and ½ inch apart from each other.
2. On the bottom of the board, hammer 4 more nails in line with the top nails, but lower each nail about a ½ cm lower than the previous one. This will make the "strings" different lengths. This will allow you to play different sounding notes.
3. Cut the rubber bands or thread and tie/attach them to the nails so they are different lengths on the "harp."
4. Play the harp!

CHAPTER 18
David and Goliath

Again the Philistines sent their army to attack Saul, so the Israelites went out to meet them. A man named Goliath came out from the camp of the Philistines. He was a giant, over nine feet tall and weighing hundreds of pounds. He wore a helmet and thick armor made of bronze, and he wielded a large spear.

Goliath came into the valley and cried out, "Choose a man for yourselves, and let him come down to me. If he is able to fight with me and kill me, then we will be your servants; but if I prevail against him and kill him, then you shall be our servants and serve us."

When Saul and his army saw Goliath and heard his challenge, they were terrified. No soldier was brave enough to fight Goliath, even though Saul had offered his daughter in marriage to anyone who would slay him.

At this time, David's father sent him to the camp with food for his brothers stationed with the king's army. While David was there, Goliath came out into the valley between the camps and repeated his challenge. David quickly decided that he would fight Goliath. He told his brothers this and they laughed at him.

But David persisted and went to tell King Saul that he would fight the giant. Saul said, "You are not able to go against this Philistine to fight with him, for you are but a youth, and he has been a man of war."

"Your servant used to keep sheep for his father," David replied. "Your servant has killed both lions and bears; and this Philistine shall be like one of them, seeing he has defied the armies of the living God. The Lord delivered me from the hand of this Philistine."

Saul consented, saying, "Go, and the Lord be with you." Then he placed his own helmet and armor on David.

But David said, "I cannot go with these; for I am not used to them." Instead, he took a sling and five smooth stones, and he went out to meet the Philistine giant.

When Goliath saw David, such a tiny boy compared to his own massive stature, he laughed and cursed him. "Come to me," he shouted, "and I will give your flesh to the birds of the air and to the beasts of the field."

David answered the Philistine, "You come to me with a sword and with a spear and with a javelin; but I come to you in the name of the Lord of hosts, the God of the armies of Israel, whom you have defied. This day the Lord will deliver you into my hand, and I will strike you down, and cut off your head; that all the earth may know that there is a God in Israel, and that all this assembly may know that the Lord saves not with the sword and spear; for the battle is the Lord's and he will give you into our hand."

David then took his sling and whirled a stone at Goliath, striking him directly between the eyes and sending him tumbling to the ground. David ran up to the stunned giant, took his sword, and cut off his head.

The rest of the Philistines were shocked as they fled in terror. The Israelites pursued and killed many of them. When they returned from the pursuit, they sang the praises of David, who was now the nation's hero. Saul then became jealous of David for the praise he received. Even so, Saul insisted that David come live with the royal family in the palace.

QUESTIONS FOR REVIEW:

1. When David said he could fight Goliath, how did his brothers react?

2. How did David defeat Goliath?

3. When the Israelites praised David for his defeat of Goliath, what was Saul's reaction?

ACTIVITIES

CRAFT PROJECT: DAVID'S MARSHMALLOW SLINGSHOT

Materials:
- ☐ 2 empty toilet paper rolls
- ☐ 2 large rubber bands (do not need to be thick)
- ☐ pencil
- ☐ strong tape (such as duct tape)
- ☐ hole punch reinforcements
- ☐ mini marshmallows

Directions:

1. Cut the toilet paper roll in half lengthwise.

2. Roll half the toilet paper roll into a tight cylinder.

3. Completely wrap the cylinder with strong tape.

4. Make a small hole completely through the diameter of the cylinder and insert the pencil into this hole.

5. Cut the rubber band in half and attach to one end of the pencil.

6. Repeat with second rubber band and other side of the pencil.

7. Cut a 3"x 5" rectangular section from the remaining toilet paper roll and fold in half so that it now measures 1 1/2"x 2 1/2".

8. Place a small piece of duct tape to hold together the open side.

9. Hole punch each end and place hole punch reinforcements around the holes.

10. Attach the free ends of the rubber bands to the "pouch" and knot in place.

11. Load with marshmallows.

12. Enjoy!

COLORING PAGE: DAVID AND GOLIATH

CRAFT PROJECT: TOILET PAPER ROLL DAVID AND PAPER TOWEL ROLL GOLIATH

Materials:
☐ Templates below and on page 137
☐ coloring pencils
☐ craft glue
☐ scissors
☐ empty paper towel roll
☐ empty toilet paper roll

Directions:

1. Remove the templates from the Activity Book and color the David and Goliath figures.

2. For David, cut along the dotted lines to fit size of toilet paper roll.

3. For Goliath, just use the page as is. Minimal trimming or none at all should be needed.

3. Use craft glue to attach David and Goliath to the rolls.

4. Enjoy!

WORD SEARCH: DAVID

Find the following words.
Anointed, Armor, Bethlehem, David, God, Goliath, Harp, Helmet, Jonathan, King, Lord, Music, Philistine, Samuel, Saul, Servant, Sling, Spear, Stones, Sword

```
T  J  M  R  E  M  S  G  O  D  K  F
E  O  U  A  N  O  I  N  T  E  D  G
M  N  S  E  I  D  C  S  M  C  O  B
L  A  I  P  T  D  L  E  L  L  W  G
E  T  C  S  S  K  H  E  I  I  P  Y
H  H  I  C  I  E  I  A  U  A  N  X
K  A  N  H  L  D  T  N  S  M  D  G
D  N  A  H  I  H  T  E  G  N  A  E
G  R  T  A  H  T  N  A  V  R  E  S
P  E  O  D  P  O  D  A  V  I  D  G
B  J  Y  W  T  R  O  M  R  A  Y  J
L  U  A  S  S  L  O  R  D  O  Y  H
```

Note: Some words may appear backwards.

CHAPTER 19
David's Reign

Later on, Saul and his sons were caught and killed by the Philistines. When David became king, his army captured the city of Jerusalem from the Canaanites. He then made Jerusalem the capital city.

The next thing he did was retrieve the Ark of the Covenant to bring it into Jerusalem. Thinking himself unworthy and having great reverence for the Ark, he first offered sacrifices. Then David and the Israelites came dancing and singing into the city, celebrating the joyous return of the Ark of the Covenant. David went on to write and compose many songs, called the Psalms, and was a just king loved by the Israelites. The Lord blessed him.

It was not much later that David took interest in a woman named Bathsheba. But she was the wife of one of his soldiers, a man named Uriah. David yearned for her so badly that he would stop at nothing to make her his own. So David committed a grave sin. He gave orders for Uriah to be placed in the front line of battle. Then he commanded Uriah's fellow soldiers to fall back and leave him there alone to be killed. His devious plan worked: Uriah was killed, leaving Bathsheba free to marry David.

Seeing the evil that had infected David's heart, God sent Nathan, the prophet, to talk to him. Nathan approached David and told him a story.

"There were two men in a certain city," Nathan began, "the one rich and the other poor. The rich man had very many flocks and herds; but the poor man had nothing but one little ewe lamb, which he had bought. And he brought it up, and it grew up with him and with his children; it used to eat of his morsel, and drink from his cup, and lie in his bosom, and it was like a daughter to him. Now there came a traveler to the rich man, and he was unwilling to take one of his own flock or herd to prepare for the wayfarer who had come to him, but he took the poor man's lamb, and prepared it for the man who had come to him."

When David heard this, he was angry. He didn't realize the story was a fable that symbolized his own actions. David himself was the rich man who had come and stolen the poor man's lamb. Nathan replied, "You are the man. You have struck down Uriah with the sword, and have taken his wife to be your wife. Now therefore the sword shall never depart from your house."

In that moment, David realized the evil of his actions. "I have sinned against the Lord!" he exclaimed. When Nathan saw that David was sorry for his sins and asked God for forgiveness, he said to him, "The Lord has put away your sin; you shall not die. Nevertheless, because by this deed you have utterly scorned the Lord, the child that is born to you shall die."

Not long after, David and Bathsheba had a son. The child fell sick, and his life was in danger. David prayed and fasted, but on the seventh day, the baby died. This fulfilled the warning Nathan had given him. Yet some years later, a second son was then born to David and Bathsheba, whom they named Solomon. He was destined to succeed his father on the throne and to rule over the chosen people of God. We will learn more about Solomon in the next chapter.

QUESTIONS FOR REVIEW:

1. How did Jerusalem become the capital city?

2. What did David bring back into the city?

3. What was David's grave sin?

ACTIVITIES

MAZE: HELP DAVID BRING THE ARK BACK TO JERUSALEM

START

FINISH

COLORING PAGE: DAVID WITH HIS HARP

CRAFT PROJECT: KING DAVID'S CROWN

Materials:
- ☐ gold poster board
- ☐ stapler
- ☐ craft gems OR markers
- ☐ craft glue OR hot glue gun

Directions:

1. Cut a 5 in. strip lengthwise from the poster board.
2. Decorate by gluing gems to the crown or by using markers to create your own gems.
3. Fashion around child's head and staple to the appropriate size.
4. Enjoy!

CHAPTER 20
Solomon

When David eventually died, his son Solomon became king. He loved God and strived to follow all of the Commandments. God appeared to him in a dream and asked him what he would desire to have. Solomon told God that he wished he could be a better king to rule the people, so he asked for wisdom. God was pleased that Solomon had not asked for great wealth or a long life, so not only did he grant him the wisdom that he desired, but God also gave him great wealth and a long life as well.

The wisdom he received from God was put to good use. One day two women came to Solomon to settle a dispute. Both of them had infants about the same age. In the middle of the night, the baby that belonged to one of them died. The mother of the dead child took the living child and left the other in its place. The next morning, the other woman discovered what had happened and demanded that her living child be given back to her.

Both women argued in front of the king, exclaiming that the living child was her own. Solomon then asked for a sword in order to cut the child in half and give half to each woman. When the true mother heard this command, she cried out "Give her the living child, and by no means slay it!" But the other woman said, "It shall be neither mine nor yours; divide it."

Solomon knew at once which woman was telling the truth. The true mother was willing to give up her child to the other woman rather than see it die. But the other woman was content to see both children dead. So Solomon commanded to give the living child to the true mother. This was one of many wise actions of Solomon.

Other than his wisdom, King Solomon was known for overseeing the construction of a grand temple where the Ark of the Covenant would be housed, and where the Israelites could worship God. It took many years to finish the temple, and when it was complete, it was adorned in gold and the walls smelled of beautiful cedar wood. The Ark of the Covenant, containing the Ten Commandments, was brought in, Solomon blessed the people, and a great celebration that lasted for seven days began.

Solomon had a long and peaceful reign for many years. It was this reign of peace that made his days the golden age of the kingdom of Israel. But eventually his heart was corrupted. He built a large palace and had many other expenses. To pay for these, he taxed the people unfair amounts. He also married women from foreign countries and built temples to their false gods to please him. God saw how Solomon had turned away from him and so decided that the next king would not come from his lineage.

QUESTIONS FOR REVIEW:

1. When God asked Solomon what he desired, what did he ask for and what did he receive?

2. How did Solomon decide the case of the two women who claimed the same child?

3. In what ways did Solomon turn from God?

ACTIVITIES

SNACK PROJECT: KING SOLOMON'S TEMPLE RICE KRISPIE TREAT

Ingredients:
- ☐ Rice Krispie bars already prepared
- ☐ Canned frosting
- ☐ Small, thin pretzel rods

Instructions:
1. Cut the Rice Krispie bars into squares.
2. Stack the squares into a cube to make the temple, leaving a space for the doorway.
3. Put frosting all around the "temple."
4. Attach small pretzel rods all around the "temple" to serve as columns.
5. Enjoy!

CROSSWORD: KING SOLOMON

Across

3. David's son
4. The Temple was adorned in _____.
6. To pay for his palace, Solomon _____ the people unfair amounts.
9. Was held inside the Ark

Down

1. Solomon's heart eventually became _____.
2. The Temple housed the Ark of the _____.
5. God appeared to Solomon in a _____.
6. Solomon asked God for _____ to govern his people well.
8. Solomon helped oversee the construction of the _____.

COLORING PAGE: KING SOLOMON AND THE TEMPLE

CHAPTER 21
Jeroboam and Rehoboam

After the death of Solomon, his son, Rehoboam, went to Shechem, where he hoped to be anointed king. The people told him that they would only recognize him as their king if the taxes his father had imposed on them were reduced. But instead of lightening their taxes, he decided to increase them! This led the people to revolt. Rehoboam sent his servant to calm them, but they stoned him to death.

Rehoboam, realizing that his life was in danger, fled to Jerusalem. He intended to raise an army and force the rebels to obey him. But the voice of God came to the prophet Shemaiah, telling Rehoboam that he was not to attack. So Rehoboam, fearing the Lord, obeyed the prophet's warning.

The tribes of Judah and Benjamin remained loyal to Rehoboam. But the other ten tribes chose as their king Jeroboam, the leader of the rebellion against Solomon. The Levites aligned themselves with Rehoboam when they saw that Jeroboam was leading his people into idolatry, worshipping false gods.

Jeroboam would not allow the people of his ten tribes to worship in the Temple at Jerusalem. He set up a golden calf in each of them, much like the golden calf that the Israelites had worshipped in the wilderness many years before.

To recruit priests for this idolatrous worship, Jeroboam allowed any man to fulfill the role if he could provide a young bull and seven rams for sacrifice. In addition, the king allowed altars to be built to false gods throughout his kingdom.

One day Jeroboam was worshipping the golden calf at Bethel when a prophet from the kingdom of Judah prophesied to him. The prophet foretold that a future king, Josiah, would burn the false priests of Jeroboam on an altar, and that a sign would occur to let the people know this prophecy had been fulfilled. The prophet also said that the altar of worship was about to be broken, and the ashes would be scattered about on the ground.

When he heard these threatening words, Jeroboam called for his men to take the prophet captive. Suddenly, the hand with which he was pointing became withered, the altar was broken in two, and the ashes were scattered on the ground. Jeroboam was terrified and asked the prophet to pray on his behalf. The prophet did so, and Jeroboam's hand was healed.

Later, Jeroboam's son became very ill. Jeroboam sent his wife to see the prophet Ahijah in Shiloh, to inquire about their son's health. But he told her to disguise herself so the prophet wouldn't know she was the queen.

When she knocked at his door, God told the prophet who she was, that she was the queen and the wife of Jeroboam, and that she had come to ask about her sick son. So the prophet saw right past her disguise and addressed her as the wife of Jeroboam.

He gave her a message to deliver to her husband. "Thus says the Lord, the God of Israel: 'I made you leader over my people Israel, and tore the kingdom away from the house of David and gave it to you; and yet you have not been like my servant David, who kept my commandments, but you have done evil above all that were before you and have gone and made for yourself other gods, and molten images, provoking me to anger, and have cast me behind your back; therefore behold, I will bring evil on the house of Jeroboam.'"

The prophet reported that Jeroboam would be rooted out of the land, and his son would die. The Kingdom of Israel would be overthrown by the Assyrians, who would lead the people into captivity. The queen left frightened and returned to her city to find that her son had died, just as Ahijah had prophesied.

For three years, Rehoboam remained a just and God-fearing ruler. But eventually he followed evil advice and built altars to pagan gods in various parts of the kingdom. Rehoboam set an example of idolatry, just as Jeroboam had done, and the people followed it. Because of this idolatry, God permitted the Pharaoh of Egypt at that time to invade the Kingdom of Judah.

QUESTIONS FOR REVIEW:

1. What did Rehoboam do to provoke a rebellion against his rule?

2. Why did Jeroboam's hand wither?

3. How did the prophet Ahijah know that the disguised woman was really the queen? What did he tell her?

ACTIVITIES

MAP ACTIVITY: JEROBOAM AND REHOBOAM

(map located on next page)

1. Locate the cities of Shechem and Jerusalem and, using a red pencil, draw a line between the two cities to show that Rehoboam went to Shechem to be anointed king, but because of his foolishness and arrogance he instead had to flee to Jerusalem to avoid being killed.
2. Now shade the land of Judah, the land Rehoboam ruled, in red.
3. Locate the land of Israel, the land Jeroboam ruled, and shade it blue.
4. Note that the kingdom that was united under David and Solomon became divided.

THE DIVIDED KINGDOM OF ISRAEL AND JUDAH

Damascus

Sidon

PHOENICIA

Tyre

Dan

KINGDOM OF DAMASCUS

Sea of Galilee

MEDITERRANEAN SEA

Samaria

ISRAEL

Shechem

Jordan River

Joppa

Bethel

PHILISTIA

AMMON

Gaza

Jerusalem

Dead Sea

Beersheba

MOAB

JUDAH

King's Highway

EGYPT

JUDAH

EGYPT

EDOM

Kadesh Barnea

Elat

Ezion Geber

© 2014 Good Will Publishers, Inc

WORD SEARCH: JEROBOAM AND REHOBOAM

Jeroboam and Rehoboam Word Search Clues

1. Solomon's son.
2. The city where Solomon's son hoped to be anointed king.
3. The people demanded their _____ be reduced.
4. Rehoboam fled to Jerusalem in his _____.
5. The leader in the rebellion against Solomon.
6. The people following Jeroboam were worshiping _____ gods.
7. The name of the Southern Kingdom.
8. The name of the Northern Kingdom.
9. Jeroboam did not allow his people to worship at the _____ of Jerusalem.
10. Jeroboam built two new temples each containing a _____ calf.
11. The prophet reported to Jeroboam that Israel would fall to the _____.

(word search located on next page)

```
L  E  A  R  S  I  D  F  S  W  N  J
R  V  Y  S  B  P  E  N  S  C  E  S
R  E  H  O  B  O  A  M  H  I  D  E
B  B  J  L  V  I  Q  A  E  C  L  I
G  J  H  U  R  E  R  Y  C  V  O  X
Z  V  E  Y  D  I  L  G  H  R  G  X
U  O  S  R  O  A  S  P  E  K  W  N
S  S  D  T  O  E  H  M  M  O  E  E
A  G  Q  V  X  B  U  D  J  E  Z  T
C  Z  T  A  Q  E  O  U  O  W  T  R
E  D  T  H  N  O  H  A  Y  D  D  Q
F  A  L  S  E  D  G  Z  M  U  Q  C
```

Note: Some words may appear backwards.

If you have trouble figuring out the words from your clues, see if you can find the words from this list:
Assyrians, Chariot, False, Golden, Israel, Jeroboam, Judah, Rehoboam, Shechem, Taxes, Temple

CHAPTER 22
Elijah the Prophet

After the death of Jeroboam, a man named Ahab eventually became king. He was wicked, building in Samaria a temple to the pagan god Baal.

God then sent to the king a man named Elijah, a prophet and a brave and fearless man. The prophet told Ahab that because of his sins of idolatry, the land would suffer a great drought. For three years no rain would fall.

After Elijah had foretold the drought, God directed him to go to the brook called Cherith. "You shall drink from the brook," God told him, "and I have commanded the ravens to feed you there."

So the prophet went there, and each morning and evening a raven would bring him bread and meat to eat.

But soon the brook dried up, for just as Elijah himself had predicted, a drought had begun to plague the land. God then directed him to go a city near Sidon, where a widow would feed him. When Elijah came to the gate of the city, he called to her and said, "Bring me a little water in a vessel and a morsel of bread."

But the woman told Elijah that she had no food to spare. She barely had enough to feed her son and herself. She told him that soon they would die of starvation.

Elijah told the woman not to be afraid. She should still share whatever food she had with him, because the Lord would maintain their food supply until the drought was over. She went and did as Elijah had said, and from that day forward until the end of the famine, her food supply remained steady.

One day, however, the son of the widow became ill and died. She shouted at Elijah, "What have you against me, O man of God?"

Elijah was grateful to the woman who had fed him and was sad over her son's death. He took the boy away from her and begged God to bring him back to life. The Lord heard Elijah's prayer, and he raised the boy from the dead.

Because of the drought, Ahab wanted to kill Elijah, but he could not find him.

In the third year of the drought, God said to Elijah, "Go, show yourself to Ahab; and I will send rain upon the earth."

When the two of them met, Elijah told Ahab to gather the people of Israel together at Mount Carmel, including the priests of the false god Baal. Ahab did so, and when the people assembled, Elijah spoke to them, hoping to lead them back to the one true God.

"If the Lord is God, follow him; but if Baal, then follow him."

Elijah went on. "Let two bulls be given to us; and let them choose one bull for themselves, and cut it in pieces and lay it on the wood, but put no fire to it; and I will prepare the other bull and lay it on the wood, and put no fire to it. And you call on the name of your god and I will call on the name of the Lord; and the God who answers by fire, he is God."

The people were willing to make this test of their god, to see which bull would be consumed by fire: the bull of Baal or the bull of the true God. So the prophets of Baal called on the name of Baal from morning till noon, begging for fire, even leaping over the altar they had made. But it was all in vain; there was no answer.

At noon, with the sun high in the sky, Elijah mocked them. So they cried out even louder, egged on by his taunts, and cut themselves with their knives till they were covered with blood. But no answer came to their prayers.

Then Elijah said to the people, "Come near to me." So the people approached him.

He built an altar to the Lord with twelve stones, one for each of the twelve tribes of Israel. Then he made a trench for water. He placed his bull on the wood and he had twelve buckets of water poured over the bull. The water ran around the altar and filled the trench.

When it was time to offer the sacrifice, Elijah came near to the altar and said, "O Lord, God of Abraham, Isaac, and Israel, let it be known this day that you are God in Israel, and that I am your servant, and that I have done all these things at your word. Answer me, O Lord, answer me, that this people may know that you, O Lord, are God, and that you have turned their hearts back."

At that moment, the fire of the Lord fell and consumed the offering. The fire was so great that it even dried up the water in the trench! When all the people saw this, they fell on their faces and cried, "The Lord, he is God; the Lord, he is God."

QUESTIONS FOR REVIEW:

1. What did the prophet Elijah tell Ahad would happen because of his idolatry?

2. What did Elijah do when the widow's son died?

3. How did the people come to believe that God was the one true God and not Baal?

ACTIVITIES

COLORING PAGE: ELIJAH BEGGING GOD

COLORING PAGE: THE FIRE OF GOD FROM HEAVEN

ELIJAH FINDS THE WIDOW MAZE

Help Elijah find the widow who takes him in and feeds him.

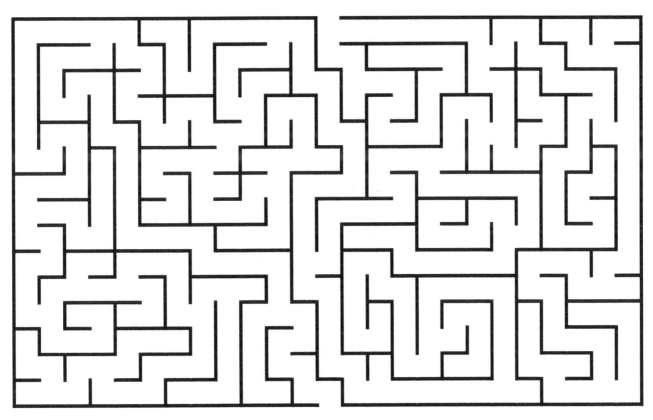

CRAFT PROJECT: PAPER PLATE RAVEN

Materials:

- ☐ 3 paper plates
- ☐ black marker
- ☐ scissors
- ☐ stapler
- ☐ googly eyes
- ☐ yellow construction paper
- ☐ black construction paper
- ☐ metal round paper fasteners

Directions:

1. Color all 3 paper plates black.
2. Leave one plate full size, cut the center circle from one of the plates and discard the outer ring, and cut the third plate in half.
3. The full size plate is the body of the raven.
4. Staple the small inner circle to the top of the full size plate. This small circle will be the head of the raven.
5. Use brackets to attach the half plates to the sides of the full size plate. These are the wings of the raven.
6. Cut a triangle that is 2 in. on each side out of the yellow construction paper. Glue onto the head of the raven so that one point faces down.
7. Glue the googly eyes above the triangle.
8. Use the black construction paper to fashion two feet for the raven. These can be small triangles with the point stapled to the body.
9. Use extra black construction paper to cut "feathers" to be stapled on top of the raven's head.
10. Enjoy!

CRAFT PROJECT: ALTAR AT BAAL PROVING GOD IS THE ONE TRUE GOD

Materials:
- ☐ white construction paper
- ☐ brown construction paper
- ☐ blue marker
- ☐ orange and yellow tissue OR construction paper
- ☐ craft or popsicle sticks cut into 3 in. segments.
- ☐ craft glue

Directions:

1. The white construction paper is the background for the altar.

2. Cut the brown construction paper into 12 rock-like shapes.

3. Paste the rocks in a pyramid formation hallway up the pieces of white construction paper.

4. Take the 3 in. segments of popsicle or craft sticks and paste them like logs on top of the rocks.

5. Draw a trench of blue water along the base of the altar.

6. Add small squares of crumpled tissue paper or construction paper and paste them to be the flames on top of the altar built to God.

SNACK PROJECT: THE RAVEN BRINGS BREAD AND MEAT

Ingredients:
- ☐ bread (any type desired)
- ☐ deli meat (any type desired)

Directions:

Today is a great day for a deli sandwich for lunch with a discussion of how the ravens were commanded by God to feed Elijah bread and meat at the brook.

CHAPTER 23
The Story of Job

Job was a holy and wealthy man from the land of Uz. He lived in a house with his seven sons and three daughters. He had many servants and owned sheep, camels, oxen, and donkeys.

On a certain day, when the angels came to stand before God, Satan was present among them. The Lord said to Satan, "Have you considered my servant Job, that there is none like him on the earth, a blameless and upright man, who fears God and turns away from evil?"

Satan answered the Lord claiming that Job loved God only because he was a blessed man. The Lord then agreed to let Satan test Job, but told him not to kill him. So Satan left the presence of the Lord and set his sights on Job.

Great disasters then came upon Job. One day, a servant came to Job to tell him that raiders had rushed into the fields where his oxen were plowing and taken them all away. Then, the raiders had killed all the servants, except this one messenger who had escaped.

While this servant was speaking, another servant came to tell him that lightning from the sky had killed all his sheep and the servants who were tending them. Only this one servant had escaped to tell Job about it.

While he was speaking, yet another servant came to say that more hostile men had come and taken Job's camels away. They had killed the servants, except for this one servant who had gotten away.

While he was speaking, still another servant came in and told Job that a violent wind had shaken the house of his eldest son, where his sons and daughters were feasting. The house fell on his children and killed them all. Only this one servant had managed to get out before the house collapsed.

In that brief span, Job had lost his oxen, sheep, camels, dozens of servants, and most importantly, his children, but he did not sin or blame God.

Meanwhile, Satan returned to stand before God. God said to him, "Have you considered my servant Job, that there is none like him on the earth, one who fears God and turns away from evil? He still holds fast his integrity, although you moved me against him."

Satan answered, "All that a man has he will give for his life. But put forth your hand now, and touch his bone and his flesh, and he will curse you to your face."

The Lord said to Satan, "He is in your power; only spare his life."

So Satan went forth with plans to destroy Job's health. He struck him with ulcers that covered him from the sole of his foot to the top of his head. Job was in terrible pain, but he didn't blame God. Job's wife ridiculed him because he actually blessed God in his suffering.

But Job pointed out that up until now, they had received many blessings from the Lord. So why shouldn't they accept these hardships as well? He famously said, "Naked I came from my mother's womb, and naked I shall return." Meaning, he came into the world with nothing that was not from God, and that is how he would return to God at the end of his days. Everything he had came from God.

Job cried out in sorrow and pain, and his friends came to him. But instead of consoling him, they rebuked him and told him he was being punished for his sins. But Job knew that this was no punishment. He told his friends that even though he suffered, he still trusted in God.

In the end, Job held tightly to his love and faith in God. Job pleased God by his patience in suffering. So the Lord rewarded him. He restored Job's health and doubled his wealth, and gave him seven more sons and three more daughters.

QUESTIONS FOR REVIEW:

1. What were some of the things that Job lost as part of his trials?

2. How did Job please God?

3. How did the Lord reward Job?

ACTIVITIES

SNACK PROJECT: CANDY TRIALS OF JOB

Ingredient:
☐ bag of candy-coated chocolates or other favorite candy

Directions:

1. Begin your story of trials of Job with, "Job found favor with God and received many blessings from him. Job was healthy and happy and glorified God." **Place 2 candies before the child.**

2. "Job lived in a house built of stone with his seven sons and three daughters." **Place 10 candies before the child.**

3. "He had many servants to wait on him." **Place another 10 candies before the child.**

4. "He owned seven thousand sheep, three thousand camels, five hundred yoke of oxen, and five hundred donkeys." **Place 7, then 3 more, then 5 more, then 5 more candies before the child.**

5. "God allowed Satan to test Job. Job lost all of his livestock." **Take away 20 of the candies.**

6. Continue, "Job lost all of his servants." **Take away 10 more candies.**

7. "Job lost all of his children." **Take away another 10 of the child's candies.**

8. "Then Satan took away Job's health. Job was filled with sorrow and pain." **Take away the last 2 candies.**

9. **Place all of the candies out of sight.**

10. "Job was ridiculed by his wife and friends and told his troubles were a punishment. Still, Job told his friends that even though he suffered greatly, he still trusted in God. In the end, Job held tightly to his love and faith in God. Job pleased God by his patience in suffering. So the Lord showed that He was pleased with him by rewarding him. He restored Job's health and doubled his wealth, and Job had seven more sons and three more daughters." **Give back the candies in handfuls showing that God gave abundantly to Job because of his trust in Him.**

CROSSWORD: JOB

Across

3. What killed Job's sheep.
4. Job's friends told him he was being _____ for his sins.
5. A holy and wealthy man from the land of Uz.
7. Satan claimed Job only loved God because he was a _____ man.
8. God _____ Job by doubling his wealth and giving him seven more sons and three more daughters.

Down

1. After destroying Job's flocks and his family, Satan tried to destroy Job's _____.
2. Satan set his sights on Job and great _____ came upon him.
4. God was pleased with Job's _____ in suffering.
6. Job did not _____ God for all the hardships.
8. "Naked I came from my mother's womb, and naked I shall _____."

SCIENCE PROJECT: SATAN TRIES TO PULL JOB IN

Materials:
- ☐ glass Erlenmeyer flask OR glass bottle with the opening smaller than body of the bottle
- ☐ water
- ☐ water balloon
- ☐ match
- ☐ scrap of paper

WARNING!
This experiment uses fire. Children should be supervised closely to avoid injury.

Directions:

1. Fill the water balloon with water to where it is slightly larger than the opening to the glass.
2. Light the paper on fire and place it in the bottom of the glass.
3. Place the balloon on top and steady it with your hand (while the flame is still lit the balloon will wobble as air is escaping around the sides of the balloon).
4. When the flame goes out, the balloon will be sucked into the flask.
5. To get the balloon out, blow into the glass. This will force the balloon to begin to come out of the opening. You can pull it out the remainder of the way.

In this lesson, the balloon is Job and the flame is Satan. Job does not allow the flame to tempt him. He does not allow the flame to burn in his life. Therefore he can rest easily on top of the glass bottle. If, however, he were to allow the temptation to take root in his life, it would push him in as the balloon is pushed into the glass bottle. Once inside, it's very difficult to get back out. We need to blow on the bottle in order to get the balloon back out (this represents God's help).

The physics behind this experiment: Warmer air takes up more space than cooler air. Once the fire is out, the air cools rapidly, thus condensing. This makes the atmospheric pressure outside the bottle greater than that inside the bottle. The balloon is therefore pushed inside the bottle.

CHAPTER 24
Jonah

Nineveh was the great city of the Assyrians. Its inhabitants worshiped false gods, and they were brutal and wicked.

One day, the Lord spoke to Jonah, a prophet. "Go to Nineveh, that great city, and cry against it," God commanded; "for their wickedness has come up before me."

But Jonah was afraid of the cruel Assyrians. So he tried to flee from God's presence. He boarded a ship in Joppa that was bound for a city located in the opposite direction.

The Lord knew exactly were Jonah was. So he sent a great storm across the sea, and the ship was in danger of being destroyed. The men cried out to their gods for help.

The shipmaster found Jonah fast asleep. He woke him and told him to get out of bed. "Call upon your god!" he insisted. "Perhaps the god will give a thought to us, that we do not perish!"

Jonah finally admitted that God had sent the storm because of the prophet's disobedience. He said, "Take me up and throw me into the sea; then the sea will quiet down for you; for I know it is because of me that this great tempest has come upon you."

The crew was reluctant to throw Jonah overboard. But the storm only grew fiercer, threatening to drown them all. So at last they did as Jonah had told them. They cast him into the sea—and the sea became calm.

The Lord then sent a great fish to swallow Jonah, and Jonah remained in the belly of the fish for three days and three nights. He prayed to the Lord to be rescued, and God caused the fish to cast him up on the shore.

A second time God spoke to Jonah. "Go to Nineveh, that great city," he instructed, "and proclaim to it the message that I tell you."

This time Jonah obeyed. He went to Nineveh as the Lord had instructed him. When he entered the city, he cried out, "Yet forty days, and Nineveh shall be overthrown!"

The people of Nineveh believed that Jonah was a messenger from God. They began a great fast to show that they were sorry for their wickedness. The king and all the people, from the greatest to the least, put on sackcloth (clothing that makes you itch) and did penance. They even put sackcloth on their animals! When God saw that they wanted to repent and change their ways, he had mercy and spared them.

QUESTIONS FOR REVIEW:

1. Why did God send Jonah to Nineveh? Why did Jonah head the opposite direction?

2. Why was Jonah thrown from the sea? How was he saved from the sea?

3. What did the people of Nineveh do in response to the Jonah's preaching?

ACTIVITIES

MAP ACTIVITY: JONAH DISOBEYS GOD

(Map located on next page)

Directions:

1. Locate Joppa on the map. In blue draw a line from Joppa out into the Mediterranean Sea.

2. Draw a whale in the middle of the Mediterranean Sea to indicate that Jonah was thrown overboard and swallowed by the whale.

3. Using blue, draw a line from the whale back to shore.

4. Now use yellow to draw a line from here to Nineveh. This shows that Jonah finally did what God asked of him.

MAP ACTIVITY: JONAH DISOBEYS GOD

COLORING PAGE: JONAH AND THE WHALE

CRAFT PROJECT: STYROFOAM CUP WHALE

Materials:

- ☐ styrofoam cup
- ☐ blue paint
- ☐ silver OR white pipe cleaner
- ☐ googly eyes
- ☐ stapler
- ☐ craft glue OR hot glue gun
- ☐ Lego figure or other small "man" figure
- ☐ Template from page 177

Directions:

1. Cut a small hole in the bottom of the cup (the pipe cleaner will thread through here).
2. Paint the entire cup blue.
3. Cut pipe cleaner into 6 in. segments and thread through the hole.
4. Set the cup face down on a hard surface (the rim of the cup is on the surface and the bottom of the cup is in the air with the pipe cleaner coming out of it).
5. Bend the pipe cleaner at the ends (this is the spray coming from the whale's spout).
6. Cut 2 fins and 1 tail out of blue construction paper to fit the size of the cup you are using. Staple the fins to the bottom sides of the whale and the tail to the back. Cut a mouth out of red construction paper and glue onto the cup.
7. Glue on the googly eyes.
9. Place the "man" figure under the whale.
10. Enjoy!

SNACK PROJECT: GOLDFISH CRACKERS

Today is a great day to have goldfish crackers alongside your Jonah and the whale craft.

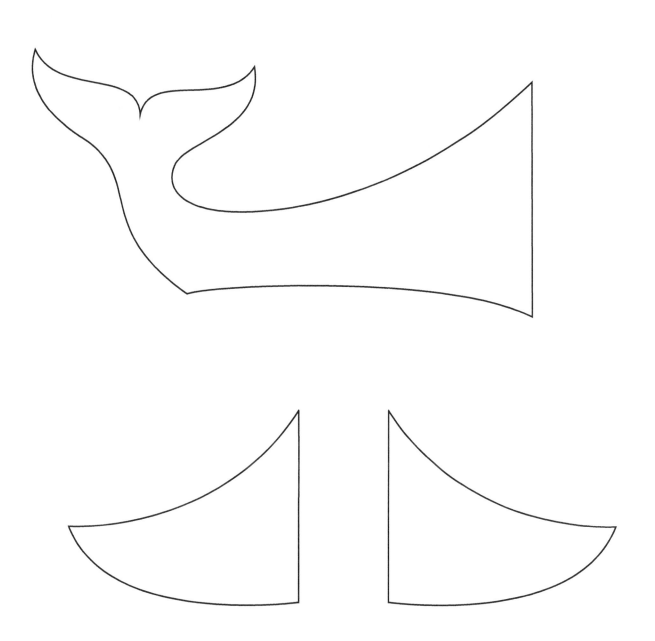

CHAPTER 25
Tobit

Tobit was an upright man who obeyed the Law of Moses. When a cruel king had put several prisoners to death, Tobit took the time to bury them. Tobit was always doing kind acts like this. The king did not like his acts of charity, and so ordered Tobit to be put to death. Tobit went into hiding until that king died.

Under the new king, the Israelites enjoyed more liberty and freedom. Tobit returned and was able to live a normal life again, continuing with his works of charity. One night, after a hard day of labor, he lay on the ground beside the wall of his courtyard, and there he rested.

While he was lying there, the droppings from birds sitting above him on a wall fell into his eyes and blinded him. As a blind man, he was unable to work as he had before, so he became poor. His family's only income was from the work his wife did as a weaver of cloth.

Toward the end of his life, when Tobit believed that death was near, he called for his son, Tobias. Then he gave him these words of wisdom: "My son, when I die, bury me, and do not neglect your mother. Honor her all the days of your life; do what is pleasing to her, and do not grieve her."

"If you have many possessions, make your gift from them in proportion; if few, do not be afraid to give according to the little you have. . . . Practice charity, for it is an excellent offering in the presence of the Most High."

After saying this, Tobit thought of some money he had let a friend borrow many years ago when he had been rich and before he went blind. The friend's name was Gabael and he lived in the city of Rages. Tobit told his son to seek out a faithful man as a companion to go with him to collect the debt from Gabael.

Young Tobias prepared for the journey, but before leaving, he followed his father's advice to seek out a faithful man to join him. He found a young stranger in the city and requested his services as a guide. The man agreed, and they set out on the journey together.

On the way, they came to a river. Tobias went to wash his feet, and as he did, a monstrous fish leapt out of the water to devour him. His companion told him to catch the fish by the gills and pull it ashore. Then he instructed him to cut out the heart, the gall, and the liver, and to save them for medicine. When Tobias asked his guide what they were good for, the guide told him that the gall was good for anointing and curing eyes.

Tobias was led by his guide to a distant relative, whose daughter, Sarah, he married. Sarah's father gave her and Tobias, as a wedding present, one half of his property, with the promise that they would inherit the rest when he died. The wedding feast lasted two weeks. Tobias was unable to leave, for it wouldn't have been right to abandon his bride. So the guide set out alone to collect the debt from Gabael. When Tobias and Sarah finally departed, Tobias recalled that the guide had claimed the gall they retrieved from the fish was good for anointing and curing eyes. So Tobias ran to his blind father and placed the gall in his eyes.

Tobit immediately recovered his sight!

When Tobit and his son sought to pay the guide for his great services, he revealed his identity. The guide said, "I am Raphael, one of the seven holy angels who present the prayers of the saints and enter into the presence of the glory of the Lord."

After prophesying about events to come, the old man Tobit died at a good old age.

QUESTIONS FOR REVIEW:

1. Why did Tobit go into hiding?

2. What happened to Tobit's eyes and how did this affect him?

3. Who was disguised as the guide that accompanied Tobit's son and what did the guide do?

ACTIVITIES

COLORING PAGE: RAPHAEL, TOBIT, AND TOBIT'S SON

CRAFT: PAPER PLATE ANGEL RAPHAEL

Materials:
- ☐ White paper plate
- ☐ White scrap sheet of paper
- ☐ Scissors
- ☐ Glue
- ☐ Yellow marker or yellow glitter
- ☐ Black marker

Instructions:
1. Cut out a one quarter section of the paper plate into a wedge shape by cutting toward the center of the paper plate.
2. Cut out a small circle from your scrap sheet of paper. This is the angel's head. Draw a face with the black marker.
3. Glue the circle face to the tip of the wedge you cut out, creating the angel's gown below her head.
4. Glue the angel to his "wings" (the plate with the wedge cut out).
5. Decorate with the yellow marker or glue and glitter.

WORD SEARCH: TOBIT AND TOBIAS

Find the following words.

Tobit, Tobias, Raphael, Hiding, Israelites, Charity, Gabael, Sarah, Journey

```
Q  L  P  T  G  X  P  V  C  W  S  K  A  T  W
G  N  I  D  I  H  A  L  Q  H  C  P  F  I  F
C  M  H  E  W  M  P  Q  E  V  A  X  O  B  D
J  A  G  B  K  I  L  O  X  A  Y  R  H  O  Y
O  I  R  A  P  H  A  E  L  F  B  S  I  T  I
U  W  Z  D  D  R  V  U  S  X  E  A  V  T  A
R  P  Q  O  P  W  Z  H  E  T  X  V  G  J  Y
N  M  X  M  H  N  Q  P  I  Y  V  D  C  Y  Q
E  M  Y  A  V  T  V  L  R  Q  G  G  L  F  F
Y  T  R  C  O  B  E  L  X  K  F  Z  K  U  R
A  A  O  B  W  A  Y  W  C  B  D  L  E  N  W
S  U  I  O  R  N  Y  V  E  R  Q  N  Z  U  X
F  A  W  S  T  I  B  Y  U  R  C  C  W  G  D
S  R  I  J  F  C  P  E  G  T  O  T  I  I  P
Q  E  T  T  C  D  X  G  E  N  F  O  W  Q  L
```

Note: Some words may appear backwards.

CHAPTER 26
Judith

A man named Holofernes, an Assyrian general, had an enormous army of one hundred and twenty thousand footmen and twenty-thousand horsemen. Once, it happened that he attacked the city of Bethulia. The people defended the city bravely, but when the Assyrians cut off their water supply, they begged their leader to surrender. They could not survive without their water, so they held a council of war and decided that if no help came within five days, they would give up the city.

Suddenly, a woman spoke up to rebuke the elders of the city for putting a time limit on the power of God. She was angered that they would test God this way. Her name was Judith, a rich, beautiful, and virtuous widow of the city of Bethulia.

Judith promised to put an end to the battle. She prayed for success and then set out to visit the Assyrian camp. She was brought before the general Holofernes.

Judith told him that she fled from the city to escape the inevitable attack of his cruel soldiers. Instead of being a victim of his attack, she wanted to flee and find him, and tell him the best routes into the city where he could overcome them without losing a single soldier. Holofernes was pleased with her and gave her maid's a tent.

Four days later, Holofernes hosted a great feast for his officers and invited Judith. At the feast, Holofernes became drunk with wine and fell into a deep sleep. The officers left him alone in his tent. Judith then took the sword of Holofernes, cut off his head, hid it in a pouch, and hurried to Bethulia.

When she returned, the people were shocked at her bravery and welcomed her with great joy. At daybreak, the soldiers of the town attacked the Assyrians. But the enemy was panic-stricken when they discovered that their leader had been killed in the night. So they fled to the hills, and the people of Judah followed them and defeated the invaders.

QUESTIONS FOR REVIEW:

1. Why did Judith feel the need to speak out to the elders?

2. After Judith promised to put an end to the battle herself, what did she do?

3. How did her own people welcome her home?

ACTIVITIES

COLORING PAGE: JUDITH

MAZE: HELP JUDITH FIND HER WAY TO ATTACK HOLOFERNES

START

FINISH

CRAFT PROJECT: JUDITH'S SWORD

Materials:
- ☐ empty wrapping paper tube
- ☐ 9 in. by 3 in. strip of cardboard
- ☐ aluminum foil
- ☐ scissors
- ☐ markers
- ☐ craft jewels (if desired)
- ☐ hot glue (if using craft jewels)

Directions:

1. Flatten one end of the wrapping paper tube and shape to be the point of the sword.

2. Cut a hole in both ends of the 9 in. x 3 in. cardboard piece. The hole should be just large enough to slip over the end of the wrapping paper tube.

3. Slip both holes onto the end of the wrapping paper tube that hasn't been flattened. This will be the hilt for the sword.

4. Cover the sword and hilt with aluminum foil.

5. Color with markers if desired.

6. Hot glue jewels onto hilt of sword if desired.

7. Enjoy!

DRAWING ACTIVITY: JUDITH

Instructions: Practice your drawing by copying the coloring page from earlier in this chapter. Then, under your drawing of Judith, write a sentence or two that you remember from her story.

CHAPTER 27
The Babylonian Captivity

Egypt and Babylonia were now at war with each other. In Judah, the people were divided: One group favored Egypt, while the other favored Babylonia. Jehoiakim was king at the time, and Jeremiah, the priest and prophet, warned him to obey God and to trust in him rather than trust in an alliance with the king of Egypt.

Jeremiah prophesied the evils that would come to the people of Judah if they relied on Egypt. Since Jehoiakim favored the Egyptians, he ordered Jeremiah's arrest. The prophet was imprisoned several times.

But Jeremiah's enemies could not silence him as he spoke God's message to the people. His words were soon fulfilled.

Nebuchadnezzar, son of the king of Babylon, attacked Jerusalem because of its alliance with Egypt. He captured the city and took many of the men there as captives. He carried off the sacred vessels of the Temple and put King Jehoiakim in prison. After a short time in prison, Jehoiakim was released and restored to his throne, but only because he was made to swear allegiance to the king of Babylon and become his subject.

Three years later, Jehoiakim rebelled against the Babylonians. But the Babylonian army entered Jerusalem to put down his rebellion, and he and his men were killed. The city was conquered and the son of Jehoiakim was placed on the throne in his place.

After three months, Nebuchadnezzar himself came to Jerusalem, still angry about the rebellion. He burned the Temple and carried off the king and his family. He took with him seven thousand Jewish soldiers and every skilled workman he could find. Then he placed on the throne of Judah as his subject the uncle of the king, whom he named Zedekiah.

For a time, Zedekiah listened to Jeremiah, asking for his counsel and even for the prayers of the man of God. Thus, Jeremiah enjoyed freedom under Zedekiah. He walked the streets of the city with a yoke on his neck as a warning of what was in store for the people if they continued their wicked lives and their trust in Egypt, rather than in God. He wrote letters to those already taken captive and urged them to be patient and to await the time when they would be free.

After a while, however, Zedekiah no longer listened to Jeremiah. He joined the Egyptians against the Babylonians. Nebuchadnezzar came to Jerusalem for the fourth time to attack. During the siege, Jeremiah preached in the city and told the people that all who joined Nebuchadnezzar and the Babylonians would be saved. For this message, he was cast into prison.

The siege of the city continued for two years. Finally, a breach was made in the walls, and the city was taken by the Babylonians. Zedekiah fled, but the enemy pursued and captured him. He and his children were brought to Nebuchadnezzar. His children were put to death right in front of him, then his eyes were plucked out, and he was taken as a prisoner to Babylon.

Everything of value was taken from the houses of Jerusalem. The important buildings were destroyed, including the beautiful Temple that Solomon had built. Even the walls of the city were torn down. But Jeremiah was spared and allowed to remain in Jerusalem.

While the Babylonians were plundering the city and before they reached the Temple, Jeremiah and some Levites secretly removed the Ark of the Covenant and the altar of incense. They carried them across the Jordan and hid them in a cave in Mount Nebo. The place where they hid them was not marked in any special way, so the treasure would not be found by the enemy.

QUESTIONS FOR REVIEW:

1. What did Jeremiah prophesy about the people of Judah?

2. What did Jeremiah do as a warning of what was in store for the people of Jerusalem if they continued their wicked lives?

3. What did Jeremiah and some Levites do to protect the Ark of the Covenant?

ACTIVITIES

MAP ACTIVITY: THE BABYLONIANS ATTACK JUDEA

1. Draw two red lines from the Babylonian Empire (Babylon) to Jerusalem to represent the two attacks on the city.
2. Beside one of the lines near the city of Jerusalem write the words "two years" indicating that the second attack lasted for two years.
3. Using yellow, draw a line from Jerusalem to Mount Nebo, showing that Jeremiah got the Ark of the Covenant out of the city.
4. With blue, draw a line from Jerusalem to the city of Babylon, showing that the captives of Jerusalem were taken to Babylon.

Black Sea

HITTITES

ASSYRIA

MEDITERRANEAN
SEA

•Haran

Ninevah•

Tigris

Euphrates

•Damascus

▲ MT.
CARMEL

Joppa•
Jerusalem•

▲ MT. NEBO

•Babylon

Beersheba•

Ur•

▲ MT. SINAI/
MT. HOREB

ARABIAN DESERT

Nile River

EGYPT

Red Sea

CROSSWORD: THE BABYLONIAN CAPTIVITY

Across

4. King of Babylon.
5. The priest and prophet
7. The final siege of Jerusalem lasted for _____ years.

Down

1. Place where the Ark was hidden
2. _____ was the leader of Judah and favored the Egyptians. He threw Jeremiah in prison.
3. Nebuchadnezzar placed him on the throne.
6. Jeremiah warned of evils if the people relied on _____.

GAME PROJECT: HIDE THE ARK

Materials: An empty shoe box to use as the Ark of the Covenant. Decorate it if you wish or place some kind of treasure in it.

Instructions: Pretend you are hiding the Ark of the Covenant and need to keep the enemy from finding it. Then have a friend, sibling, or parent try to find it.

CHAPTER 28
Daniel in the Lions' Den

One of Nebuchadnezzar's successors was King Darius. He selected a man named Daniel to be one of his three presidents, a high position of authority in Babylon. Darius was so impressed with Daniel that he planned to give him authority over the entire kingdom. This was unusual because Daniel was Jewish.

The Babylonian officials grew angry that a Jewish man would be placed over them. Worse yet, Daniel had demonstrated to the king that the priests of the Babylonian gods were frauds. So the prophet had many enemies, and they sought to bring some charge against him.

Daniel was blameless in performing his duties, so they couldn't accuse him of any wrongdoing. But they knew that Daniel carefully obeyed the laws that God had given to the Jewish people. So they found a way to trap him.

The Babylonian officials persuaded Darius to make a new law: for thirty days, no one was to make a petition to anyone, whether a man or a god, except Darius himself. That meant they were forbidden even to pray! If they did, they would be thrown into a den of hungry lions.

The officials knew that Daniel prayed faithfully three times a day. They also knew that he would disobey the king's command in order to follow the Law of God. So they spied on him, and when they found him praying, they went to the king, demanding that Daniel be put to death as the new law required.

The officials threatened to revolt and kill the king if he didn't sentence Daniel to death. In fear, the king gave in to their demands. He commanded that Daniel be arrested and thrown into a den of hungry lions.

Darius had been reluctant to act against Daniel. He had great respect for the prophet and his God, and he realized that he had acted foolishly when he made the law against praying. So as the prophet was being dragged off, the king said to him, "May your God, whom you serve continually, deliver you!"

For six days the lions received no food, because the Babylonians were hoping to starve them. That way, their great hunger would drive them to rip Daniel apart right away.

But Daniel remained firm, placing his trust in God. And when he was thrown into the lions' den, his faith was rewarded: Despite their hunger, the lions refused to harm him. God had sent an angel to protect Daniel.

At that time, back in the land of Judah, there was a prophet named Habakkuk. He had just prepared a meal when an angel appeared. The angel instructed him to take some of the dinner to Babylon and give it to Daniel in the lions' den.

Habakkuk protested that he had never been to Babylon and knew nothing about the lions' den. So the angel carried him to Babylon, right to the den, so he could give Daniel the food. Then the angel carried him back home. The next morning, Darius came to find out what had happened to the prophet. He shouted into the den, "O Daniel, servant of the living God, has your God, whom you serve continually, been able to deliver you from the lions?"

Daniel shouted back, "My God sent his angel and shut the lions' mouths, and they have not hurt me, because I was found blameless before him."

When the king learned that Daniel had not been harmed by the lions, he commanded that the prophet be released. Then he commanded that those who had unjustly persecuted Daniel should suffer the same fate they had intended for the prophet. The Babylonian leaders were cast into the very same den of lions. Immediately, the hungry beasts devoured them.

QUESTIONS FOR REVIEW:

1. Why was Daniel thrown into the lion's den?

2. How did he keep from being eaten while in the lion's den?

3. Who was Habakkuk and what did he do?

ACTIVITIES

COLORING PAGE: DANIEL IN THE LION'S DEN

CRAFT PROJECT: DANIEL AND THE LION WOODEN SPOONS

Materials:
- ☐ 2, 10 in. wooden spoons
- ☐ Templates from page 201
- ☐ small piece of neutral fabric
- ☐ brown yarn
- ☐ markers
- ☐ colored pencils
- ☐ hot glue gun

Directions:

1. Cut out and color Daniel's body from Activity Book. Hot glue onto the spoon.
2. Cut a small scrap of fabric and fashion over top of Daniel's head. Hot glue into place.
3. Cut a piece of brown yarn to wrap around the cloth hat.
4. Use markers to add eyes, nose, and mouth to Daniel.
5. Cut out and color the lion's body from the Activity Book and hot glue to the second wooden spoon.
7. Cut as many pieces of 1–2 in. brown yarn as you can fit around the face of our lion and hot glue them into place
8. Use markers to create eyes, a rectangular nose, and scary teeth.
9. Enjoy!

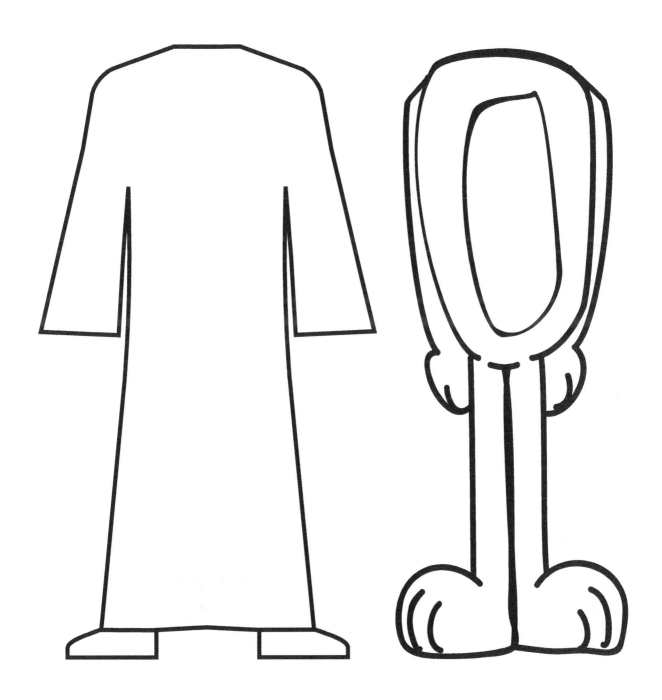

CHAPTER 29
The Prophets Isaiah, Jeremiah, and Ezekiel

What is a prophet?

Prophet is a word you hear a lot when reading the Bible. We have already heard this word a few times here already. Do you know what a prophet is?

Sometimes people think a prophet is just a person who predicts the future, and there is some truth to this. The prophets of the Old Testament would often speak of things that waited in the future, many of which came true.

However, the main thing a prophet did was try to bring people back to God. They spoke about the evils of worshipping false gods and pointed out when the Jewish people had sinned. They instructed their people in paths to holiness and begged for them to repent. Many of the things they predicted were merely warnings. In other words, they might predict a bad thing happening down the road, but said it would only happen if the people did not turn back to God. In many cases, the people did not listen to the prophet, and bad things did happen. So in that sense they did predict future events, but the people had control over keeping them from happening.

We have already met a few prophets, including Elijah, Samuel, Daniel, and others. But let's meet a few more.

Isaiah

Daniel was a great prophet. But there were three more great prophets among the Jewish people. The first we will discuss is Isaiah, born many years after Solomon. When the child grew older, he had a vision while he was praying. Angels were chanting, "Holy, holy, holy, Lord God of Hosts. The earth is filled with his glory." And God was sitting on the throne surrounded by these angels. Isaiah became so overwhelmed by this beautiful vision that he was mourning in sorrow for his sins. Then suddenly an angel flew down and touched Isaiah's lips with a burning coal. "Your sins are forgiven," said the angel.

God then spoke. He wanted to send a message to the Hebrews. Immediately, Isaiah begged God to send him. It was then that Isaiah became a great prophet revealing God's words to his people. He often spoke of repenting from sin and turning their hearts to God. He also revealed that God would send the Messiah, the Christ. This had been promised years ago to Adam and Eve, but then the Jews had referred to him as the Savior.

Isaiah also predicted that Christ would come from the lineage of Jesse and David and that truly awesome things would happen once the Christ was born, but that there would also be great suffering and that the Christ would be despised and would offer his life as a ransom for many.

Jeremiah

It was about the year 586 BC that the Jews were carried off into captivity by the Babylonians. For forty years the prophet Jeremiah had been warning them that this terrible punishment would come upon them unless they repented of their sins and returned to God. But they refused to listen to him.

The terrible day came when the people and the vessels of the Temple were carried off by the king of Babylon. Jeremiah was left behind in the ruins of the Temple and the city to mourn for his people. At this time, he wrote the book of Lamentations, which is found in the Bible.

The heart of Jeremiah was bowed down with grief and loneliness. Yet he didn't lose his hope in God. He knew that the day would come when God would deliver his people from bondage.

Ezekiel

Ezekiel was among those who had been carried away from Jerusalem by the Babylonians. He prophesied for many years after the death of Jeremiah. His message was one of hope and of victory, saying that God would be true to his promises and deliver his people from the hand of the enemy.

Ezekiel prophesied in parables, which are sometimes hard to understand. In one vision, for example, he saw a great whirlwind and a great cloud surrounded by fire. In the midst of the cloud and fire he saw what looked like four living creatures: a man, a lion, an ox, and an eagle.

The symbols of the four Evangelists, or Gospel writers, come from this vision. St. Matthew is represented as a man, St. Mark as a lion, St. Luke as an ox, and St. John as an eagle.

QUESTIONS FOR REVIEW:

1. What is a prophet?

2. How was Isaiah purified of his sins?

3. What did Jeremiah warn the people about?

4. What were the four creatures Ezekiel saw in his vision that became the symbols of the Gospel writers? Did you remember which creature represents each writer?

COLORING PAGE: PROPHET

ACROSTIC POEM: PROPHETS

Instructions:

Write the word "prophets" vertically in the space provided, writing one letter per line.

Think of different ways to describe a prophet and write them in a line that contains one of the letters in the word "prophet." For example, you might use the word "brave." You would write that word using the line that contains the letter "e" in "prophet."

CRAFT ACTIVITY: THE PROPHET EZEKIEL'S VISION OF THE APOSTLES

Materials:
- ☐ Poster board
- ☐ Ruler
- ☐ Pencil/Markers/Crayons/Coloring
- ☐ Pencils

Instructions:
1. Use the ruler to measure and draw lines, dividing the poster board into four equal sections.
2. Draw the four symbols Ezekiel saw that point to the four Gospel writers: A man, a lion, an ox, and an eagle.
3. Label each at the bottom with the name of the apostle it matches.

CHAPTER 30
Summary of the Old Testament

Throughout the many stories of the Old Testament, we can see that God has constantly revealed his overflowing love and mercy for mankind. In the beginning, he authored the book of nature with Adam and Eve, who, even when they disobeyed him, he forgave. Noah and his family were likewise spared from the great flood when the rest of the people of world had turned away from God.

Then, through the lives of Abraham, Isaac, and Jacob, we learned about the courage of men and God's plan for the future of the Hebrews. God tested Abraham by asking him to sacrifice his son, Isaac, and Abraham did not hesitate to obey. Yet his son was spared. Isaac's son Jacob tricked his other son, Esau, into giving up his birthright, a lesson to teach us the importance of what God has given us.

Jacob had twelve sons, one of whom was destined for greatness. Although his son Joseph was scorned by his brothers and sold as a slave, he eventually grew up in favor of the pharaoh of Egypt, who made him a governor. In this we can see how God can turn even the most insufferable events into one that would shape the future of his Chosen People. God's mercy and forgiveness are reflected in this story when his brothers were sorry for what they had done to Joseph.

Along came the great prince of Egypt, Moses, who, like Joseph, became such an influential figure despite coming from humble beginnings. He was saved from being murdered as a baby when his mother placed him in a basket and floated him down a river. He landed into an Egyptian princess's arms, where he would become the one to lead the Hebrews out of slavery. After Moses, Joshua showed that even a city can crumble if God wills it, while Samson showed that only one man's strength is enough to conquer the enemy, even if it means dying along with them.

Samuel showed great courage by reminding his soldiers that the Ark of the Covenant was not a good luck charm, that God would help them defeat their enemies if they just trusted in him alone. He anointed David as king, after which God sent David to conquer a giant. The little shepherd boy slew Goliath and lived to write beautiful psalms that are still sung today.

King Solomon exemplified the virtue of humility by asking God for wisdom. God rewarded him not only with wisdom but with great wealth and good health. Unfortunately, Solomon turned away from God, and God declared that the next king would not come from his lineage.

After Solomon, the kingdom would split. Solomon's son, Rehoboam, had the loyalties of the tribes of Judah and Benjamin, while a man named Jeroboam recruited the other ten tribes to worship false idols. And although Rehoboam loved God, and Jeroboam was given tribes by God, in time, both of these men turned away from him.

Then the great prophet Elijah performed a miracle, which brought worshippers of the false god, Baal, to fall on their knees to worship the one true God. Certainly, Job faced one of the greatest tests when he lost everything, even his children. But Job pleased God by his patience in suffering. So the Lord rewarded him.

He restored Job's health and doubled his wealth, and gave him more sons and daughters.

All by herself, the brave Judith killed an Assyrian general with his own sword! As a result, the people of Judah defeated his army as they fled. Later, Jonah survived in the belly of a fish because he needed to repent from disobeying God. Tobit was a man who obeyed the Law of Moses and always did kind acts. He became blind and poor, but was rescued from his sufferings through the help of an angel in disguise, Raphael!

Jeremiah prophesied the evils that would come to the people of Judah if they relied on Egypt. Although imprisoned, he was spared of harm. He then carried the Ark of the Covenant to safety. Through the story of Daniel in the lion's den, God revealed his love and mercy again by sparing Daniel from getting eaten alive.

Ezekiel prophesied for many years after the death of Jeremiah. His message was one of hope and of victory, reminding us that God will be true to his promises and deliver his people from the hand of the enemy.

Throughout the many events and people of the Old Testament, from Adam and Eve, Abraham to Moses, to all of the prophets, God's plan for the salvation of mankind and his utter love and mercy is clearly evident. It will become even more evident when he finally sends the Savior to redeem us all. The New Testament will tell that story. This is where we will turn next!

ACTIVITIES

QUIZ ACTIVITY: OLD TESTAMENT FLASHCARD WAR

Materials:
☐ Index cards
☐ 2 people

Instructions:

1. Use this chapter and other chapters as needed to create flashcards. On one side of the flashcard, write the name of one of the people you learned about. On the other side of the flashcard, write down something about them. Repeat with as many flashcards as you wish.

2. Distribute the cards evenly with the other person.

3. Question your opponent by reading either side of the flashcard, as they guess what is on the other side of the flashcard. If they get it right, they keep the card. If they are incorrect, you keep the card. Then have your opponent do the same thing, taking turns.

4. Keep score by tallying up who has the most cards at the end.

QUIZ ACTIVITY: OLD TESTAMENT TIMELINE

Instructions:

In the space provided, rewrite the names below in the order in which they appeared in the Old Testament (chronological order). Or, simply put numbers beside their names ordering them from 1–10.

Joseph

Noah

Adam and Eve

Abraham

David

Jacob

Solomon

Saul

Moses

Isaac

THE NEW TESTAMENT

CHAPTER 31
The Annunciation

The angel Gabriel was sent from God into a city of Galilee called Nazareth. His mission was to speak to a virgin engaged to a man whose name was Joseph, a descendant of David. The virgin's name was Mary, and she was a relative of Elizabeth.

The angel said to Mary, "Hail, full of grace! The Lord is with you; blessed are you among women." When Mary heard these words, she was troubled, and wondered what kind of greeting this could be.

But the angel said to her, "Don't be afraid, Mary, for you have found grace with God. You will conceive in your womb and bear a Son; and you will call his name Jesus. He will be great, and will be called the Son of the Most High. And the Lord God will give him the throne of David his forefather; and he will reign as king over the house of Jacob forever. And of his kingdom there will be no end."

Mary said to the angel, "How will this happen, since I don't have relations with a man?"

The angel said to her, "The Holy Spirit will come upon you, and the power of the Most High will overshadow you. So the Holy One to be born will be called the Son of God. See! Your relative Elizabeth has also conceived a son in her old age . . . because nothing is impossible with God."

Then Mary said, "I am the handmaiden of the Lord; let it be done to me according to your word." And the angel departed from her.

The knowledge that she was to be the Mother of God filled Mary's heart with happiness, but she didn't forget the great joy that had come to Elizabeth. She set out right away on the journey from Nazareth to the Judean hill country to visit her relative. It was a journey of four or five days, and she probably made it on foot.

Entering the house of Zechariah, Mary greeted Elizabeth affectionately. In that moment the Holy Spirit revealed to Elizabeth that Mary was the Mother of God, and she cried out with a loud voice, "Blessed are you among women, and blessed is the fruit of your womb. And how have I deserved to have the mother of my Lord come to me? For behold, when the voice of your greeting came to my ears, the child in my womb leaped for joy. And blessed is she who believed, because the things promised her by the Lord will be accomplished."

When Mary heard these words, the joy in her heart knew no bounds. There burst from her lips the song we call the *Magnificat*, a prayer of praise and thanksgiving to the Lord. She said, "My soul magnifies the Lord, and my spirit rejoices in God my Savior; because he has regarded the lowly estate of his handmaiden. From now on, all generations will call me blessed, because he who is mighty has done great things for me, and holy is his name. And his mercy is from generation to generation on those who fear him.

"He has shown might with his arm; he has scattered the proud in the conceit of their hearts. He has put down the mighty from their thrones, and has exalted the lowly. He has filled the hungry with good things, and the rich he has sent away empty.

"He has given help to Israel his servant, mindful of his mercy—just as he spoke to our fathers, to Abraham and to his posterity forever."

Mary stayed with Elizabeth about three months, and then she returned to her home in Nazareth.

QUESTIONS FOR REVIEW:

1. What did the angel Gabriel say to Mary when he visited her?

2. How did Mary respond to the angel?

3. What happened when Mary visited her cousin, Elizabeth?

ACTIVITIES

COLORING PAGE: THE ANNUNCIATION

CRAFT ACTIVITY: THE ANNUNCIATION PRAYERCARD

Materials:
- ☐ Scissors
- ☐ Glue
- ☐ Pencil/Pen/Crayons/Markers

1. On the template below, draw the angel Gabriel visiting Mary to tell her she is going to become the Mother of God. On the other template, write out the words to the Hail Mary.

2. Cut them out and glue them together to make it a front and back prayer card.

SNACK PROJECT: EDIBLE ANGEL

Ingredients:

☐ Ice cream cone (cone shaped)
☐ White frosting
☐ Sprinkles
☐ Large marshmallow
☐ 2 candy fruit slices (or Vanilla Wafers or other small cookies)

Instructions:

1. Place the cone pointy side up.

2. Insert the large marshmallow into the pointy side of the cone for the angel's head.

3. Frost the cone with the white frosting. Make sure to put enough on the back that it can support the wings.

4. Decorate with sprinkles by holding the cone from within and dripping the sprinkles on.

5. Place the candy fruit slices on the back of the angel for the wings. You can use Vanilla Wafers or other small cookies if you wish.

6. Enjoy!

CHAPTER 32
The Nativity

After Mary had returned to her home in Nazareth, Joseph learned that she was to become the mother of the Savior. An angel appeared to him in his sleep and said, "Don't be afraid, Joseph, son of David, to take Mary as your wife, for the Child conceived in her is of the Holy Spirit. She will bear a Son, and you will call his name Jesus; for he will save his people from their sins."

In this way the prophecy of Isaiah was fulfilled: "Behold, the virgin will be with child, and will bear a son, and they will call his name *Emmanuel,* which means, 'God with us.'"

Now in those days, Augustus, the Roman emperor, issued a decree ordering that a census must be taken of his whole empire. Rome had reached the height of her power, and the emperor wanted to know more exactly the extent of his rule. The census would also reveal to him the resources of the various provinces, so he could decide how much to tax them.

Whenever the Jews took a census, they left their place of residence and went to the city from which their ancestors had come. So Joseph and Mary left the city of Nazareth in Galilee, and went to Bethlehem in Judea. Bethlehem was King David's birthplace, and Rachel, the wife of Jacob, Abraham's grandson, was buried there.

When they reached the little town of Bethlehem, they found it crowded with visitors. There was no room for them in the inn. They sought in vain for a place to stay, but the best shelter they could find was a stable for animals.

So Joseph and Mary made preparations to remain there for the night. And it was during that night, and in that humble stable, that the Son of God was born into the world. Mary wrapped the divine Infant in swaddling clothes and laid him in a manger, where the animals were fed.

Not far away a group of shepherds were keeping watch over their flocks at night to protect them from wolves and robbers. Suddenly, an angel of the Lord appeared to them, and the brightness of heaven shone around them. The shepherds were terrified!

But the angel said to them, "Don't be afraid. Look! I bring you good news of great joy that will be to all the people. For today in the town of David a Savior has been born to you, who is Christ the Lord. And this will be a sign to you: You'll find an Infant wrapped in swaddling clothes and lying in a manger."

He had no sooner spoken than the shepherds saw with him a great multitude of angels, and heard them praising God: "Glory to God in the highest, and on earth peace among men of good will!" Then the angels disappeared.

The hearts of the shepherds were filled with wonder, and they said one to another, "Let's go over to Bethlehem and see this thing that has come to pass, which the Lord has made known to us."

They hurried to Bethlehem, and there they found Mary and Joseph, and the Baby lying in a manger. Kneeling down, they adored their Savior. Then the shepherds returned to their flocks, glorifying and praising God for all the things they had heard and seen.

The shepherds were not the only visitors Jesus, Mary, and Joseph would receive. The Magi, the three wise men or three kings, as they are often called, also came to adore the Christ Child, bringing with them gifts of gold, frankincense, and myrrh. These three gifts were seen as symbols for Jesus's life: the gold to represent his kingship, the frankincense to represent his royal priesthood, and the myrrh which pointed to his sacrificial death (myrrh was often used to anoint people's bodies after they died).

QUESTIONS FOR REVIEW:

1. Why did Joseph and Mary leave the city of Nazareth in Galilee and go to Bethlehem in Judea, the City of David?

2. Why did Joseph and Mary have to stay in a stable and have Jesus there?

3. Who did the angels appear to, asking them to go and adore the Infant?

ACTIVITIES

MAZE: HELP THE WISE MEN FIND JESUS

Help the Wise Men travel the right path to find Jesus

START

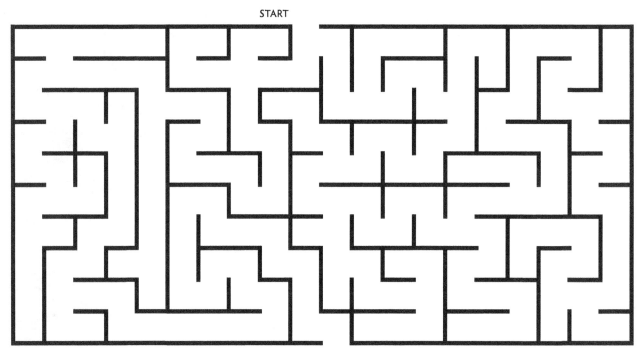

FINISH

COLORING PAGE: THE HOLY FAMILY

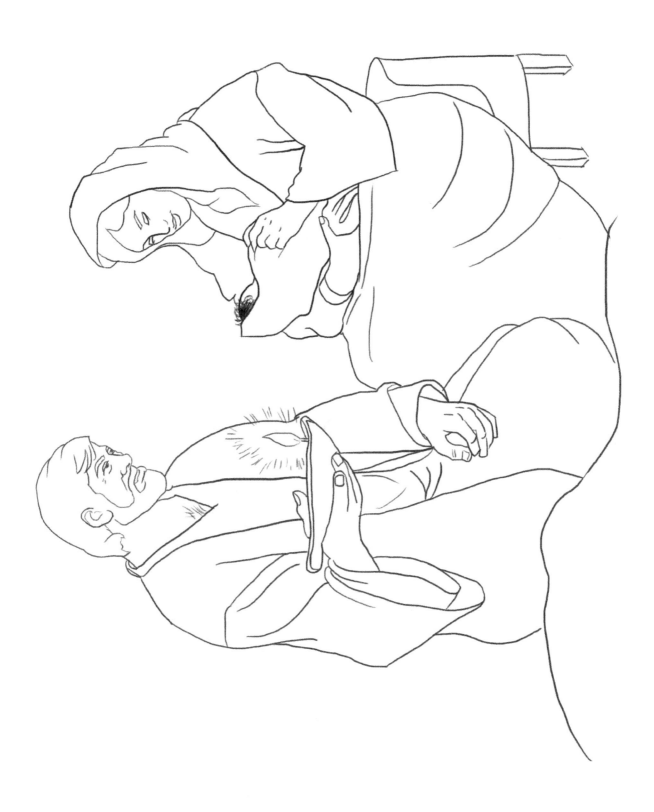

COLORING PAGE: THE WISE MEN

WORD SEARCH: THE BIRTH OF JESUS

Answer the below questions and then find the answers in the Word Search on the next page.

1. Jesus was born in the city of _____.

2. _____ was born in a stable.

3. _____ was the Mother of God.

4. Another name for the Wise Men: _____

5. Angels appeared to the _____ to tell them about Jesus.

6. _____ was Jesus's foster father.

7. Jesus was born in a _____.

8. A name which means "God with us": _____

9. Joseph and Mary could find no room at the _____.

10. Joseph and Mary had to travel to Bethlehem for the _____.

```
K  V  D  M  C  D  H  B  E  S  M  P  F  W  R
O  X  B  O  X  I  W  L  K  Y  A  S  M  I  A
I  H  C  F  H  A  B  J  G  S  R  J  V  T  B
J  X  P  Q  Y  A  Z  H  V  B  Y  V  I  U  G
F  E  I  N  T  B  C  B  E  D  X  Q  I  C  Y
L  W  S  S  X  M  V  T  N  A  F  Y  M  U  D
P  E  P  U  A  E  H  Z  O  K  A  Z  Z  X  N
V  T  U  G  S  L  S  D  R  E  H  P  E  H  S
N  N  I  N  E  Y  J  J  B  S  O  H  U  A  F
C  B  V  H  A  N  J  E  Y  R  H  P  J  S  K
C  Z  E  Z  G  M  T  F  S  M  N  E  S  B  G
A  M  D  G  J  X  M  J  K  V  C  S  I  D  B
C  E  N  S  U  S  K  E  L  U  H  O  I  A  Z
B  E  D  D  J  G  N  Q  L  O  W  J  U  O  S
K  N  I  S  R  Y  T  R  K  H  J  B  X  F  O
```

Note: Some words may appear backwards.

If you have trouble figuring out the words from your clues, see if you can find the words from this list:
Bethlehem, Census, Emmanuel, Inn, Jesus, Joseph, Magi, Mary, Shepherds, Stable

CRAFT PROJECT: NATIVITY WITH POPSICLE STICKS

Materials:
- ☐ 7 popsicle sticks
- ☐ acrylic paint
- ☐ pipe cleaners (gold or yellow)
- ☐ hot glue gun
- ☐ yarn or string (optional)
- ☐ scissors

Directions:

1. Paint the popsicle sticks.
   a. Paint 5 sticks brown for the stable.
   b. Cut 1 stick in half and paint each to represent Mary and Joseph.
   c. Cut 1 stick into thirds. Paint 1/3 brown (to be cut in half to make sticks for manger). Paint 1/3 as baby Jesus. Paint 1/3 as an angel.

2. After drying, use 5 sticks to create a stable. Use 1 whole stick for the base and 1 whole stick for each side of the roof. Cut 1/3 off the top of remaining 2 sticks to be the sides of the stable. Glue all pieces together to construct stable outline.

3. Glue baby Jesus to 2 sticks in "x" shape and then glue that to the center of the base of the stable.

4. Glue Mary and Joseph to either side of the manger.

5. Glue the angel to top peak of stable.

6. Use pipe cleaners to create halo and wings for the angel.

7. Optional: Use hot glue gun to glue yarn loop to the backside of the stable peak to hang as decoration or as a Christmas tree ornament.

8. Enjoy!

CHAPTER 33
John the Baptist

About thirty years after the birth of Jesus, out in the desert, John, the son of Zechariah, was getting ready for the great work to which God had called him. He wore a rough garment made of camel's hair, with a leather belt around his waist. The only food he ate was locusts and wild honey. When God revealed to him that the time had come for him to begin his work, he came to the Jordan River and began to preach to the people. He would yell out, "Repent, for the kingdom of heaven is at hand!"

In the beginning, John's audiences were small. But soon the story of this strange preacher traveled throughout the land, and great crowds came to the Jordan to hear him. Many were converted by his words. They went out and stood in the river, where he baptized them as a sign of their repentance and their resolution to live a better life. This baptism did not wash away their sins, but it prepared their hearts for the coming of the Savior.

Many of the people began to wonder in their hearts whether John might perhaps be the Savior. But John said to them, "I baptize you with water. But there will come One mightier than I am, and I am unworthy even to loosen the strap of his sandals. He will baptize you with the Holy Spirit and with fire."

When Jesus was thirty years old, he left Nazareth and came to the Jordan where John was preaching. He asked to be baptized. Knowing that Jesus was the Messiah and was without sin, John said to him, "I ought to be baptized by you, yet you come to me?"

Jesus explained to John that he must be baptized because it was part of God's plan for redeeming the human race. Humbly John obeyed, and he baptized the Savior of the world.

When Jesus came out of the water, the heavens were opened and the Holy Spirit came down on him in the form of a dove. A voice from heaven was heard, saying, "This is my beloved Son, in whom I am well pleased. Listen to him!"

The ruler of Galilee during this time was named Herod Antipas. He had unlawfully married Herodias, the wife of Philip, his half-brother. John the Baptist rebuked him publicly for this sin, so Herod ordered him thrown into prison.

At this time, Jesus had begun his public life, preaching to the people and working a number of miracles. John the Baptist had been in prison about a year when Herod Antipas held a great celebration on his birthday. Salome, the daughter of Herodias, danced. Herod was quite pleased with her, so he made an oath to give her whatever she wanted, even if it were half of his kingdom.

Salome asked permission to consult with her mother. Now Herodias hated John the Baptist, because he had publicly condemned her sinful behavior. So she told her daughter to ask for the head of John the Baptist on a dish. Salome returned to the king and said to him, "Give me, on a dish, the head of John the Baptist." When Herod heard this, he was very sad. He knew that John was a holy man, for he had visited him in prison. But because of the oath he had made before all his guests, he ordered that John must be beheaded.

The head was brought to him on a dish and he gave it to Salome, who took it to her mother. In this way Herodias had her revenge. The disciples of John took the body of their master and buried it.

In the meantime, Jesus had a mission to fulfill. But we will pick up there in the next chapter!

QUESTIONS FOR REVIEW:

1. When John questioned Jesus about why he needed to be baptized, what did Jesus say?

2. In what form did the Holy Spirit appear after Jesus was baptized? What did God say at this time?

3. Who hated John the Baptist and what did she tell her daughter to do?

ACTIVITIES

COLORING PAGE: JOHN THE BAPTIST

SNACK PROJECT: LOCUSTS AND HONEY

Ingredients:
☐ pecans (halved)
☐ pretzels
☐ mini chocolate candy bars (or full sized candy bars, cut into small pieces)
☐ mini chocolate chips
☐ sandwich bag

Ingredients for honey frosting:
☐ 3/4 cup powdered sugar
☐ 1 Tbsp. milk or water
☐ 1 Tbsp. honey

Directions:

1. In small bowl, mix powdered sugar, milk, and honey to make frosting. The frosting's texture should be sticky but smooth.

2. Using a rubber spatula, scoop frosting into the sandwich bag. Seal bag removing all air. Snip a tiny triangle off the tip of one side of the bag.

3. Squeeze a dime sized drop of frosting toward the back of each candy bar. Glue pecan on top and toward the back, slightly hanging off, so that it is parallel with the candy bar.

4. Cut pretzels in half for the wings, and use frosting to glue each wing to the side of the candy bar with the curved part facing down.

5. Glue a second pecan half to the front of the candy bar at a vertical angle to create the face of the locust (this may slightly overlap with the back pecan).

6. Finally, use the frosting to glue on mini chocolate chips to the front for the eyes.

7. Enjoy!

CRAFT PROJECT: PAPER PLATE DOVE

Materials:
- ☐ paper plate
- ☐ scissors
- ☐ pencil
- ☐ markers or crayons
- ☐ glue

Directions:

1. Draw a bowling pin shape in the middle of the paper plate, leaving the rim on the bottom. Cut this shape out and set aside.
2. Cut the sides of the paper plate off for the wings.
3. Glue the wings to the back of the body.
4. Draw a beak, eyes, and feet on your dove.
5. Enjoy!

CHAPTER 34
Jesus Calls His Apostles

At the start of Jesus's mission, he went into the desert to fast and pray for forty days and do battle with the devil. When he returned, he went back to the Jordan, where John was still baptizing. When John saw Jesus coming toward him, he cried out, "Behold the Lamb of God! Behold the One who takes away the sin of the world!"

The next day John was with two of his *disciples*—that is, his followers—and Jesus passed by again. Pointing to him, John said again, "Behold the Lamb of God." The two disciples left John and started to follow Jesus.

Jesus turned and said to them, "What is it that you seek?"

They answered, "*Rabbi*," which means "Teacher," "where do you live?" Jesus replied, "Come and see." So they went along and stayed with him all that day. Their names were John and Andrew. Now Andrew had a brother named Simon. He went to look for him, and when he found him, he said, "We have found the Messiah." Then he took him to Jesus.

When Jesus saw Simon, he said, "You are Simon; you will be called *Cephas*." *Cephas* is the Aramaic word for "Peter," which means "a rock."

On the following day, Jesus went into Galilee and met there a young man named Philip. He said to him, "Follow me." Shortly after this, Philip met his friend, Nathanael, and told him that he had found the Messiah, who was Jesus of Nazareth.

When Jesus saw Nathanael coming to him, he said, "Look! A true Israelite in whom there is no deceit!"

Nathanael said to him, "How do you know me?" Jesus answered, "Before Philip called you, when you were under the fig tree, I saw you." Nathanael replied, "Rabbi, you are the Son of God; you are the King of Israel."

Jesus began to preach to the people, saying, "Repent, for the kingdom of heaven is at hand." Soon, great crowds were following him wherever he went. Many of the people believed in him and tried to live according to his teachings.

One day, when Jesus was walking by the Sea of Galilee, He saw the two brothers Simon and Andrew. They were casting a net into the sea, for they were fishermen. He said to them, "Come, follow me, and I'll have you fishing for men." Immediately, they left their nets and followed him.

Going a little farther on, he saw John in a boat with his brother, James, and his father, who was called Zebedee, mending their nets. He called them, and immediately James and John left their nets and their father and followed him.

Another day, as Jesus was passing by the tax office, he saw a tax collector named Matthew collecting taxes. Jesus said to him, "Follow me." Right away, Matthew got up and followed him.

One day, when they were in Galilee, Jesus went alone up a mountain to pray. Then he chose twelve of these men who followed him to be his *apostles*. These twelve men would have a special mission in establishing his Church and were to remain with him always.

So here were their names: Simon, the fisherman to whom Jesus gave the name Peter; James and John, the sons of Zebedee, whom he nicknamed the "Sons of Thunder"; Andrew, Peter's brother; Philip; Bartholomew, known also as Nathanael; Matthew, the tax collector; Thomas, whose name means "the twin"; James, the son of Alpheus; Thaddeus, also called Jude; Simon, called the Zealot; and Judas Iscariot. All except Judas, who came from Kerioth, a town in Judea, were Galileans. From this time forward the twelve apostles gave all their time to the service of the Savior and followed him wherever he went.

QUESTIONS FOR REVIEW:

1. What does *Rabbi* mean?

2. What did Jesus call Simon?

3. Which apostle was the tax collector before being called by Jesus?

ACTIVITIES

MAP ACTIVITY: JESUS FINDS HIS DISCIPLES

(map located on page 242)

1. Jesus called his first two disciples, John and Andrew, who were disciples of John the Baptist. He called them from the banks of the Jordan River. Trace the Jordan River with blue.

2. Jesus traveled to Galilee where he met Philip and then Nathanael. Circle Galilee with red.

3. Jesus was walking by the Sea of Galilee when he called the brothers, Simon and Andrew. Circle the Sea of Galilee in green.

4. Judas came from Kerioth, a town in Judea. Circle Judea in orange.

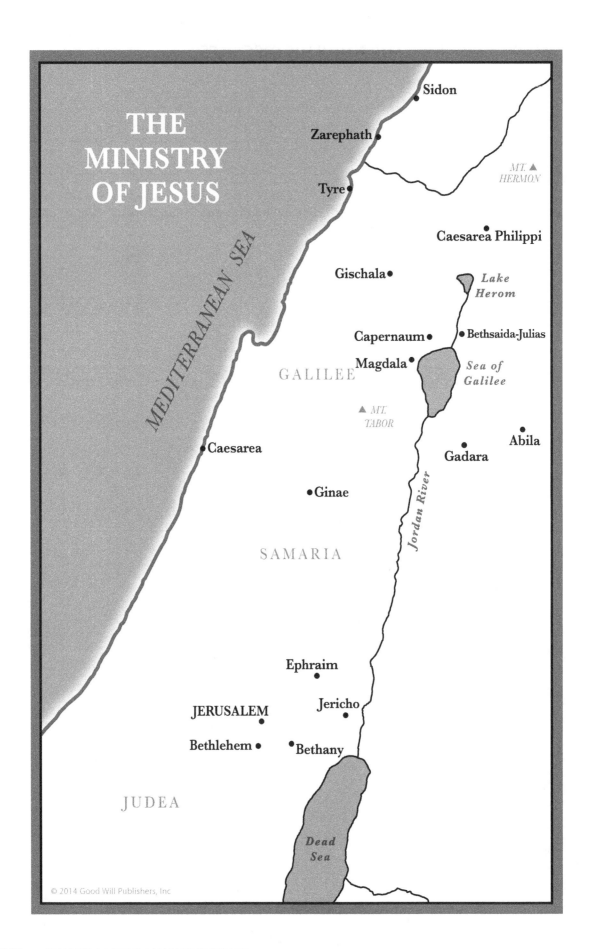

THE MINISTRY OF JESUS

MEDITERRANEAN SEA

Sidon

Zarephath

MT. HERMON

Tyre

Caesarea Philippi

Gischala

Lake Herom

Capernaum

Bethsaida-Julias

Magdala

GALILEE

Sea of Galilee

MT. TABOR

Abila

Caesarea

Gadara

Jordan River

Ginae

SAMARIA

Ephraim

JERUSALEM

Jericho

Bethlehem

Bethany

JUDEA

Dead Sea

© 2014 Good Will Publishers, Inc

WORD SEARCH: THE APOSTLES OF JESUS

Answer the below questions and then find the answers in the Word Search on the next page.

1. A tax collector. _____

2. Older brother of John and son of Zebedee. _____

3. His name means "the twin." _____

4. Younger brother of James and son of Zebedee. _____

5. The brother of Simon Peter. _____

6. Was known first as Simon, the fisherman. _____

7. Friend of Nathaniel (Bartholomew). _____

8. Son of Alphaeus. _____

9. Betrayed Jesus. _____

10. Called the Zealot. _____

11. Also called Nathaniel. _____

12. Also called Jude. _____

WORD SEARCH: THE APOSTLES OF JESUS

```
N  W  W  Z  T  K  D  P  O  G  B  C
S  U  E  D  D  A  H  T  S  A  O  P
M  W  R  H  D  I  G  T  R  I  I  J
Q  W  D  H  T  W  J  T  T  L  R  U
A  O  N  J  A  T  H  A  I  J  J  D
P  N  A  Q  X  O  A  H  M  Y  N  A
Y  S  H  G  L  L  P  M  B  E  G  S
J  A  O  O  P  D  N  O  M  I  S  T
B  A  M  E  J  K  O  F  F  Z  G  B
G  E  T  L  O  M  S  E  M  A  J  Y
W  E  E  U  K  T  H  O  M  A  S  U
R  R  G  I  I  Q  Z  L  G  D  X  S
```

Note: Some words may appear backwards.

If you have trouble figuring out the words from your clues, see if you can find the words from this list: Andrew, Bartholomew, James, John, Judas, James, Matthew, Peter, Philip, Simon, Thaddeus, Thomas

CRAFT PROJECT: FISHING POLE

Materials:
- ☐ construction paper
- ☐ stick or twig (12–18 in. long)
- ☐ scissors
- ☐ markers or crayons
- ☐ tape
- ☐ hole punch
- ☐ hole punch reinforcement
- ☐ string (18 in. per pole)

Directions:

1. Draw a fish onto construction paper so it is about 10 in. long.

2. Cut out the fish and hole punch through the tip of its mouth. Use the hole punch reinforcement to secure the hole.

3. Draw on fins, a tail, and a face, and color.

4. Wrap the 18 in. piece of string around one end of the stick several times and tie off (leaving the majority of the string hanging off the end). Tape around the string to secure it.

5. Tie the other end of the string through the mouth.

6. Enjoy!

CHAPTER 35
The Wedding at Cana

As the days passed, the people flocked to Jesus to hear his gracious teaching. But how could they know that he was truly speaking for God? The miracles he performed were the evidence God provided to show that Jesus was his divine Son, in whom he was well pleased.

The first of those miracles took place at the very beginning of his public life. Jesus didn't hold himself aloof from the people, but was always ready to take part in their innocent pleasures. So he was pleased to accept an invitation to attend a wedding feast at Cana, in Galilee.

Mary, his mother, was also invited. Taking with him his first disciples, Jesus left the Jordan and made the long journey into Galilee so he could attend the feast.

During the festivities, Mary noticed that the servants were greatly worried. She asked them what was the matter, and they told her that the wine had run out. So Mary came to Jesus and said, "They have no wine."

Jesus answered, "What would you have me do? . . . My hour has not yet come."

But Mary knew that Jesus loved these people, and he wanted them to be happy on their wedding day. Running out of wine for the guests would be an embarrassment. So she said to the waiters, "Do whatever he tells you."

Six large stone water jars were standing nearby. Jesus said to the waiters, "Fill the jars with water." They obediently filled them to the brim.

Then he said, "Draw some out, now, and take it to the chief steward of the feast." They did as he commanded. The water had been changed into wine, and when the chief steward tasted it, he found it much better than the wine he had already been serving.

He didn't know where it came from, and he thought that the bridegroom had made a mistake in serving the best wine last. So he called him and said, "Every man at first sets out the good wine, and when the guests have drunk freely, then the wine of lesser quality. But you've kept the good wine until now."

This was the first miracle that Jesus worked. He performed it at the request of his Blessed Mother so that these friends of his could celebrate their wedding day without embarrassment.

QUESTIONS FOR REVIEW:

1. How did the people know Jesus was truly speaking of God?

2. Where did Jesus perform his first miracle?

3. What prompted Jesus to perform this miracle?

ACTIVITIES

CRAFT PROJECT: WATER INTO WINE

Materials:
☐ 6 toilet paper rolls
☐ markers or paint
☐ blue tissue paper
☐ purple or red tissue paper
☐ glue

Directions:

1. Decorate the toilet paper rolls with markers or paint (these will be the pots).
2. Write "water" toward the top of one side of the toilet paper rolls. Turn them upside-down and write "wine" toward the top of the other side.
3. Cut pieces of tissue paper in half. Stuff blue tissue paper into "water" side of toilet paper roll (glue to sides). Let dry and repeat with purple tissue paper on "wine side."
4. Once both sides are dry you can tell the story of Jesus changing water into wine and turn pots from water side to wine side.
5. Enjoy!

DRAMA PROJECT: THE WEDDING AT CANA

Materials:

Use the completed craft project for the water and wine vessels.

Instructions:

Act out the scene of Jesus and his Mother at the wedding at Cana. Rolls include: Jesus, Mary, the couple, the servants, and the chief steward. People can play several rolls if need be.

CHAPTER 36
Jesus Teaches: The Prodigal Son

Jesus taught his followers many lessons on how to live justly, honor God, and reach heaven. Often to teach these lessons he would speak in parables, meaning he would tell stories. These stories had moral lessons that, by telling them in the context of a story, remained with his listeners longer than if he had just told them the lesson alone.

One of the most famous of Jesus's parables is the story of the prodigal son. Jesus told it like this:

"A certain man had two sons. The younger of them said to his father, 'Father, go ahead and give me now my share of your property.' So the father divided his property and gave the son the portion that he would one day have inherited. Not many days later, the younger son gathered up all his wealth and journeyed into a faraway country.

"There he squandered his fortune by living a wild and wicked life. After he had spent everything he had, there came a terrible famine in that country, and he began to be in need. So he went and hired himself out to one of the citizens there, who sent him to his farm to feed the pigs. He was so hungry that he would gladly have eaten the slop that the pigs were eating, but no one would let him have even that.

"At last he came to his senses. He said to himself, 'How many hired men in my father's estate have an abundance of bread, while I'm perishing here with hunger! I'll get up and go to my father, and say to him: Father, I have sinned against heaven and against you. I'm no longer worthy to be called your son. Make me one of your hired servants.'

"Getting up, he went home to his father. When he was still a long way off, his father saw him and was moved with compassion. Running to meet him, he kissed him on his neck.

"The son said, 'Father, I have sinned against heaven and against you. I'm not worthy to be called your son.'

"But the father said to his servants, 'Hurry and bring out the best robe and put it on him, and put a ring on his finger, and sandals on his feet. Then bring out the fattened calf—the one we've long been preparing for a grand feast—and kill it, so that we can eat and celebrate. Because this, my son, was dead, and has come to life again; he was lost, and now is found.' And they began to celebrate.

"Now his elder son was in the field. When he came near the house, he heard music and dancing. So he called one of the servants and asked what this meant. The servant said to him, 'Your brother has come home, and your father has killed the fattened calf, because he's gotten him back safe.'

"Hearing this, the elder son became angry and refused to go into the house. So his father came out and began urging him to come in. But the elder brother said to his father, 'Look! For all these many years I've been serving you, and I've never disobeyed you. Yet you've never given me even as much as a little goat to have a party with my friends! But as soon as this son has come home—the one who has squandered his fortune in sinful living—you've killed the fattened calf for him.'

"But his father said to him, 'Son, you are always with me, and all I have is yours. But we had to celebrate and rejoice, for this brother of yours was dead, and has come to life again; he was lost, and now is found.'"

This powerful story of forgiveness should remind us that God's mercy has no end. The father in the story represents God, and the wayward son is all of us who sin against God. Even if we have committed serious sins, God waits for us to repent and come to the sacrament of Reconciliation so that we can be forgiven and start over.

QUESTIONS FOR REVIEW:

1. What is a parable?

2. How did the younger son squander his fortune? How did his father react when he returned?

3. What is the main lesson of the story of the Prodigal Son?

ACTIVITIES

COLORING PAGE: THE WAYWARD SON

MAZE: THE WAYWARD SON

START

FINISH

CRAFT PROJECT: DUCT TAPE RING

Materials:
- ☐ toilet paper roll
- ☐ scissors
- ☐ duct tape (preferably in fun colors or prints)
- ☐ glue
- ☐ glitter
- ☐ craft jewels

Directions

1. Cut toilet paper roll down one side and flatten out. Cut the rectangle into 1/2 in. strips across the width of the roll.
2. Wrap around finger to estimate size and mark with a pen (it is okay if it wraps around twice).
3. Cut duct tape into narrow strips and wrap around ring until all cardboard is covered.
4. Using glitter paint and jewels decorate duct-taped ring as desired.
5. Enjoy!

CRAFT PROJECT: PIGGY BANK SAVINGS

Materials:
- ☐ Empty can with plastic lid (for example, Smokehouse Almonds)
- ☐ Construction paper
- ☐ Scissors
- ☐ Tape
- ☐ Markers

Instructions:

1. Cut a slit in the lid large enough to fit coins in.
2. Cut a strip of construction paper and tape it around the can.
3. Decorate the can with markers.
4. Start adding coins to save up. When the piggy bank is full, empty it into your parish poor box. Recall the story of the prodigal son and how he squandered, rather than saved, all his wealth.

CHAPTER 37
Jesus Teaches: The Good Samaritan

Our Lord knew that love is the most important and powerful force that could guide our lives, not only in our families, but in our relationships with everyone. So he told a parable one day to emphasize that truth and to explain it in a practical way.

While Jesus was preaching, one of the scribes stood up and interrupted him with a question. "Teacher," he said, "what must I do to gain eternal life?" This may have sounded like an honorable question, but the man was not being sincere. He was simply testing Jesus to see what he would say.

Knowing this, Jesus said to him, "What is written in the Law? What do you read there?"

The scribe answered, "You will love the Lord your God with your whole heart, and with your whole soul, and with your whole strength, and with your whole mind; and you shall love your neighbor as you love yourself."

"You have answered rightly," said Jesus. "Do this, and you will live."

But the scribe wasn't satisfied with that answer. He pressed further. "Well, then," he said, "who *is* my neighbor?"

Then Jesus replied with this parable about love:

"A certain man was going down from Jerusalem to Jericho, and he fell among robbers. They stripped him and beat him and went their way, leaving him half dead.

"But as it happened, a certain priest was going down the same way. Seeing the wounded man, the priest passed him by. In the same way a Levite, when he was near the place and saw him, also passed him by. But a certain Samaritan came nearby on his journey."

You can imagine at this point what the people were thinking as they listened to Jesus. After all, the Jews did not like the Samaritans. If even a priest and a Levite refused to help the man, what would they expect of a Samaritan, whom they looked down upon? But the story had a surprise ending.

Jesus continued, "And when the Samaritan saw the wounded man, he was moved with compassion. Going up to him, he bound up his wounds, pouring oil and wine on them to cleanse them and help them to heal. Then he set the wounded man on his own animal to ride, brought him to an inn, and took care of him.

"The next day the Samaritan took out two denarii and gave them to the innkeeper, saying, 'Take care of him, and whatever more you spend, I will repay you on my way back.'"

Then Jesus asked the scribe, "Which of these three, in your opinion, proved himself a neighbor to the one who fell among the robbers?"

The scribe answered, "The one who showed mercy to him."

Jesus said to him, "Go and do the same."

Jesus could simply tell us to love our neighbor, and he did, but it helps us understand what this means to hear it in a story. As we listen to it, we put ourselves in the place of the injured man, and we know in such a situation we would want someone to help us. We then understand how compassionate the good Samaritan was and we admire him for it and want to be like him. This inspires us to go out and live like we are also good Samaritans, helping our neighbors who are in need.

QUESTIONS FOR REVIEW:

1. Why did Jesus tell the parable of the good Samaritan?

2. What was surprising about this parable?

3. How do you think this story teaches us about loving our neighbor?

ACTIVITIES

DOUBLE PUZZLE: THE GOOD SAMARITAN

Unscramble the words. Copy the letters in the numbered blocks with the corresponding numbers at the bottom to help answer the question.

HOIGEBNR

SAAMIRNAT

BERORB

RPSITE

LIVTEE

BIRCES

DEOWUND

VLEO

SSJEU

JSEW

Jesus often used _____ to teach important lessons.

CRAFT PROJECT: HELPING HANDS

Materials:

☐ 2 pieces of construction paper or
   cardstock
☐ 5 pieces of computer paper
☐ scissors
☐ markers
☐ stapler

Directions:

1. Trace child's hand on 2 pieces of construction paper or cardstock.

2. Cut the hand out and then place the stencil on a stack of five pieces of computer paper and re-trace.

3. Cut out all the hands and staple them together (with the cardstock as the front and back) on the pinky side.

4. Write child's name on the front and color or design their hand.

5. Have child draw or write an example of helping others just as the Good Samaritan did on each page.

6. Enjoy!

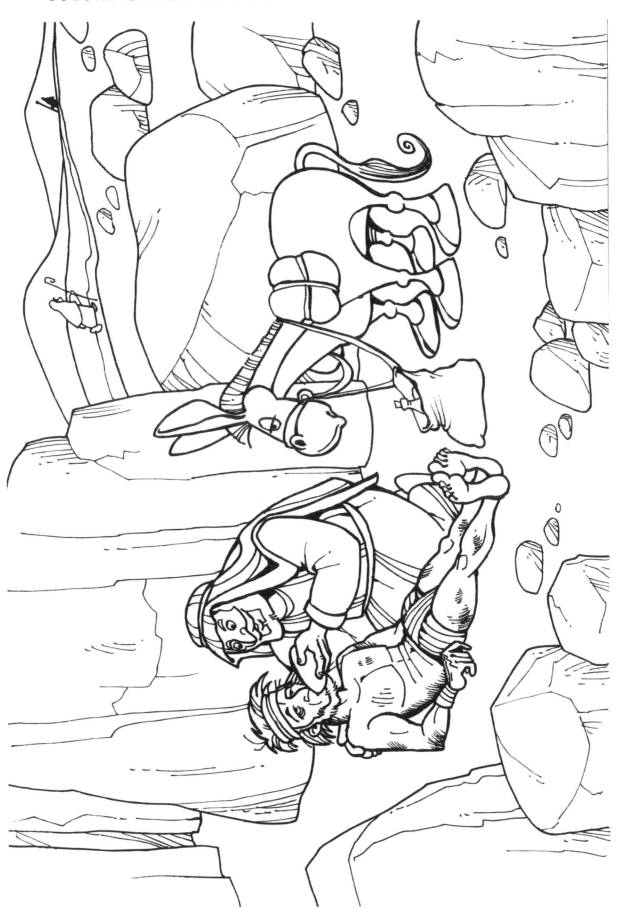

CHAPTER 38
Jesus Teaches: The Kingdom of Heaven

Jesus often told parables in order to teach about the kingdom of heaven.

"The kingdom of heaven," he said, "is like a man who sowed good seed in his field. But while everyone was sleeping, his enemy came and sowed weeds among the wheat, and went away. When the plants came up and bore grain, then the weeds appeared as well.

"The servants of the man's house came to him and said, 'Sir, didn't you sow good seed in your field? Then why does it have weeds?'

"He said to them, 'An enemy has done this.'

"The servants said to him, 'Do you want us to go and pull up the weeds?'

"He replied, 'No. When you pull up the weeds, you may uproot the wheat together with it. Let both grow until the harvest, and at harvest time I'll say to the reapers, pull up first the weeds and bind them into bundles to burn. But gather the wheat into my barn.'"

His disciples said to him, "Explain to us the parable of the weeds in the field."

Jesus said, "The One who sows the good seed is the Son of Man. The field is the world, and the good seed are the children of the kingdom, while the weeds are the children of the wicked one. The enemy who sowed them is the Devil. The harvest is the end of the world, and the reapers are the angels."

On another occasion, Jesus spoke a parable about the tiny mustard seed. "What is the kingdom of God like, and to what will we compare it?" He asked. "It's like a grain of mustard seed that a man took and sowed in his field. It's the smallest of all seeds, but when it grows up it's larger than any herb and becomes a tree, so that the birds of the air come and live in its branches."

In another parable about the kingdom of heaven, Jesus said, "The kingdom of heaven is like a treasure hidden in a field. A man finds it and hides it again. Then in his joy he goes and sells all he has to buy that field.

"Again, the kingdom of heaven is like a merchant in search of fine pearls. When he finds a single pearl of great price, he goes and sells all he has and buys it."

The mere fact that we belong to the Church doesn't in itself make us fit for the kingdom of heaven. It's necessary to live a holy life. Our Lord compares our good works to the fruit of a tree. A good tree produces good fruit. A bad tree produces bad fruit.

Jesus illustrated this truth for his listeners by the parable of the barren fig tree. He said, "A certain man had a fig tree planted in his vineyard. He came looking for fruit on it, but he found none. Then he said to the vinedresser, 'Look! For three years I've come seeking fruit on this tree, and I've found none. So cut it down. Why let it use up the ground?'

"The vinedresser said to him, 'Sir, let it alone this year, too, till I dig around it and fertilize it. Perhaps it will bear fruit then. If not, I'll cut it down.'"

This story reminds us that God is merciful, giving us every opportunity to bear fruit. But if we continue to reject his grace, eventually we'll face his judgment. To remain in his kingdom, we must bear good fruit.

These are the parables Jesus told about the kingdom of heaven that we all hope to one day reach.

QUESTIONS FOR REVIEW:

1. Try to explain the first parable of the wheat and weeds in the field. What did each thing symbolize: The man sowing seeds, the wheat, the weeds and the enemy who sows those, the harvest, the reapers (or workers), the barn, the fire?

2. How does Jesus compare the kingdom of God to the mustard seed? What was this comparison trying to show?

3. Do these images of the world and heaven help you understand them? How so? Why do you think Jesus used stories like this to explain difficult teachings?

ACTIVITIES

SCIENCE PROJECT: CHILDREN OF THE KINGDOM GOOD SEEDS

Materials:
- ☐ Styrofoam cup
- ☐ Potting soil
- ☐ Pencil
- ☐ Marker
- ☐ Seeds (3 of any variety)
- ☐ Ziplock bag (large)
- ☐ Small plate

Instructions:
1. Poke two holes in the bottom of the cup with the pencil (this will help the germination process).
2. Fill the cup with the soil.
3. Place the seeds into the soil, following directions on the package as to how deep.
4. Place the cup on the small plate.
5. Water the plant until the soil is moist.
6. Wrap the plate and the cup with the Ziplock bag and place in a sunny spot (sealing plants in a plastic bag helps seeds to germinate more quickly).
7. Check your plant often over the next two weeks. When they sprout, remove the Ziplock bag.
8. Optional: Once the plant has leaves that are about 3 inches, you can replant it into a garden or large planter.
9. Discuss how the children of the kingdom are the good seeds.

GAME ACTIVITY: HIDDEN TREASURE HUNT

Materials:
- ☐ Small box
- ☐ Small wrapped candy
- ☐ Two people

Instructions:
1. Place the candy in the box.
2. One person hide the box for the other person to find.
3. When the box is found, eat a piece of candy.
4. Switch roles and repeat steps 1–3.

WORD SEARCH: THE KINGDOM OF HEAVEN PARABLES

Find the following words.
Merchant, Kingdom, Mustard, Pearls, Treasure, Parable, Vinedresser, Heaven, Weeds, Wheat

```
M W W L P N N X U T P V Q O G
L E Z H E E M L R X X I B R L
R Z R V E T G E N S S N P S J
Q U A C L A A O K Z L E S C R
Q E Q B H S T G X Y R D X I W
H T Q X U A A Y Q R A R W D A
Y B V R E I N Y L V E E H J M
V W E C F L I T Q E P S W T J
W E E D S F B I K X U S U K M
S F S C K P M A K I B E C T K
D R A T S U M T R L N R A D I
Q S O A C F S S T A E G C Z U
U I C D S Z K T S U P U D Q F
Y O P M W R V N A U Y V B O B
L V E W X B U Y Z F N Q J R M
```

Note: Some words may appear backwards.

CHAPTER 39
Jesus Teaches: The Sermon on the Mount and the Beatitudes

One of Jesus's sermons is known as the Sermon on the Mount because it was preached on the side of a small mountain, or hill. We can imagine our Savior seated on a rock, high on the side of the hill, with the people gathered below him.

It was in this sermon that Jesus gave us the Beatitudes, which tell us the actions and attitudes that God blesses. The sermon offers us what might be called the laws of the kingdom of heaven that Christ came to establish on earth. Jesus said:

"Blessed are the poor in spirit, for theirs is the kingdom of heaven.

"Blessed are the meek, for they will possess the earth.

"Blessed are those who mourn, for they will be comforted.

"Blessed are those who hunger and thirst for justice, for they will be satisfied.

"Blessed are the merciful, for they will obtain mercy.

"Blessed are the pure in heart, for they will see God.

"Blessed are the peacemakers, for they will be called children of God.

"Blessed are those who suffer persecution for the sake of justice, for theirs is the kingdom of heaven.

"Blessed are you when men reproach you, and persecute you, and—speaking falsely—say all kinds of evil against you, for my sake. Be glad and rejoice, for your reward is great in heaven."

Jesus himself was the perfect example of each of these Beatitudes. For this reason, not only every word, but also every action of Christ is a lesson for us. That's why he said of himself, "I am the way, the truth, and the life."

Each of these Beatitudes has a deeper lesson that shows us a way Jesus wants us to live. These lessons are too much to go into here, but we can discuss one of them.

Jesus began his wonderful Sermon on the Mount with the words, "Blessed are the poor in spirit, for theirs is the kingdom of heaven." The poor in spirit are those whose hearts are not set on the things of this world. They may be terribly poor and have scarcely enough to survive. But if they bear their circumstances patiently, their reward will be the kingdom of heaven.

Other people are poor because they have willingly given up all that they own for the love of Jesus. They too will possess the kingdom of heaven. But even those who possess great wealth may be poor in spirit if they use their riches well: not merely for their own comfort and enjoyment, but for the glory of God and the good of their fellow human beings. Theirs, too, will be the kingdom of heaven.

QUESTIONS FOR REVIEW:

1. What did Jesus teach us from his Sermon on the Mount?

2. Why is it called the Sermon on the Mount?

3. What does it mean to be "poor in spirit"?

ACTIVITIES

COLORING PAGE: JESUS TEACHING

SNACK PROJECT: SERMON ON THE MOUNT CUPCAKES

Ingredients:
- ☐ 1 1/2 cups all-purpose flour
- ☐ 1 tsp. baking powder
- ☐ 1/2 tsp. salt
- ☐ 1/2 cup (1 stick) softened butter
- ☐ 1 cup of sugar
- ☐ 3 eggs
- ☐ 1 1/2 tsp. vanilla extract
- ☐ 3/4 cup milk
- ☐ whipped cream
- ☐ toothpick
- ☐ string

Directions:

1. Preheat oven to 350° F. Line a cupcake pan with twelve paper liners and set aside.
2. Mix flour, baking powder, and salt in medium bowl by hand.
3. Beat butter and sugar until fluffy. Add eggs one at a time, then beat in vanilla.
4. Add flour mixture and milk alternately, mixing until batter is smooth.
5. Distribute mixture evenly among the cupcake liners.
6. Bake 18–22 minutes. Remove and let cool.
7. Once fully cooled, use whipped cream for frosting in order to create a "mountain look."
8. Using string, attach toothpicks to each other to create a cross.
9. The cross represents Jesus, and the cupcake with whipped cream represents the mountain.
10. Enjoy!

CRAFT PROJECT: THE MOUNT OF BEATITUDES POSTER

Materials:
- ☐ Large white poster board
- ☐ Markers/Pencil/Pen

Instructions:

1. On the poster, draw a mountain. Then draw Jesus on top of it.
2. Going up the slopes and within the mountain, write out the Beatitudes (and try to commit them to memory). After you have written all of them, verbally give your mom or dad an example of how you could live out each beatitude in your everyday life.

CHAPTER 40
Jesus Teaches: The Rich Young Man

One day, a rich young man came to Jesus. He belonged to a noble family, and his character was beyond reproach. He kept the commandments of God and lived an upright life.

But he wasn't satisfied with himself. His heart was on fire with holy ambitions, and he wanted to make better use of his talents and his wealth. He thought that Jesus could advise him on what to do.

Coming to the Savior, he asked, "Teacher, what good work must I do to have eternal life?"

Jesus answered, "If you want to enter into life, keep the commandments."

The young man said to him, "Which ones?"

Jesus answered, "You shall not kill. You shall not commit adultery. You shall not steal. You shall not bear false witness. Honor your father and your mother. And you shall love your neighbor as yourself."

The young man replied, "Teacher, all these commandments I have kept since I was young. What do I still lack?"

Jesus looked at him lovingly and called him to the perfect life. "Only one thing is lacking for you," he said. "Go, sell all that you have and give to the poor, and you'll have treasure in heaven. Then come and follow me."

When the young man heard these words, he became very sad, because he did not want to give his possessions away. Turning around, he went away in silence. He had great possessions, and although he felt a great desire to follow Jesus, he didn't have the courage to give them up.

After he had gone, Jesus said to his disciples, "How hard it is for those who have riches to enter the kingdom of God!"

Hearing these words, the apostles were astonished. Though they were poor themselves, it seemed that they had not yet learned to love the freedom that comes from being poor for the sake of the kingdom of God. Perhaps deep down in their hearts, they still envied the rich.

So Jesus repeated what he had said to them: "How hard it is for those who trust in riches to enter the kingdom of heaven! It's easier for a camel to squeeze through the eye of a needle, than for a rich man to enter the kingdom of heaven."

But the apostles were more deeply puzzled than before. They said among themselves, "Who, then, can be saved?" Jesus replied, "With men it is impossible. But not with God. For all things are possible with God."

Jesus meant this: As long as a rich man depends only upon himself and puts his faith in what he possesses, he may be able to purchase for himself all the finest things of this world, but he won't be able to gain the happiness of heaven. If God gives him the grace, however, he may understand the foolishness of his ways before it's too late. If he becomes generous with what he possesses, God will have mercy on him.

Our Lord knew, however, that people with great riches are often so taken up with their money and the things it will buy, they easily forget that all they are, and all they have, belong to God. They think they can live without him, and they pay little attention to the inspirations of his grace.

Peter said to Jesus, "We've left behind everything to follow you."

Jesus answered, "Truly, I say to you, everyone who has left behind a house, or brothers, or sisters, or mother, or father, or children, or lands for my sake and for the gospel, will receive in this life a hundred times as much . . . and in the age to come, eternal life."

QUESTIONS FOR REVIEW:

1. Why did the rich young man turn to Jesus?

2. Why did the rich young man go away sad from Jesus?

3. What do you think Jesus meant when he said: "How hard it is for those who trust in riches to enter the kingdom of heaven!"

ACTIVITIES

DRAWING PROJECT: THE RICH YOUNG MAN COMIC STRIP

Materials:
- ☐ Poster board
- ☐ Ruler
- ☐ Markers/Pencil/Pen

Instructions:
1. On the poster board, use the ruler to divide it into 8 even boxes
2. Draw and write a comic strip that re-tells the story of the rich young man.

MAZE: FINDING OUR WAY TO HEAVEN

Go through the maze to make it to heaven!

FINISH

START

CROSSWORD PUZZLE: THE RICH YOUNG MAN

Across

2. Jesus said it is easier for a _____ to pass through the eye of a needle than for a rich man to enter the kingdom of heaven.
3. All things are _____ with God.
6. Jesus said to keep the _____.

Down

1. The rich young man wanted this.
4. Giving away his possessions made the young man _____.
5. Jesus said to give his possessions to the _____.

CHAPTER 41
Miracles: Jesus Heals

In addition to teaching us, one of the other big aspects of Jesus's ministry while he walked the earth was performing miracles. And some of the most beautiful miracles that he performed were miracles of healing. Let's hear a few of these amazing stories now!

One evening, Jesus and his disciples were staying in Capernaum. The townspeople brought to him all who were ill or possessed by demons. In fact, the whole town had gathered together at the door. That night he healed many who were afflicted with various diseases, and he cast out many demons.

The news spread throughout Capernaum that Jesus was in the city and was staying at a certain house. Immediately, the people stopped whatever they were doing and hurried there to see him and listen to his teaching. Soon, a great crowd gathered that filled the house and spilled out the door. Outside in the street were many more who strained their ears to hear the Savior's voice and tried to see him over the heads of those in front of them.

Several men came along who were carrying on a paralyzed man on a bed. They tried to push their way through the crowd so they could enter the house and ask Jesus to heal him. But the people wouldn't make way for them.

So they climbed up on the roof of the house, removed some tiles to make a hole in it, and lowered the bed with the sick man through the opening. In this way, they were able to lay him down in front of Jesus.

Our Lord admired their faith and their perseverance. He said to the paralyzed man, "Son, your sins are forgiven."

Hearing this, some of the scribes and Pharisees sitting there were outraged, thinking to themselves, "Why does this man speak like this? It's blasphemy! Who can forgive sins but God alone?"

Knowing their thoughts, Jesus said to them, "Why do you question in your hearts? Which is easier to say to the paralytic: 'Your sins are forgiven you,' or to say to him, 'Get up, pick up your bed, and walk'? But so that you can know that the Son of Man has power on earth to forgive sins"—then he turned and said to the paralyzed man—"I say to you, get up, pick up your bed, and go home."

Right then, the man got up, picked up the bed where he had been lying, and carried it home, glorifying God as he walked along.

The crowds, seeing what had happened, were filled with amazement. They praised God, saying, "We've seen astounding things today!"

Another day, Jesus was walking along the road that leads from Jericho to Jerusalem, with a great crowd following him. A blind man sat by the roadside, begging, because he couldn't work to make a living. His name was Bartimaeus.

Hearing all the voices of the crowd, Bartimaeus called out to ask what was happening. They told him that Jesus of Nazareth was passing by. He knew that Jesus could work miracles of healing, so when he heard this, he began to cry out, "Jesus, Son of David, have mercy on me!"

Some of the people were annoyed by his cries and told him to be quiet. But he cried out even louder, "Son of David, have mercy on me!"

Hearing his cry, Jesus stopped and said, "Tell him to come to me."

So the people called the blind man and said to him, "Get up. Take heart! He's calling you." Bartimaeus jumped up, threw off his cloak, and came to Jesus.

Our Lord asked him, "What do you want me to do for you?"

Bartimaeus answered, "Rabbi, let me receive my sight."

"Go your way," Jesus replied. "Your faith has healed you."

Immediately, the blind man received his sight and joined the crowd that was following Jesus.

QUESTIONS FOR REVIEW:

1. What did Jesus do one evening while staying in Capernaum with his disciples?

2. How was the paralyzed man able to get to Jesus?

3. Why were the Pharisees angry that Jesus forgave the sins of the paralyzed man?

ACTIVITIES

COLORING PAGE: JESUS HEALING THE PARALYTIC

CRAFT PROJECT: JESUS HEALS THE PARALYTIC DIORAMA

Materials:
- ☐ shoe box
- ☐ brown paper, paper bag, or construction paper
- ☐ scissors
- ☐ (2) 3x4 in. pieces of fabric
- ☐ hole punch
- ☐ yarn or string
- ☐ 4 craft sticks
- ☐ markers
- ☐ 4 Lego, Playmobil, or other small people
- ☐ glue

Directions:

1. Cover the outside of shoebox in brown paper. Set the shoe box so that the opening is facing you. Draw a door on the long side adjacent to the open side and a large rectangular opening on the top.

2. Cut door so it swings open and cut out the opening on the rooftop. Hole-punch all four corners around the edge of the opening on the rooftop.

3. Hole-punch all four corners of one piece of fabric.

4. Tie pieces of yarn or string (about 12 inches each) to each corner of the hole-punched fabric. This is the mat to be lowered through the opening in the roof.

5. Glue craft sticks to other piece of fabric along long side of fabric so there are two on top and two on bottom parallel to the top ones. Let dry. This is the stretcher.

6. Designate one figure to be the paralytic, one to be Jesus, and two to be the paralytic's friends.

7. Lay the paralytic man on the stretcher and set the stretcher on the mat to be lowered.

8. Tie the stretcher and mat with string to holes in the opening on the rooftop.

9. Place the Jesus figure inside the house and the two friends on the rooftop.

10. Enjoy!

CRAFT PROJECT: BLIND MAN FACE PUPPET

Materials:
- ☐ Templates
- ☐ crayons or markers
- ☐ scissors
- ☐ straw

Directions:

1. Cut out the face and half face from the template from page 281.
2. Using crayons or markers have child color both faces.
3. Glue googly eyes on the full face.
4. Cut two circles out of black paper or felt and glue those onto the half face.
5. Lay the half face on the full face and secure with tape at the hairline.
6. Tape straw to the backside near the chin. Face puppet is complete!
7. Enjoy!

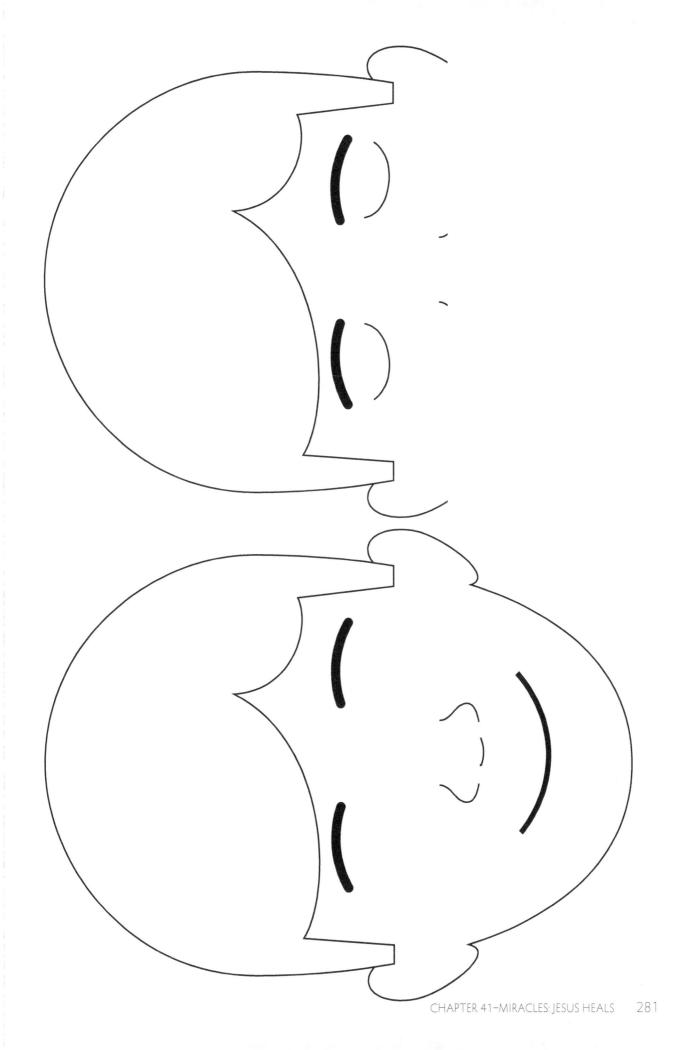

CHAPTER 42
Miracles: The Loaves and the Fishes

Jesus performed many other miracles that had nothing to do with physical healings.

One day, he and the apostles found a great number of people waiting for them. Walking on through the crowd, they went on into the wilderness. Soon they came to a grass-covered hill where they sat down on the ground to rest.

But there was to be no rest for them that day. The crowds followed after them, and soon they were surrounded by about five thousand people.

Jesus felt compassion for the crowds. He couldn't send them away, because they were like sheep without a shepherd, and they had come to him to learn about the love of God. So he laid aside his own weariness. He taught them all day long about the kingdom of God, and he healed all their sick.

When the day was almost done, the shadows of the evening began to close in on them. The apostles came to Jesus and said, "This is a remote place, and the hour is late. Send the people away, so they can go into the villages to buy food for themselves."

But Jesus replied, "They don't need to go away. Give them something to eat."

The apostles were skeptical. "Are we to go and buy two hundred denarii worth of bread, and give it to them to eat?"

Jesus asked, "How many loaves do you have? Go and see."

One of the apostles, Andrew, the brother of Simon Peter, said, "There's a boy here with five barley loaves and two fishes, but what are these among so many?"

Jesus said, "Have the people sit down on the grass in groups of fifty." The apostles did as Jesus instructed, and soon that great multitude was sitting down on the green grass.

Then Jesus took the five loaves and the two fishes. Looking up to heaven, he blessed the loaves, broke them, and distributed them to his apostles to give out to the multitude, along with the fish.

The people were very hungry. Many of them had left home the night before, and they had been listening to Jesus all day long. So they all ate as much as they wanted, until they were satisfied.

Then Jesus said to his apostles, "Gather up the fragments that are left over, so that nothing will be lost." The apostles did this, filling twelve baskets with the leftover pieces of the five barley loaves.

When the people saw the great miracle that Jesus had performed, they said, "This is truly the prophet who is to come into the world."

Knowing that they had it in mind to take him by force and make him king, Jesus went away up the mountain by himself, for this was not the kind of kingdom he had come to establish.

QUESTIONS FOR REVIEW:

1. When the apostles came to Jesus to tell him to send the 5,000 people away so they could go into the villages to buy food for themselves, how did Jesus reply?

2. How many loaves and fishes did the apostles realize they had to give to the crowd of 5,000?

3. What miracle did Jesus perform?

ACTIVITIES

COLORING PAGE: THE BOY WITH THE LOAVES AND FISHES

CRAFT PROJECT: LOAVES AND FISHES NECKLACE

Materials:
- [ ] pasta (rigatoni, penne, or some kind with a hole large enough to string)
- [ ] construction paper
- [ ] yarn or sting
- [ ] hole punch
- [ ] scissors
- [ ] markers
- [ ] paint (optional)

Directions:

1. (Optional) Paint the noodles your favorite color.

2. On the construction paper, draw a fish slightly bigger than your pasta noodle, then use this as a template to cut out 8–10 fish.

3. Hole-punch each fish's mouth.

4. Draw eyes and fins on the fish.

5. Cut yarn to desired length for necklace (tape one end for easier stringing). Then, string the noodles and fish on the yarn in an alternating manner.

6. Tie necklace off.

7. Enjoy!

DOUBLE PUZZLE: THE LOAVES AND THE FISHES

Unscramble the words. Copy the letters in the numbered blocks with the corresponding numbers at the bottom to help answer the question.

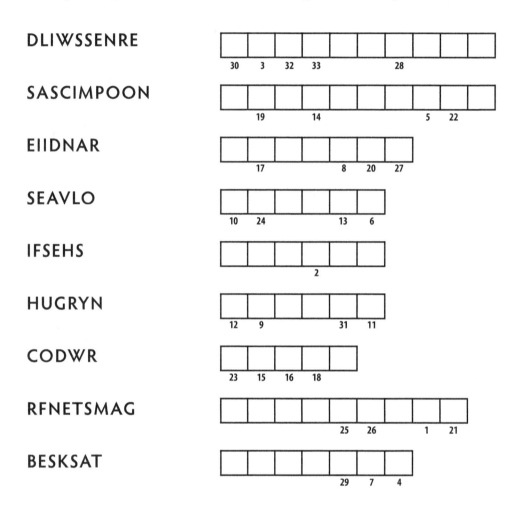

DLIWSSENRE

30 3 32 33   28

SASCIMPOON

19   14   5   22

EIIDNAR

17   8   20 27

SEAVLO

10 24   13   6

IFSEHS

2

HUGRYN

12   9   31 11

CODWR

23 15 16 18

RFNETSMAG

25 26   1 21

BESKSAT

29   7   4

When the people saw the great miracle that Jesus had performed, what did they say?

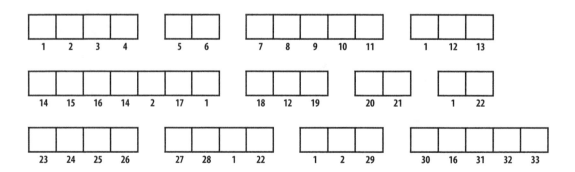

1 2 3 4   5 6   7 8 9 10 11   1 12 13

14 15 16 14 2 17 1   18 12 19   20 21   1 22

23 24 25 26   27 28 1 22   1 2 29   30 16 31 32 33

CHAPTER 43
Miracles: Walking on Water

Yet another time Jesus performed a miracle to show his apostles who he really was so they could put their faith in him.

This occurred in Galilee where Jesus was preaching to the people on the eastern shore of the Sea of Galilee. In the evening, he dismissed the people and told the apostles to get into the boat and row back to Capernaum. Then he went up on a mountain alone to pray.

The sea was rough, and the apostles had a hard time rowing the boat because the wind went against them. They were still far from shore in the early morning hours before dawn, when they suddenly saw someone coming toward them, walking on the water. They were terrified, crying out, "It's a ghost!"

But the figure walking on the water spoke to them, saying, "Take courage! It's Jesus; don't be afraid."

Peter said, "Lord, if it's really you, tell me to come to you on the water."

Jesus said to Peter, "Come on!"

Peter immediately got out of the boat and started to walk toward Jesus on the water. But when Peter saw how strong the winds were blowing, he began to be afraid. At once he felt himself sinking.

Peter cried out, "Lord, save me!"

So Jesus reached out his hand and caught him, saying, "You of little faith! Why did you doubt?"

When they got into the boat, the wind ceased. Then those who were in the boat worshipped Jesus, saying, "Truly, you are the Son of God."

Our Lord's miracle had helped them to understand more clearly who he was, and to put their trust in him. But God's plan of salvation was still in many ways a mystery to them. They had much yet to learn, and they would see and hear much that would require of them a firm faith in God.

QUESTIONS FOR REVIEW:

1. What did the apostles think was coming toward them on the water?

2. What did the figure on the water say to them?

3. Why did our Lord tell Peter he had little faith?

ACTIVITIES

CROSSWORD PUZZLE: JESUS WALKS ON WATER

Across

4. Jesus spoke saying, "Take _____."
5. Apostles thought this was coming toward them.
6. He wanted Jesus to make him walk on the water.

Down

1. Jesus said to Peter: "You of little _____."
2. Jesus went here to pray.
3. Jesus was preaching on this shore.
7. The sea was_____.

CHAPTER 44
Miracles: Raising the Dead

Some of the most powerful miracles Jesus performed were when he raised the dead to life! Three times Our Lord showed that he had power over life and death.

One day, as he and his disciples were entering a little town in Galilee called Nain, the body of a young man was being carried out. He had been the only son of his mother, who was a widow.

Seeing the bereaved widow, Jesus had compassion on her and said to her, "Don't weep." Then turning, he touched the wooden frame on which the body was being carried, and those who carried it stood still. Jesus said, "Young man, I say to you, get up."

At once the dead man sat up and began to speak. Jesus gave him to his mother. Great fear gripped all those who saw what had happened. They glorified God, saying, "A great prophet has arisen among us, and God has visited his people!"

On another occasion, the only daughter of Jairus, the ruler of the synagogue at Capernaum, was dying at the young age of twelve. Jarius fell at Jesus's feet and begged him to come to his house and cure his daughter.

Jesus started at once for the house of Jairus, but the people crowded around him, and his progress through the streets was slow. Suddenly a messenger came to Jairus, saying to him, "Your daughter is dead. Why trouble the Teacher any further?"

But when he heard this, Jesus said, "Don't be afraid. Only believe, and she will be well."

When he came to the house, he wouldn't allow anyone to enter with him except Peter, James, and John, and the parents of the little girl. Inside, many people were standing about, weeping and wailing loudly.

Jesus said to them, "Don't weep. The girl isn't dead, but only sleeping." But they knew that she was dead, and they laughed at him with scorn.

He sent them all outside and took the child's parents and his three apostles into the room where the girl was lying. Taking her by the hand, he said, "Little girl, I say to you, get up." Immediately she got up and began walking around. Then Jesus told her joyful and astonished parents to give her something to eat.

The third person to be raised from the dead was a man named Lazarus, a close friend of Jesus.

He lived in Bethany with his sisters, Mary and Martha.

One day Lazarus grew deathly ill, so his sisters sent a message to Jesus, saying, "The one you love is sick." Now, in spite of the great love that Jesus had for Lazarus, he didn't go right away to Bethany. He stayed where he was for two days longer.

His apostles wondered why he delayed so long, but finally he said to them, "Lazarus, our friend, is asleep, but I'm going to awaken him from his sleep."

The apostles said, "Lord, if he's only sleeping, he'll get well." Now Jesus had actually spoken of his death, but they thought he meant that Lazarus was just asleep.

Then Jesus said to them plainly, "Lazarus is dead. And I'm glad for your sakes that I wasn't there, so that you will believe. But let us go to him."

They set out for Bethany, and when they arrived, they found that Lazarus had been in his tomb four days. When Martha, the sister of Lazarus, saw Jesus, she said, "Lord, if you had been here, my brother wouldn't have died."

Jesus said to her, "Your brother will rise again."

Martha replied, "I know that he will rise again in the resurrection at the end of the world."

Jesus said to her, "I am the resurrection and the life. Whoever believes in me, even if he dies, he will live. And whoever lives and believes in me will never die. Do you believe this?"

"Yes, Lord," Martha answered. "I believe that you are the Christ, the Son of God, who has come into the world."

Jesus had not yet come into the village, but was still at the place where Martha had met him. Getting up, Mary ran out to meet him. When she came to him, she fell down at his feet and said, "Lord, if you had been here, my brother wouldn't have died."

When Jesus saw Mary and her friends weeping, he was deeply moved. He asked, "Where have you laid him?"

They replied, "Lord, come and see."

Then Jesus, too, began to weep. Those nearby said, "See how he loved him!"

So they came to the tomb. Like many tombs of that day, it was a cave cut out of a rock, and a stone was placed in front of it. Jesus said, "Take away the stone."

Martha said, "But Lord, by this time there will be an odor, for he has been dead four days."

Jesus answered, "Didn't I tell you that if you believe, you'll see the glory of God?" So they took the stone away.

Then Jesus, lifting up his eyes, prayed, "Father, I give you thanks that you've heard me. I knew that you always hear me, but I've said this for the sake of the people standing nearby, so that they can believe that you have sent me."

Then, crying out with a loud voice, he said, "Lazarus, come out!"

Suddenly, Mary and Martha and their friends, and the disciples of Jesus who were gathered around, saw an amazing sight: Lazarus came out of the tomb, still bound hand and foot with bandages, and his face tied up in a cloth! Jesus said, "Unbind him, and let him go." Then he gave Lazarus back to his sisters.

QUESTIONS FOR REVIEW:

1. What did Jesus do to raise the widow's son back from the dead?

2. What did Jesus say to the people who were standing about weeping for the daughter of Jairus, and what was their reaction to his words?

3. How long was Lazarus in the tomb? Describe him as he came out.

ACTIVITIES

CRAFT PROJECT: JESUS HOLDS MY HAND

Materials:
☐ construction paper (2 colors)
☐ scissors
☐ glue
☐ pencil
☐ marker

Directions:
1. Draw a heart to fill the whole piece of construction paper and cut it out.
2. Using a different color of construction paper, trace child's hand and cut it out.
3. Use a marker to write child's name on the hand.
4. Glue the hand to the heart. Explain that just as Jesus raised the daughter of Jairus by taking her hand, He holds you too by the hand, ready to heal you.
5. Enjoy!

SNACK PROJECT: GINGERBREAD MUMMIES

Ingredients:
- ☐ 2 2/3 cups all-purpose flour
- ☐ 1 tsp. baking soda
- ☐ 1/2 tsp. salt
- ☐ 2 tsp. ground ginger
- ☐ 1/2 tsp. cinnamon
- ☐ 1/2 tsp. nutmeg
- ☐ 1/2 tsp. allspice
- ☐ 1/2 cup butter, softened
- ☐ 1 egg
- ☐ 3/4 cup packed brown sugar
- ☐ 1/3 cup molasses
- ☐ 2 Tbsp. water
- ☐ white icing

Directions:

1. Preheat oven to 350° F.
2. In a large bowl, cream the butter and brown sugar with an electric mixer until light and creamy.
3. Add egg, molasses, and brown sugar with mixer.
4. In a medium sized bowl, sift flour, baking soda, salt, ginger, cinnamon, nutmeg, and allspice.
5. Add dry ingredients to wet ingredients and mix well.
6. Divide dough in half, cover each half, and refrigerate for 30 minutes.
7. Roll out each portion of dough until it is 1/8 in. thin and use gingerbread cookie cutter to cut out men.
8. Place two inches apart on greased baking sheet or parchment paper and bake for 8–10 minutes.
9. Once cooled, frost cookies with white icing to look like mummies.
10. Enjoy!

CRAFT PROJECT: LAZARUS TOILET PAPER ROLL MUMMY

Materials:
- ☐ toilet paper roll
- ☐ white yarn
- ☐ googly eyes
- ☐ glue
- ☐ tape

Directions:

1. Tape a long piece of white yarn to the inside of the toilet paper roll. Begin wrapping upward around the outside of the roll (leaving room for the face) to look like a mummy.

2. Tape the end of the yarn in place.

3. Glue the googly eyes onto the toilet paper roll.

4. Enjoy!

SNACK PROJECT: HOTDOG LAZARUS

Ingredients:
- ☐ 1 package of hotdogs
- ☐ 1 can of ready-make croissant dough
- ☐ mustard
- ☐ pizza cutter

Directions:

1. Preheat oven to 375° F.

2. Lay out croissant dough and push together any seams.

3. Using pizza cutter, cut dough into 1 in. long strips.

4. Wrap dough strips around hot dogs, starting at bottom and leaving 2 in. at the top. Using remaining strips of dough, wrap the headdress around the top of the hotdog leaving room for eyes.

5. Set on cookie sheet and place in preheated oven for 12–15 minutes or until dough is golden brown.

6. Remove and let cool for a few minutes. Then, use mustard to add the eyes to your Lazarus hotdog.

7. Enjoy!

WORD SEARCH: THE WIDOW'S SON AND JAIRUS'S DAUGHTER

Find the following words.
Believe, Capernaum, Daughter, Death, Jairus, Life, Raise, Sleeping, Teacher, Widow

V E B M Z U W K G J M R P R T

L Y S G U I L N P A C E E E U

H D Y I D A I C V I E T F C F

F H E O A P N Z A R W H I T L

K J W M E R Z R U U U G L Y Q

H T A E D C D B E S Y U C M L

Y D L Q J E U A M P H A J R M

S S Y T O E Q I H T A D C O S

F Q O H E F U X D C D C E U C

N C Y W M A L P I Z P J O H C

X C G Q B N C T A O E I V S E

B E L I E V E H F S S R N Q P

J R Q H I D T X E W H Z L B U

U K Y V V D O Z R R X T D A P

R R C P Z V I U Y Q E W F P G

Note: Some words may appear backwards.

CHAPTER 45
Peter the Rock

Toward the end of his public life, Jesus and the apostles were walking one day through the country to the east of the Jordan River. They were near the town of Caesarea Philippi when Jesus turned to them suddenly and said, "Who do people say that the Son of Man is?" He was speaking, of course, of himself. They answered, "Some say you're John the Baptist; others, that you're Elijah; still others, Jeremiah or one of the prophets."

"But who do *you* say that I am?" Jesus asked.

Simon answered on behalf of all the rest: "You are the Christ, the Son of the living God."

Then Jesus said to him, "Blessed are you, Simon, son of John, because no man has revealed this to you, but rather my Father who is in heaven. And I say to you: You are Peter, the rock, and on this rock I will build my Church. The gates of hell will not prevail against it. And I will give to you the keys to the kingdom of heaven. Whatever you will bind on earth will be bound also in heaven; and whatever you will loose on earth will be loosed also in heaven."

By calling Peter "the rock" our blessed Savior meant that Peter would be the foundation on which he would build his Church. He was to become the first pope! Jesus also revealed to Simon Peter and to the rest of the apostles the great work that they were to do in the world. Peter would receive the keys to the kingdom of heaven. He would be the one to tell men what they must do to please God and to be saved.

Together with the rest of the apostles, Peter would have the authority from Christ to say what was right and what was wrong, what was true and what was false. God would watch over him and protect him from error, and whatever he commanded would be the law for the Church.

QUESTIONS FOR REVIEW:

1. Which apostle did Jesus make the rock of his Church? What was his name originally and what did Jesus change it to?

2. Why did Jesus call him "the rock"? What did this mean?

3. What role would he go on to play and what was his authority?

ACTIVITIES

CRAFT PROJECT: KINGDOM OF HEAVEN PAPER KEY

Materials:
☐ construction paper
☐ string or yarn
☐ old key

Directions:
1. Cut a tag for the key from construction paper and write "Kingdom of Heaven."
2. Attach the paper tag to the key with a string or piece of yarn.
3. Discuss Our Lord saying to Peter that He would give him the keys to kingdom of heaven.
4. Enjoy!

SNACK PROJECT: MARSHMALLOW CHURCH

Materials:
☐ Marshmallows (preferably small)
☐ Toothpicks

Instructions:
1. Attach marshmallows to each end of the toothpick to build a church of your own design.

CHAPTER 46
Jesus, the Good Shepherd

One way Jesus explained the Church was to say it was like a flock of sheep. This was a useful comparison because raising sheep was one of the principal occupations of the people in the days of Our Lord. No figure was more familiar than that of the shepherd watching over his sheep.

All day long the shepherd would lead his flock across the countryside in search of good pasture. He would watch over them with loving care, driving them gently with his crooked staff. The sheep would learn to know his voice, and when he called, they would come scampering to his feet.

When nighttime came, he would lead them to the sheepfold. This was a kind of yard, surrounded by a stone wall. There was a narrow gate where the sheep would enter while the shepherd stood and counted them as they went in, making sure that none had been lost. Once they were inside, the shepherd would close the gate and bar it for the night.

Then, stretching out on the ground in front of it, the shepherd would go to sleep. But even while asleep, he was alert. If there was even so much as the sound of a stranger's footstep or the rustle of a prowling animal, at once he would be wide awake, ready to protect his sheep.

Sometimes the shepherd didn't own the sheep, but hired himself out to take care of them for someone else. He was known as a hireling. In that case, he might not be very careful about his work. Maybe he would neglect them, or in time of danger he might run away, because the sheep didn't belong to him, and he had little to lose if anything happened to them. This is an important distinction from a good shepherd, and Our Lord pointed out this difference when he compared his Church to a sheepfold and himself to a shepherd. He said:

"Truly, truly, I say to you: Whoever enters the sheepfold, not by the door but by climbing in another way, is a thief and a robber. But whoever enters in by the door is the shepherd of the sheep.

"To him the gatekeeper opens. The sheep hear his voice, and he calls his own sheep by name and leads them out. And when he has let out his own sheep, he goes in front of them, and the sheep follow him because they know his voice. But they won't follow a stranger. They run from him because they don't know the voice of strangers. . . .

"I am the good shepherd. The good shepherd gives his life for his sheep. But the hireling is not the shepherd, and the sheep don't belong to him.

"When the hireling sees a wolf coming, he runs away and leaves the sheep unguarded. Then the wolf snatches and scatters the sheep. The hireling runs away because he's a hireling, and he has no concern for the sheep.

"I am the good shepherd. I know mine and mine know me, just as the Father knows me and I know the Father; and I lay down my life for my sheep. But I have other sheep as well that are not of this sheepfold. I must bring them as well, and they will listen to my voice, and there will be one fold and one shepherd."

Our Lord was teaching here that his flock of sheep would include not only the Jewish people, but the Gentiles as well. Together, they would make a single flock with one Shepherd, Jesus himself.

QUESTIONS FOR REVIEW:

1. Why did Jesus tell the story of the Church being like a flock of sheep?

2. What is a hireling and how is Jesus as the Good Shepherd different?

3. What did Jesus mean when he said, "I have other sheep as well that are not of this sheepfold. I must bring them as well, and they will listen to my voice, and there will be one fold and one shepherd."

ACTIVITIES

MAZE: JESUS FINDS HIS SHEEP

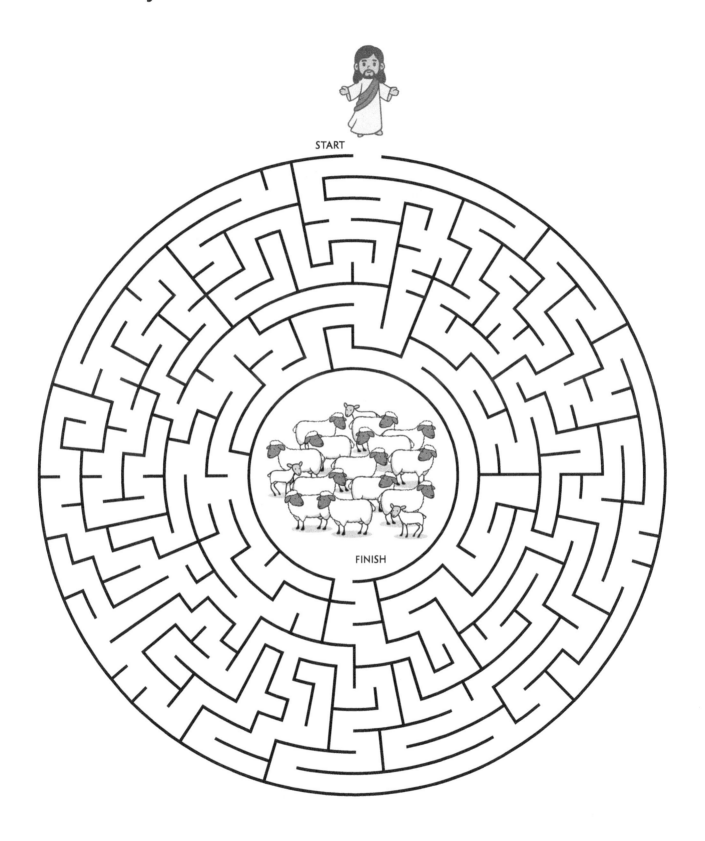

START

FINISH

CRAFT PROJECT: PAPER PLATE SHEEP

Materials:

- ☐ Small white paper plate
- ☐ Cotton balls
- ☐ Glue
- ☐ Scissors
- ☐ Black Crayon/Marker
- ☐ Templates from pages 303-305
- ☐ Small craft eyes (optional)

Instructions:

1. Cut out the sheep head, tail, and legs from pages 303 and 305.

2. Glue on the eyes to the sheep's head or draw eyes (and a mouth) with the black crayon or marker.

3. Glue all the parts of the sheep to the paper plate, which is the sheep's body.

4. Glue the cotton balls on to the paper plate.

5. Enjoy!

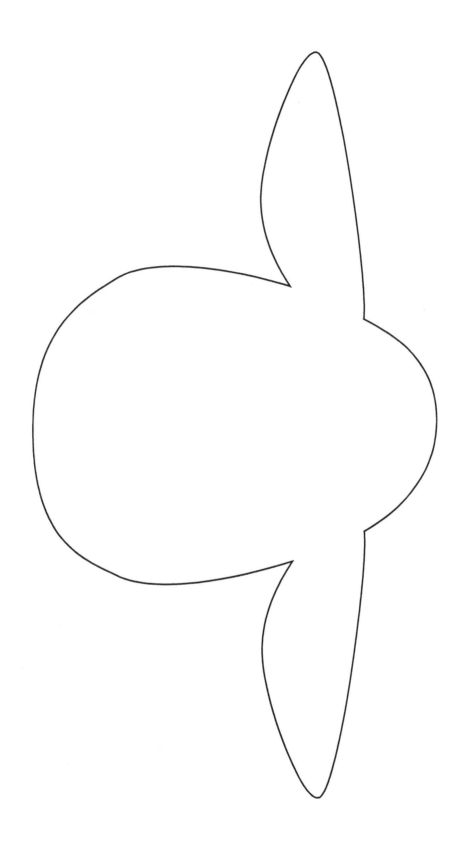

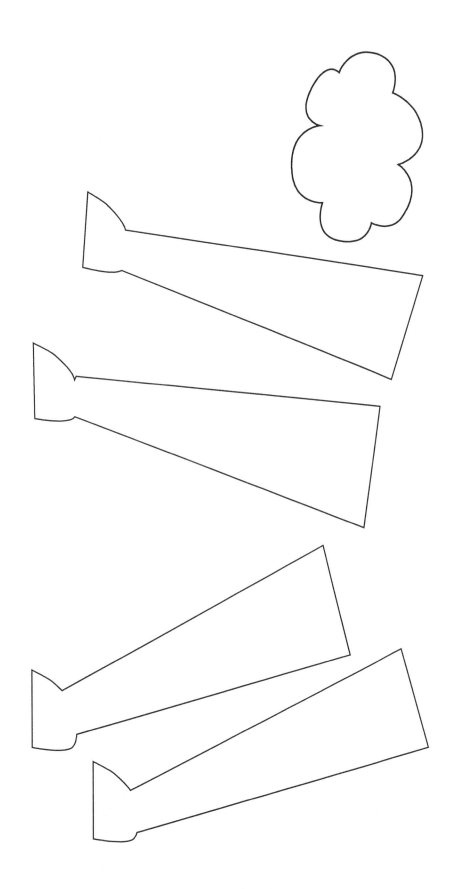

DOUBLE PUZZLE: JESUS THE GOOD SHEPHERD

Unscramble the words. Copy the letters in the numbered blocks with the corresponding numbers at the bottom to help answer the question.

FKLOC

PESHE

SAETUPR

SIAOVR

HCHUCR

KAEERPEETG

LOFW

TISLEGNE

HIWSEJ

What title did Jesus give himself?

CHAPTER 47
Jesus as the Bread of Life

Recall the miracle Jesus performed by multiplying the loaves and fishes. That amazing deed was a sign that Jesus cared about people's basic needs and wanted his disciples to help others. But it was much more than that. This particular miracle gave Our Lord the opportunity to teach about the Eucharist.

After the people had been fed, the apostles got into the boat and started back across the lake for Capernaum. It was the same night that Jesus came to them, walking on the water.

Now the people knew that Jesus had not gotten into the boat with his apostles. There was another boat near the shore, and they watched all night to see whether Jesus would take it. The next morning, they realized that it was useless for them to wait any longer, so they made their way back to Capernaum, looking for Jesus.

There they found him teaching in the synagogue, and they said to him, "Rabbi, when did you come here?"

Jesus answered, "Truly, truly, I say to you, you seek me, not because you've seen miracles, but because you ate your fill of the loaves. Don't labor for the food that perishes, but for the food that endures to eternal life."

"What are we to do," the people asked, "so that we can perform the works of God?"

Jesus answered, "This is the work of God, that you believe in the One whom he has sent."

So they said to him, "What miraculous sign, then, do you perform, so that we can see it, and believe you? Our forefathers ate the manna in the desert, just as it's written in Scripture, 'He gave them bread from heaven to eat.'"

They wanted Jesus to perform a miracle, as God had done when he gave manna to the Israelites for their wilderness journey.

Then Jesus said to them, "Truly, truly, I say to you: Moses didn't give you the bread from heaven, but my Father gives you the true Bread from heaven. For the Bread of God comes down from heaven and gives life to the world."

The people said, "Lord, give us this bread always."

Jesus answered, "I am the Bread of life. Your fathers ate the manna in the desert, and they have died. This is the Bread that comes down from heaven, so that if anyone eats of it, he won't die.

"I am the living Bread that has come down from heaven. Whoever eats this Bread will live forever. And the Bread I will give is my flesh for the life of the world."

Then the people began to murmur among themselves, saying, "How can this man give us his flesh to eat?"

But Jesus continued. "Truly, truly, I say to you: Unless you eat the flesh of the Son of Man and drink his blood, you will not have life in you. Whoever eats my flesh and drinks my blood has eternal life, and I will raise him up on the last day."

Though the people had trouble understanding what Jesus was teaching, he continued to insist that they would have to eat his flesh and drink his blood to have eternal life. In this way, he laid the groundwork for them to understand later the great gift of the Eucharist, which he would give to the Church. In the Eucharist, Jesus would continue to be with his people, even after he ascended into heaven.

QUESTIONS FOR REVIEW:

1. What lesson can we draw from Jesus multiplying the loaves and the fishes?

2. What story from the Old Testament does the multiplying of the bread and the Eucharist point to?

3. How did Jesus respond when the people said, "How can this man give us his flesh to eat?"

ACTIVITIES

CRAFT PROJECT: RAMEN AND YOGURT CUP CHALICE

Materials:
- ☐ Empty Ramen Noodle bowl cup
- ☐ Empty Chobani yogurt cup
- ☐ Toilet tissue roll
- ☐ Craft Paint
- ☐ Hot glue gun
- ☐ Sequins

Instructions:
1. Empty and clean the yogurt and Ramen noodle cups.
2. Connect the tissue roll to the bottom of the Ramen cup with hot glue. Let dry.
3. Connect the Ramen cup/tissue roll part to the bottom of the yogurt cup with the hot glue. The yogurt cup will be the bottom of the chalice. Let dry.
4. Paint and decorate the chalice with sequins.
5. Enjoy!

SNACK PROJECT: BREAD OF LIFE COMMUNION WAFERS SNACK

Ingredients:
- ☐ White sandwich bread
- ☐ Grape juice
- ☐ Rolling pin
- ☐ Shot glass

Instructions:
1. Roll out a piece of bread with the rolling pin.
2. Use the shot glass to cut out the "communion" wafers.
3. Drink the juice with the wafers as the wine.
4. Discuss Jesus as the Bread of Life.

CRAFT PROJECT: I AM THE BREAD OF LIFE BOOKMARK

Materials:
☐ White card stock
☐ Markers
☐ Scissors
☐ Yarn

Instructions:
1. Cut out a 2 in. x 6 in. rectangle from a piece of cardstock to make the bookmark.
2. Write the words, "I am the Bread of Life" at the top of the bookmark.
3. Decorate the bookmark with small images of Eucharistic symbols (chalice, bread, grapes, etc.)
4. Enjoy using the bookmark!

CHAPTER 48
The Transfiguration

Try as they might, the apostles could not bring themselves to believe that Jesus was to suffer and die. Their hearts were filled with sadness to hear him talk about what lay ahead. It was a great disappointment to them to know that all their dreams of an earthly kingdom were in vain.

Jesus knew what they were thinking. He saw the troubled looks on their faces, and he felt compassion for them. After all, most of them were just simple, hardworking men, and they had been brought up to believe that the Messiah would be an earthly king. They could not imagine a kingdom that was not of this world. So Jesus decided to show them his glory.

At one point toward the end of Jesus's ministry, the disciples happened to be with Jesus in the country around Mount Tabor, one of the highest mountains in Palestine. Taking with him Peter, James, and John, Jesus went up to the top of the mountain to pray.

While he was praying, a great change came over him. His face shone like the sun, and his clothing became white as snow, as bright as lightning. He was entirely *transfigured*; that is, his appearance was transformed. This is why this event is known as the Transfiguration.

Suddenly, two men appeared and began to talk with Jesus. One was Moses; the other was the prophet Elijah. The three apostles listened and heard them speaking about his death that would soon take place in Jerusalem.

Seeing that Moses and Elijah were about to leave, Peter cried out to Jesus, "Lord, it's good for us to be here. Let us make three tents: one for you, one for Moses, and one for Elijah."

As Peter was still speaking, a bright cloud came and overshadowed them on the mountain. Out of the cloud, they heard a voice saying, "This is my beloved Son, in whom I am well pleased. Listen to him!"

Terror filled the hearts of Peter, James, and John, and they fell upon their faces. Then someone touched them, and they heard a voice saying, "Get up. Don't be afraid." Lifting up their eyes, they saw no one but Jesus.

As they started down the mountain with Jesus, he said to them, "Don't tell anyone what you have seen here until the Son of Man has risen from the dead." In this way, he reassured them both that he would rise from the dead and that he was the Messiah.

But there was still much that they couldn't yet understand. They eagerly discussed the Transfiguration among themselves, and they puzzled over the glorious scene they had witnessed.

Though Jesus's followers often failed to grasp his message, we must not judge them too harshly. Our Lord himself told them that only later, after he returned to heaven, would the Holy Spirit enlighten their understanding. And even today, many centuries later, the Spirit continues to lead the Church into all truth, as Jesus promised.

To their credit, despite their confusion about Jesus's mission, the apostles and many others among his disciples remained faithful to him. Though many were to fall away, and even one of the apostles would betray him, in the end, those who persevered were rewarded richly—not only with understanding, but with eternal life.

QUESTIONS FOR REVIEW:

1. Where did Jesus go to pray and who went with him?

2. What happened while Jesus was at the mountaintop?

3. Who else appeared on the mountaintop and what did they do?

ACTIVITIES

CRAFT PROJECT: ACROSTIC POEM

Instructions:
1. Write the word "Transfiguration" vertically on a scrap sheet of paper or in the space provided on page 312.
2. Find words from the story that will fit horizontally with these letters. For example, for the letter T, you can write "Tabor." (If you struggle to find a word for a certain letter, write in any word that describes Jesus.)
3. The words you find do not need to begin with each letter of the word "Transfiguration," but can fall anywhere within the word.

CRAFT PROJECT: ACROSTIC POEM

MAZE: JESUS AND HIS APOSTLES HEADING FOR THE TOP OF MT. TABOR

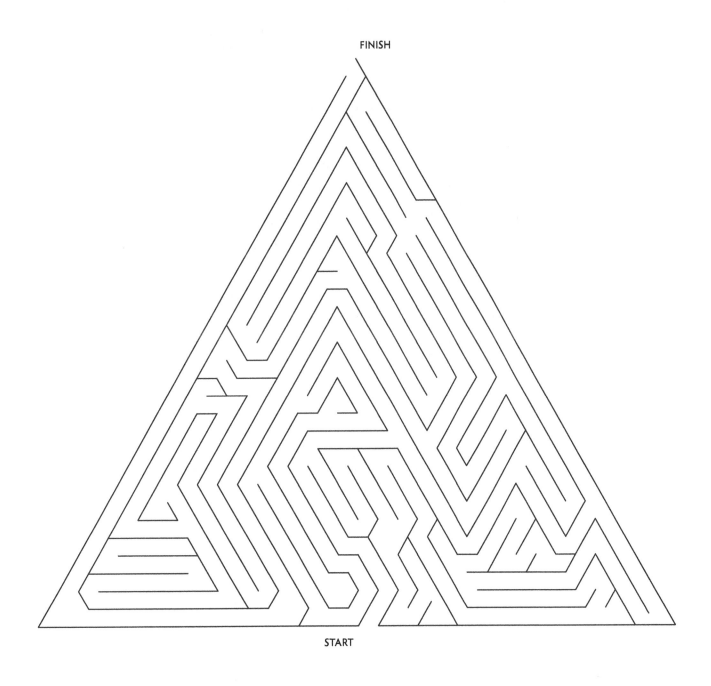

FINISH

START

CHAPTER 49
The Triumphant Entry into Jerusalem

Shortly after the Transfiguration, Jesus left Bethany and set out boldly for Jerusalem. Sending two of his apostles ahead to a little town called Bethphage, near the Mount of Olives, he said to them, "Go into the village opposite you. As soon as you enter you will find a donkey tied, and her colt with her. Untie them and bring them to me.

"If anyone says anything to you, say, 'The Lord needs them,' and he will let them go immediately."

Now all of this took place so that the words of the prophet would be fulfilled. He had said: "Tell the daughter of Zion, behold your king is coming to you, humble, and mounted on a donkey, and on a colt, the foal of a donkey." The disciples did as Jesus commanded them.

The road was crowded with throngs of people on their way to Jerusalem to celebrate the Feast of the Passover. The donkey and colt were brought to Jesus. The apostles threw their garments over them, and Jesus sat on them.

When the crowds on the road saw Jesus coming, they spread their cloaks on the ground before him and cut down branches from the trees and spread them on the road. With branches of palm trees in their hands, they crowded around him and cried out, "Hosanna to the Son of David! Blessed is the One who comes in the name of the Lord! Hosanna in the highest!"

The people were following a popular custom of their day for welcoming a king who was approaching their city. When they said, "Hosanna!"—which means "Save us!"—and they called Jesus "Son of David," they were welcoming him as the Messiah, the royal descendant of King David, who was coming to save the people from their troubles. Many of the people knew that Jesus had raised Lazarus from the dead and worked other miracles. So they now believed that he was the Christ whom God had promised to send.

QUESTIONS FOR REVIEW:

1. What did Jesus ask two of his disciples to do?

2. What feast was being celebrated at this time in Jerusalem? What present day feast do we celebrate to commemorate Jesus coming into Jerusalem (hint: remember they laid down palms before him on the road!)

3. What did the crowd yell out as Jesus was passing by on the donkey?

ACTIVITIES

CRAFT PROJECT: HANDPRINT PALM BRANCHES

Materials:
☐ parchment paper
☐ green tissue paper (a few different shades of green)
☐ glue
☐ scissors
☐ pen
☐ popsicle stick

Directions:

1. On the parchment paper, trace child's hand 6 times. Cut these out.

2. Cut or rip tissue paper into smaller pieces. Glue these to the parchment paper hands. Let dry.

3. Arrange hands so they are over lapping each other to look like a large palm branch. Glue or staple these together in palm branch form.

4. Glue or tape the entire branch to a long stick.

5. Enjoy!

COLORING PAGE: JESUS RIDING INTO JERSULAEM

CHAPTER 50
The Last Supper and the Garden of Gethsemane

It was Thursday, and the Feast of the Passover was at hand. For seven days the Jews would celebrate the anniversary of their deliverance from slavery. On the first day, they would eat the Paschal lamb. Jesus was gathered in the Upper Room of a house with his apostles. He took a piece of the unleavened bread that was part of the Paschal meal. Giving thanks to God, he blessed it, broke it, and gave it to his apostles, saying, "Take and eat; this is my body."

Then he took a chalice filled with wine and gave thanks. He passed it to them, saying, "All of you drink of this, for this is my blood of the new covenant, which will be shed for many for the forgiveness of sins." He had given his apostles his flesh to eat and his blood to drink. Then he said, "Do this in remembrance of me." By these words he gave to them and to their successors, the priests of the Catholic Church, the power to change bread and wine into his Body and Blood, and to offer up until the end of time the Holy Sacrifice of the Mass.

Then they went out to the Garden of Gethsemane to spend the night in prayer. Jesus invited Peter, James, and John to come with him farther into the garden. Then Jesus became deeply troubled. He said to them, "My soul is sad enough to die. Wait here, and stay awake with me. Pray so that you won't fall into temptation."

Then he went on alone. Falling flat on the ground, he prayed, "Father, if it is possible, let this chalice pass away from me. Nevertheless, not as I will, but as you will."

Then an angel appeared to him to strengthen him. Being in agony, he prayed even more earnestly. His sweat became like drops of blood.

Then he went back to his apostles. He found them sound asleep. He said, "Peter, couldn't you stay awake one hour with me? The spirit indeed is willing, but the flesh is weak."

Going away again, He prayed, "My Father, if this chalice cannot pass away unless I drink it, your will be done."

Coming back once more to his apostles, again he found them sleeping. Leaving them, he went again and prayed a third time, saying the same words again.

A third time he returned to his apostles, but this time he said, "The hour is at hand when the Son of Man will be betrayed into the hands of sinners." Then he added at last, "Get up, and let's go. Look! The one who betrays me is at hand."

Judas Iscariot arrived at the head of a band of soldiers and servants. Armed with swords and clubs, Judas had given them a sign, saying, "The one I kiss is the One you want. Seize him."

Jesus made no attempt to hide from the mob. Instead, he went to meet them. "For whom are you searching?" he asked.

They answered, "Jesus of Nazareth." Jesus said to them, "I am he."

As soon as Jesus had said "I am he," the mob with Judas pulled back and fell to the ground. Then Judas came forward and said, "Hello, Rabbi," and kissed him.

Jesus said to him, "Judas, are you betraying the Son of Man with a kiss?"

Again, Jesus asked them, "For whom are you searching?" They replied again, "Jesus of Nazareth."

Jesus answered, "I already told you that I am he." Then, pointing to his apostles, he said, "If I'm the One you're looking for, then let these men go their way."

This time the soldiers came up, seized Jesus, and held him, taking him off to face the Sanhedrin.

QUESTIONS FOR REVIEW:

1. What Jewish feast did Jesus and his apostles celebrate during the Last Supper and what did it commemorate?

2. When Jesus said, "Do this in remembrance of me," what did he mean? What was he establishing?

3. What did Judas do in the Garden of Gethsemane?

ACTIVITIES

COLORING PAGE: JESUS CELEBRATING THE EUCHARIST

DRAMA PROJECT: ACT OUT JESUS'S ARREST

Instructions:

Child can act out Jesus' arrest, playing the part of Peter who cut off the ear of Malchus. Optional: others can play the rolls of Jesus, Judas, the other apostles, and additional soldiers.

Judas approaches at the head of a band of soldiers.

Judas: *(Speaking to the soldiers)* The one I kiss is the one you want. Seize Him.

Jesus: For whom are you searching?

Soldiers: Jesus of Nazareth.

Jesus: I am He.

The soldiers pull back and fall to the ground.

Judas: Hello, Rabbi.

Judas kisses Jesus.

Jesus: Judas, are you betraying the Son of Man with a kiss? *(To the soldiers)* For whom are you searching?

Soldiers: Jesus of Nazareth.

Jesus: I already told you that I am He. If I'm the one you're looking for, then let these men go their way.

The soldiers seize Jesus.

Apostles: Lord, should we fight with the sword?

Simon Peter draws his sword and strikes Malchus.

Jesus: Put your sword back into its place. All those who take the sword will perish by the sword. If I asked, My Father would send ten legions of angels to defend Me. But then the Scriptures would not be fulfilled. Shouldn't I drink the chalice that the Father has given me?

Jesus touches the ear of Malchus and heals him.

Jesus: You come here to arrest me as if I were a robber. Yet I sat daily with you, teaching in the Temple, and you never laid hands on me. But this is your hour and the power of darkness.

The soldiers arrest Jesus and the apostles run away.

CRAFT PROJECT: SHOEBOX UPPER ROOM

Materials:
- ☐ Template from page 329
- ☐ Markers/Crayons
- ☐ Paint (optional)
- ☐ Glue stick
- ☐ Shoebox

Instructions:
1. Color the template of Jesus with his apostles at the Last Supper. Then cut it out (no need to color the tab at the bottom).

2. Decorate the inside of the shoebox however you like (paint it, cut out windows, etc.).

3. Fold the template at the dotted line, then glue the tab to the box so that the template is facing up.

4. Enjoy!

WORD SEARCH: THE GARDEN OF GETHSEMANE

Find the following words in the word search below:

Garden, Angel, Blood, Sweat, Sleeping, Judas, Betray, Apostles, Praying, Will

```
Q  J  B  D  U  R  A  S  E  J  F  X  A  L  G
B  G  H  X  S  E  E  N  R  H  G  N  L  X  N
X  V  A  D  B  L  K  N  M  X  G  I  J  O  I
D  T  C  R  T  M  G  I  A  E  W  P  P  K  P
Q  L  A  S  D  Y  R  B  L  T  X  Q  W  G  E
O  H  O  E  G  E  M  A  T  U  K  Y  F  Y  E
L  P  Q  C  W  Q  N  S  F  J  Y  P  C  F  L
A  J  P  N  Y  S  B  B  V  E  J  T  J  B  S
R  F  A  C  O  O  B  A  C  B  N  X  T  I  P
K  P  R  A  Y  I  N  G  B  E  G  U  I  Y  E
D  O  O  L  B  B  S  Z  X  T  K  A  C  S  S
B  I  T  D  U  M  N  L  I  R  Q  Y  Q  G  A
J  J  T  F  D  O  E  H  U  A  V  S  X  R  D
M  I  N  M  G  Q  B  X  F  Y  F  E  E  U  U
N  D  W  F  W  P  G  Y  P  A  K  N  T  W  J
```

Note: Some words may appear backwards.

CHAPTER 51
The Passion and Crucifixion of Jesus

Jesus was eventually brought before the Sanhedrin, who wanted him put to death for what they said was the sin of blasphemy. They did not believe Jesus when he said he was the Son of God.

But the Jewish leaders did not have the right by law to put someone to death. Only the Roman authorities could do that. So they brought Jesus before Pontius Pilate, a Roman governor of the province. Pilate at first did not see why Jesus should be put to death, but he was a weak man and he feared the crowd would turn on him. So he sentenced Jesus to be scourged, or whipped, and crucified.

Pilate ordered his soldiers to take Jesus away. Then they stripped him of his garments, bound him to a pillar, and scourged him with whips.

Next, they put a purple cloak on him and made a crown of thorns. They mocked him by shouting, "Hail, King of the Jews!" They spat on him and struck his head with a reed. Then the soldiers led Jesus away. First, they took the purple cloak from his shoulders. His body was bruised and torn and bleeding from the cruel scourging. They dressed him again in his own clothes. Then they placed a cross on his shoulders and led him away to be crucified on a hill named Golgotha, or Calvary.

It was now about nine o'clock on Friday morning. Jesus had had nothing to eat or drink since the Paschal supper the evening before. He had suffered terribly during his agony in the garden.

Seeing how weak our Savior had become, the four soldiers who were guarding him feared that he would die before he reached Golgotha. A man named Simon was coming into the city from the country. The soldiers grabbed him and forced him to carry the cross behind Jesus.

At last, they reached Calvary. Three crosses were laid on the ground, and Jesus and two thieves were stripped of their clothes.

Now Jesus was stretched upon the cross, and spikes were driven into his hands and his feet. They placed over the head of Jesus the board that the centurion had been carrying. On it was written his name and the offense for which he had been condemned. Pilate himself had written the title for the cross of Jesus. It read, "Jesus of Nazareth, King of the Jews."

No sooner had Jesus been raised on the cross than he opened his mouth in prayer. "Father, forgive them, for they don't know what they're doing."

Yet even during his agony, the enemies of our Savior did not spare him. Many who passed by mocked him, wagging their heads and saying, "If you're the Son of God, come down from the cross!"

The soldiers also mocked him, saying, "If you're the king of the Jews, save yourself!"

One of the robbers hanging on a cross beside Jesus began to curse and swear at him, saying, "If you're the Christ, save yourself and us!"

But the other robber rebuked him. "Have you no fear of God?" he asked. "We've received the just punishment for our deeds; but this man has done no wrong." Then he said to Jesus, "Lord, remember me when you come into your kingdom."

"Truly, I tell you," Jesus replied, "this day you will be with me in paradise."

Most of Jesus's friends and family had abandoned him, fearing they too would be forced to suffer. But some did remain. Mary, his mother, Mary Magdalene, the apostle John, and a few other women stayed and cried at the foot of the cross.

Looking down from the cross, Jesus saw his mother and his beloved disciple gazing up at him in compassion and love. Tenderly he spoke to Mary. "Woman, there is your son." Then he said to John, "Son, there is your mother." From that moment on, John took Mary as his own mother.

It was about noon when Jesus was nailed to the cross. About that time, it grew dark. At last Jesus said, "It is finished." Then with a loud voice he cried out, "Father, into your hands I commit my spirit." And bowing his head, he died.

QUESTIONS FOR REVIEW:

1. To where was Jesus lead away to be crucified?

2. Who was the Roman governor who sentenced him to be scourged and crucified? Who helped Jesus carry his cross when he was weak? Who else was crucified along with Jesus?

3. Who was the only apostle to stay at the foot of the cross, who Jesus gave his mother to?

ACTIVITIES

CRAFT PROJECT: JESUS' PURPLE CLOAK

Materials:
- ☐ purple paper or plastic tablecloth
- ☐ purple ribbon
- ☐ duct tape
- ☐ scissors

Directions:

1. From the purple tablecloth, cut a triangle with a flat top appropriate for the size of the child in the tablecloth.

2. Use a long enough piece of purple ribbon to run the width of the narrower end of the cape (leaving an extra foot of ribbon on each end).

3. Fold the cape over the ribbon four times, making sure that the ribbon stays inside the fold.

4. Tape the entire length of the fold so that the ribbon stays in place inside its "seam."

5. Enjoy!

COLORING PAGE: PILATE PRESENTS JESUS TO THE PEOPLE

COLORING PAGE: JESUS CARRYING THE CROSS

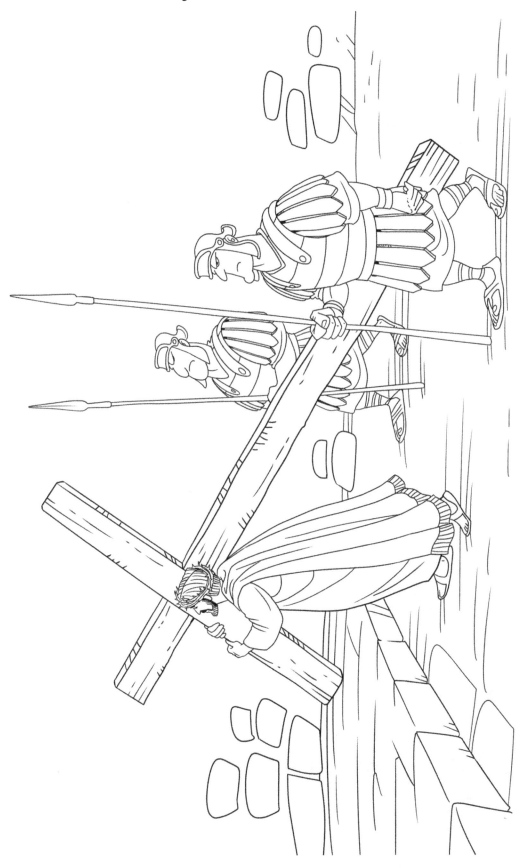

CRAFT PROJECT: JESUS PAYS FOR SINS OF THE WORLD

Materials:
- ☐ card stock
- ☐ pennies
- ☐ hot glue gun

Directions:
1. Cut the card stock into the shape of a cross.
2. Glue the pennies to the cross, symbolizing that by Jesus' suffering and death, He ransomed us and opened the gates of heaven.
3. Enjoy!

SNACK PROJECT: CROWN OF THORNS RICE CAKES

Ingredients:
- ☐ rice cakes
- ☐ peanut butter
- ☐ pretzels

Directions:
1. Spread peanut butter onto the rice cakes.
2. Break the pretzels into pieces and stick them around the rim of the rice cakes to look like a crown of thorns.
3. Enjoy!

SNACK PROJECT: PEANUT BUTTER CHOCOLATE CALVARY CUPCAKES

Ingredients:
- ☐ 1 cup sugar
- ☐ 1 1/2 cups all-purpose flour
- ☐ 1 tsp. baking soda
- ☐ 1 tsp. salt
- ☐ 1/2 cup cocoa powder
- ☐ 1/2 cup melted butter
- ☐ 1 cup water

Peanut Butter Frosting:
- ☐ 1/2 cup butter, softened
- ☐ 1 cup creamy peanut butter
- ☐ 3 Tbsp. milk
- ☐ 2 cups confectioners' sugar

Cross topping:
- ☐ 6 mini pretzel sticks
- ☐ peanut butter, small amount

Directions:

1. Preheat oven to 350° F.
2. Combine dry ingredients in large bowl.
3. Combine melted butter, water, and vinegar in a small bowl then add to dry ingredients.
4. Mix until batter is smooth and free of lumps.
5. Divide into one cupcake tray lined with cupcake liners and bake for 22–26 minutes.
6. Remove and let cool before frosting.

Frosting:

1. Mix softened butter and peanut butter with electric mixer.
2. Gradually mix in sugar.
3. When it begins to thicken, add the milk one tablespoon at a time until all the sugar is mixed in and the frosting is thick and spreadable. Mix for at least 3 minutes so that the frosting becomes light and fluffy.

Cross topping:

1. Once cupcakes are frosted, arrange them into a "mountain."
2. Place three pretzel sticks into the top cupcakes for Jesus' cross and the two thieves on his left and right.
3. Use peanut butter to stick the other three pretzel sticks to make the cross shape. You now have a cupcake Calvary scene.
4. Enjoy!

CHAPTER 52
The Resurrection

After Jesus died, a man named Joseph of Arimathea allowed Mary and Jesus's followers to bury him in a tomb cut out of a rock which Joseph owned. They wrapped his body in linen and laid him in the tomb, then rolled a large stone in front of it to seal it.

Meanwhile, the Pharisees thought that the disciples might steal the body of Jesus and pretend he is risen from the dead, so they asked Pilate to send guards to watch the tomb.

Suddenly on Sunday there was a great earthquake, and an angel of the Lord descended from heaven. He rolled back the stone and sat on it. His face was brilliant like lightning and his clothing white as snow. Seeing him, the guards were struck with terror and fell fainting to the ground.

That morning, Mary Magdalene and Mary, the mother of James and Salome, came to the tomb of Jesus, bringing spices to anoint the body. On the way they said to one another, "Who will roll away the stone for us from the door of the tomb?"

When they came to the tomb, however, they saw that the stone had been rolled away already. Entering, they found that the body of the Lord Jesus was gone.

By this time, the apostles had gathered together in the upper room where Jesus had eaten his last supper with them, when he instituted the Eucharist. Mary Magdalene hastened back to the city and found them there. Calling Peter and John aside from the others, she said, "They have taken away the Lord from the tomb, and we don't know where they have laid him."

In the meantime, Mary, the mother of James and Salome, had been joined by the other women who had been faithful to Jesus. They decided to look into the tomb again. When they did, they saw what appeared to be a young man sitting on the right side, clothed in a white robe. They were astonished.

He said to them, "Don't be afraid. You seek Jesus of Nazareth, who was crucified. He is risen; he's not here. Look at the place where they laid him. But go, tell his disciples and Peter that he goes before you into Galilee. There you'll see him, just as he told you."

Hearing this, the women fled from the tomb, trembling with fear and joy. They hurried to Jerusalem to tell the apostles. But the apostles did not believe the women.

Peter and John had left the upper room when they heard that the body of Jesus had disappeared. They ran to the tomb and saw the linens, but not Jesus. Then both of them believed that he had risen from the dead. So they returned to the other apostles and told them.

Mary Magdalene returned to the tomb and stood at the door waiting. She looked inside and saw two angels in white, sitting there on the stone where the body of Jesus had been laid. One sat at the head, and one at the feet.

They said to her, "Woman, why are you weeping?" She replied, "Because they have taken away my Lord." She turned around and saw Jesus standing there, but she didn't recognize him. He said to her, "Woman, why are you weeping?"

Thinking it was the caretaker of the garden, she said to him, "If you've taken him from here, tell me where you've laid him, and I'll take him away."

Jesus said to her, "Mary."

Then, she recognized him. Falling down at his feet, she said, "Teacher!"

Jesus said, "Don't hold on to me, because I've not yet ascended to my Father. But go to my brothers, and say to them: 'I'm ascending to my Father and to your Father, to my God and your God.'"

Then he disappeared. She stood up and hurried to Jerusalem to find the apostles. "I've seen the Lord!" she told them. Then she repeated what he had said to her.

QUESTIONS FOR REVIEW:

1. Who owned the tomb Jesus was buried in?

2. Why did Pilate send guards to watch over the tomb?

3. What was the apostles' first reaction when the women told them Jesus was not in the tomb?

ACTIVITIES

COLORING PAGE: THE EMPTY TOMB

CRAFT PROJECT: PAPER PLATE JESUS' TOMB

Materials:
- ☐ large paper plate
- ☐ small dessert sized paper plate
- ☐ gray paint
- ☐ rock, slightly larger than a golf ball
- ☐ scissors
- ☐ markers
- ☐ glue
- ☐ tissues

Directions:

1. Paint the front and back of the large paper plate gray. Let dry.
2. Draw a circle in the center of the small paper plate. Cut out four skinny triangles with the point toward the center.
3. Round off one of the points to create the angel's head. The remaining three points are the angel's wings and body. Have child color the angel.
4. Cut the dried gray paper plate in half, and on one half cut a circular opening the size of your rock.
5. Glue the two open halves of the paper plate together so there is space inside.
6. Glue the decorated angel above the opening to the tomb and roll the rock aside to show the empty tomb. Place the shredded tissues inside to represent the linen cloths Jesus had been buried in.
7. Enjoy!

SNACK PROJECT: EMPTY TOMB DONUT

Ingredients:
- ☐ mini chocolate donuts
- ☐ mini chocolate cookies
- ☐ graham crackers
- ☐ shredded coconut

Directions:

1. Use the green food coloring to color both the white frosting and shredded coconut.

2. Frost a graham cracker thickly with the green frosting so one side is completely covered.

3. Set mini donut toward the back of the graham cracker firmly into the frosting so it is standing upright.

4. Place a chocolate cookie in front of the hole of the donut and slightly to one side.

5. Cover the remaining frosted graham cracker with green shredded coconut to look like grass.

6. Cut out small rectangular pieces of paper and write "Alleluia, He is Risen." Tape one side to a toothpick so it looks like a banner. Stick the toothpick banner in each donut.

7. Enjoy!

MAGIC TRICK: JESUS DISAPPEARS FROM THE TOMB

Materials:
- ☐ Shoe Box (with top preferred)
- ☐ Scissors
- ☐ Large paper towels or tissue paper
- ☐ Tiny figurine or baby doll
- ☐ Markers/Paint/Colored Construction paper
- ☐ Tape/Glue
- ☐ Another person

Instructions:
1. Color or paint the inside of the shoebox black and the outer part gray. If preferred, tape or glue colored sheets of paper instead. This will be the tomb.

2. Cut a round hole (large enough to sneak a few fingers in and allow your figuring to be pulled out) in one of the longer sides of the shoe box. This hole will be on the bottom of the tomb.

3. Place the empty box on top of the back of the couch and have another person hide behind the couch, helping to prop it up.

4. Wrap the figurine with paper towel or tissue paper to resemble the buried body of Jesus. Recall the event by saying a few words to the audience about the burial of Jesus.

5. With your audience watching, place the buried Jesus in the box and cover the front with the shoe box top (if you do not have the top, use a dishtowel). Make sure to not allow it to fall through the hole. Say a prayer of thanksgiving for Jesus's sacrifice.

6. Recall to the audience that three days later Jesus rose from the dead. Then person hiding will remove the buried Jesus and leave the linens inside the tomb.

7. You will then open the front of the tomb to reveal only the linens, for Jesus has risen!

CHAPTER 53
The Ascension

It had been forty days since Jesus had risen from the dead. Once more the apostles were gathered together at the table with Jesus. He commanded them not to leave Jerusalem but to wait there for the coming of the Holy Spirit, whom he had promised to send.

"John baptized with water," he said, "but you will be baptized with the Holy Spirit, not many days from now."

Even at this point, the apostles didn't fully understand that the kingdom of Jesus was not of this world. They asked him, "Lord, will you now restore the kingdom to Israel?"

He answered, "It's not for you to know the times or the dates that the Father has determined by his own authority. But you'll receive power when the Holy Spirit comes on you, and you'll be witnesses for me in Jerusalem, and in all Judea and Samaria, and even to the ends of the earth.

"Everything written about me in the Law of Moses, and in the prophets, and in the psalms, must be fulfilled. It is written that the Christ must suffer, and on the third day rise again from the dead; and that penance and the forgiveness of sins must be preached in his name to all nations, beginning at Jerusalem.

"You are witnesses of these things. And I send the promise of my Father on you. But stay in the city until you're clothed with power from on high."

Then he led them out of the city toward Bethany. When they came to the Mount of Olives, he blessed them, and while they were looking at him, he was lifted up, and a cloud took him out of their sight.

They stood gazing into the sky, hoping to catch one last glimpse of him. Then suddenly they saw two angels standing beside them in white clothing, who said, "You men of Galilee, why do you stand looking up into heaven? This Jesus who was taken up from you into heaven will come back in the same way you've seen him go into heaven."

Then they worshipped Jesus and went back to Jerusalem with great joy in their hearts, praising and blessing God.

QUESTIONS FOR REVIEW

1. How many days after the Resurrection did the Ascension take place?

2. Who did Jesus promise he would send to the apostles?

3. What did the angels say who stood beside the apostles after Jesus ascended into heaven?

ACTIVITIES

SNACK PROJECT: CLOUD COOKIES

Ingredients:
- ☐ 2 egg whites
- ☐ 1/8 tsp salt
- ☐ 1 tsp vanilla
- ☐ 1/8 tsp cream of tartar
- ☐ 3/4 cup white sugar

Instructions:
1. Preheat oven to 300 degrees.
2. Line a baking sheet with parchment paper.
3. Beat egg whites, cream of tartar, vanilla, and salt until firm.
4. Gradually add sugar while stirring egg white mixture.
5. Use a teaspoon to drop on pan.
6. Bake for 25 minutes at 300 degrees. Will be slightly brown.

CROSSWORD PUZZLE: THE ASCENSION

Across

4. Jesus commanded the apostles not to leave _____.
6. They came to the Mount of _____.
7. The apostles saw two of these after Jesus ascended into the clouds

Down

1. John baptized with this
2. It is written that the Christ must ___.
3. Jesus led them out of the city toward ___.
5. A ___ took him out of sight.

COLORING PAGE: JESUS ASCENDING INTO HEAVEN

CHAPTER 54
Pentecost

The apostles returned to Jerusalem after Jesus rose into heaven. It was the Feast of Pentecost and the city was filled with visitors who had come to celebrate this joyful festival of the first fruits. In the Upper Room, the apostles and the other disciples of our blessed Savior were gathered together, united in prayer. This was the same room where they had been with Jesus at the Last Supper.

Suddenly there came a sound from heaven like a mighty wind, and it shook the whole house where they were assembled. Tongues of fire appeared to all those in the room and settled on each of them. They were all filled with the Holy Spirit. Then they began to speak in foreign languages that they had never learned, as the Holy Spirit prompted them to speak. It was the fulfillment of Jesus's promise to them: God's Spirit, the Advocate, had come to clothe them with power to be witnesses to all they had seen and heard.

The crowds who clogged the city streets included devout Jews from many nations. The noise of the great wind was heard all over the city, and crowds came running together to surround the house where the disciples were staying.

There they were witnesses to a wonderful sight. The twelve apostles were standing on the rooftop, preaching to the multitude. And a great excitement came on the people, because every person in the crowd heard them speak in his own language.

They said with amazement, "Aren't all these who are speaking Galileans? So how is it that can we listen to them speak, each of us in the language we've spoken since we were born? . . . We've heard them speak in our own languages the wonderful works of God."

Some of the listeners were perplexed and asked, "What does all this mean?" But others claimed that the apostles were drunk and babbling. They did not realize that Jesus had filled the apostles with the Holy Spirit. Peter preached to them, saying:

"They are not drunk, for it is only nine in the morning! What's happening has fulfilled what was spoken through the prophet Joel: 'And it will come to pass in the last days, says the Lord, that I will pour out my Spirit on all people; and your sons and your daughters will prophesy, and your young men will see visions, and your old men will dream dreams. And it will come to pass that whoever calls upon the name of the Lord will be saved.'"

Throughout the day many were baptized and thousands entered the Church. Today we celebrate this Feast of Pentecost as the birth of the Church.

QUESTIONS FOR REVIEW:

1. Where were the apostles gathered when the Holy Spirit descended upon them?

2. Describe what happened to the apostles in the upper room.

3. What were the twelve apostles doing on the rooftop?

ACTIVITIES

CRAFT PROJECT: TONGUE OF FIRE HEADBAND

Materials:
- ☐ red, orange, and yellow construction paper
- ☐ cardstock
- ☐ stapler
- ☐ scissors
- ☐ glitter paint

Directions:

1. Cut a long strip of cardstock that can wrap all the way around child's head.
2. Using the glitter paint, write "Holy Spirit" on one side of the strip of cardstock toward one end.
3. Cut flames of fire out of the red, orange, and yellow construction paper in a small, medium, and large size. Stack them on top of one another and staple together.
4. Staple the flame to the center of the cardstock then staple the cardstock together to fit the child's head.
5. Enjoy!

COLORING PAGE: PETER PREACHING

DRAWING PROJECT: SYMBOLS OF THE HOLY SPIRIT CREST

Instructions:

In the Bible, the Holy Spirit is symbolized in various ways, including fire, wind or the breath of God, a dove, a cloud, and water. On the crest below, draw one or several illustrations that depict these symbols to create your own symbolic "logo" for the Holy Spirit. Consider combining them in creative ways.

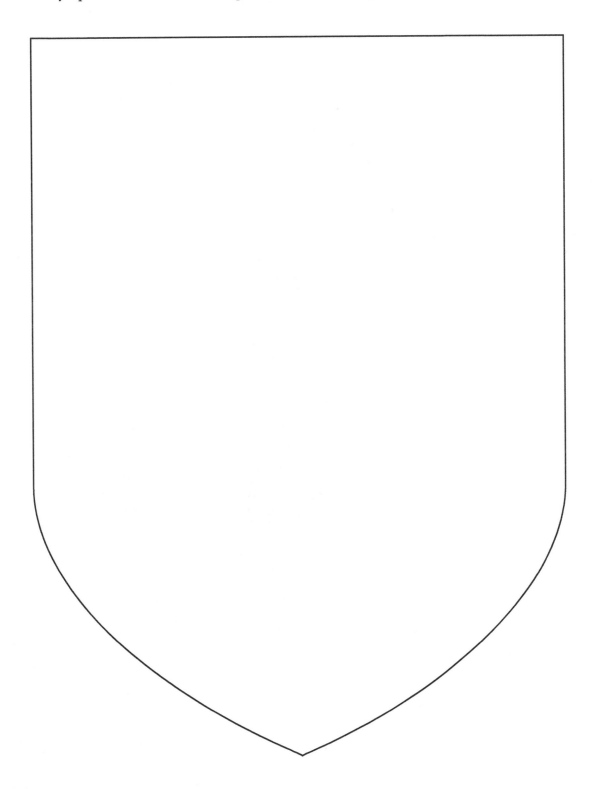

CHAPTER 55
Paul's Adventures

As time passed, the apostles baptized many, and the Church grew. They experienced many joys but also many sorrows.

One of the most famous of Jesus's followers in the years after the crucifixion was St. Paul. But he did not always go by this name. His original name was Saul, and he was at first a ferocious enemy of new Christians, arresting and persecuting many of them.

Saul once went on a journey to Damascus to bring Christians back to Jerusalem in chains. As he journeyed around hunting for Christians, a sudden bright and blinding light shone down upon him. Saul fell in terror as he heard a voice say, "Saul, Saul, why do you persecute me?"

Saul replied, "Who are you, Lord?"

"I am Jesus of Nazareth," the voice answered, "whom you are persecuting."

"What should I do?" Paul asked.

"Get up and go into the city, and you'll be told what to do. For I have appeared to you for this purpose: to appoint you to serve and bear witness to what you have seen, and to the visions you will have of me, when I deliver you from the people and from the Gentiles."

The brilliant light had blinded Saul, and for three days, he couldn't see, and he spent this time in prayer and fasting.

Then the Lord sent a man named Ananias to help Saul recover his sight. Scales fell from his eyes and he immediately recovered his sight. For many years after this, Saul preached that Jesus was the Son of God. He also preached with a man named Barnabas, and they worked together teaching people and bringing converts into the Church.

Their journeys took them far and wide. They ministered on the island of Cyprus, in the Mediterranean Sea, and in several cities of Asia Minor. Usually, they would begin a mission by preaching in the local synagogue, if there was one, so that the local Jewish population would have the chance to believe first. Then they would go out and preach to the Gentiles as well.

Saul was now going by his other name, Paul, perhaps because a Latin name would be more popular among the Gentiles. He worked miracles, just as Jesus and the other apostles had done. Again, the power of God that was displayed through these wonders helped to convince people that the gospel message was true.

When Paul and Barnabas preached in the city of Lystra, they met a man who had been crippled all his life. He listened intently to Paul's preaching. The apostle could tell that the man had the faith to be healed, so he said to him, "Stand upright on your feet." And he jumped up and began to walk around.

When the crowds, who believed in the Greek gods, saw what had happened, they cried out, "The gods have come down to us in the likeness of men!" They thought Barnabas was the Greek god Zeus, and Paul, the Greek god Hermes.

The local priest of Zeus brought oxen and flowers, prepared to sacrifice to the apostles as gods. But when they heard this, Paul and Barnabas rushed out into the crowd. "Men, why are you doing this? We are mortal human beings like you. But we bring you the good news that you should turn from these empty things to the living God who made heaven and earth and the sea, and everything in them."

Then they explained that even though they couldn't see their Creator, he had given them all the gifts of the earth as a testimony to his love for them. But even with these words, they could hardly restrain the crowds from offering sacrifices to them.

Paul had many more journeys where he would convert people to Christianity. He is known today as St. Paul and is arguably the greatest Christian writer and apologist to have ever lived. Like many of Christ's disciples, St. Paul died as a martyr for the faith.

QUESTIONS FOR REVIEW:

1. What was Paul's original name?

2. Why was he on his way to Damascus?

3. What happened to Saul on his journey? How did he change after this?

ACTIVITIES

COLORING PAGE: PAUL ON A SHIP

MAZE: PAUL'S MISSIONARY JOURNEY

FINISH

START

SNACK PROJECT: HOT DOG SWORDS

Ingredients:
- [ ] hot dogs cut into a dozen round pieces
- [ ] mini pretzel sticks

Directions:

1. Stick the pretzel stick through each hot dog piece to create the blade and hilt of the sword.

2. Discuss Saul's persecution of Christians before he converted. These swords symbolize Saul's role in punishing the Christians.

3. Enjoy!

SNACK PROJECT: APPLE SLICE BOATS

Ingredients:
- [ ] apple
- [ ] peanut butter
- [ ] rectangular corn chips

Directions:

1. Cut apple into slices and each slice will be the bottom of a boat.

2. Cut a small slit into each apple slice using a kitchen knife.

3. Using peanut butter, glue a corn chip into the slit in each apple slice for the sail.

4. Enjoy!

SNACK PROJECT: BLUE JELL-O SEA

Ingredients:
- ☐ blue Jell-o
- ☐ gold fish
- ☐ large marshmallows
- ☐ toothpicks
- ☐ post-it notes cut into triangles (leaving the sticky edge as the base of the triangle)

Directions:
1. Make the blue Jell-o according to the directions on the box.
2. Once the Jell-o is set, dish out into individual bowls to make it look like the sea.
3. Surround your "sea" with gold fish.
4. Use large marshmallows as the body of the boat. Insert toothpicks into the marshmallows and attach post-it notes as sails.
5. Discuss Paul's many missionary journeys and how they each involved sailing on the Mediterranean Sea to different cities.
6. Enjoy!

CRAFT PROJECT: SPONGE BOAT

Materials:
- ☐ kitchen sponge
- ☐ popsicle stick
- ☐ duct tape (two different colors)
- ☐ craft knife (or sharp kitchen knife)
- ☐ hot glue gun

Directions:
1. Cut a small slit, about the width of the popsicle stick, in the center of the sponge using the knife. Insert the stick. (If it does not stay, make the slit deeper.)
2. Remove the craft stick. Use duct tape to create a sail. Cut two, 3 in. pieces of one color of duct tape and tape sticky sides together so no stickiness remains. Use the other color to create designs or stripes.
3. Use the craft knife to cut the rough edges off the sail. Then cut a small slit at the top and bottom of the sail. Stick the craft stick through the front of the top slit and then through the bottom of the bottom slit. Use a small piece of tape to secure the sail.
4. Stick a drop of hot glue in the slit already made in the sponge and insert the craft stick sail into it.
5. Sail in a bucket of water or in the bathtub. Discuss Paul and Barnabas's first missionary journey and how they sailed on the Mediterranean Sea at the beginning and end of their journey.
6. Enjoy!

Answer Key

CHAPTER 1: CREATION: ADAM AND EVE

Questions for Review

1. Of what tree did God forbid Adam and Eve to eat?

The Tree of the Knowledge of Good and Evil.

2. Why did Satan want to tempt Eve?

He saw how happy Adam and Eve were, and he tried to lead them away from God because of his envy.

3. What was the last warning God delivered to the serpent?

He promised a Redeemer who would one day come.

CHAPTER 2: NOAH AND HIS ARK

Questions for Review

1. Why did God destroy the earth with a great flood?

He saw how sinful they had become and he planned to wipe out their wickedness.

2. How did Noah track when the waters had gone down?

He sent out a dove.

3. Why did God set the rainbow in the sky?

As a sign that he would never again destroy the earth by the waters of a flood.

Crossword Puzzle: Noah's Ark

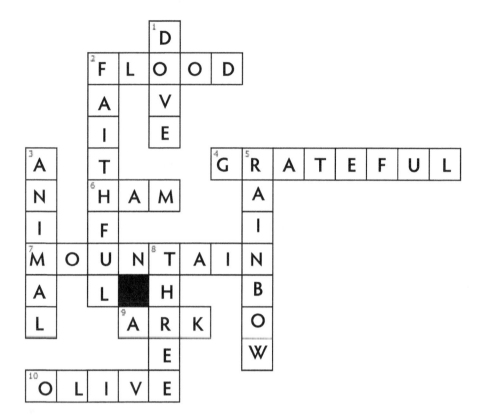

CHAPTER 3: THE TOWER OF BABEL

Questions for Review

1. What were the people trying gain from building the tower into the heavens?

They could become famous and well respected by the whole world.

2. Why didn't they complete the tower?

God dispersed them by making them suddenly speak many different languages, keeping them from being able to work together.

3. What does the word "Babel" mean?

Confusion.

Word Search: Tower of Babel

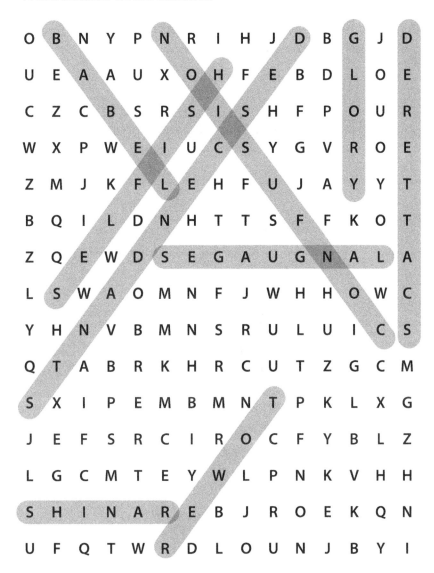

CHAPTER 4: ABRAHAM AND ISAAC

Questions for Review

1. Besides the promise of becoming the father of a great nation, what else did God promise to Abraham?

He and his wife Sarai would have a son.

2. As he was raising his knife to sacrifice his son, who appeared and prevented Abraham from sacrificing his son?

An angel of the Lord.

3. Because Abraham did not withhold his son, what was again promised?

That God will indeed bless him, and will multiply his descendants as the stars of heaven and as the sand which is on the seashore.

CHAPTER 5: ISAAC, ESAU, AND JACOB: THE BIRTHRIGHT

Questions for Review

1. What did it mean to receive the birthright?

The eldest would receive a larger portion of his father's wealth and obtain a special blessing from his father before he died.

2. How did Jacob and Rebecca deceive Isaac?

Jacob delivered Isaac's food with his neck and hands covered in animal skin so that he would seem hairy like his brother Esau.

3. How did Esau respond to Jacob receiving the birthright?

He hated Jacob and swore to kill him.

Word Search: Isaac, Jacob, and Esau

```
T H Q Y T K Q N H A K U Q Z B
S H M N A B A L U U Y L F X A
I U G Y X M E Q G S N P Z W D
X T O I S F O F X G G T P A F
G S L D R B W Z U R N F E O F
A O R S O H W P A P I F M R Y
M E W T O M T L T W S W J I F
H Z D H B N O R Z K S E A R U
T R E B E C C A I B E T C X T
B Y U H Z I O Y U B L S O B Z
D E E A S V Y Z I R B S B W H
M T X A S D E C Q A T C V A D
X X A M T E G L I D P W U W M
N C K N Y W H I O E J Q J Z H
T H M J I Q L O N Z A G R G G
```

CHAPTER 6: JOSEPH'S HUMBLE BEGINNINGS

Questions for Review

1. Give three reasons why Joseph's brothers did not like him.

- Joseph saw them doing wrong and reported it to their father.

- Joseph was shown special favor by their father and the brothers were jealous, including when their father gave him a coat of many colors.

- Joseph shared his dreams with them, which indicated he would one day rule over them.

2. What ended up happening to Joseph instead of being killed by his brothers?

The brothers offered to sell Joseph to them as a slave to some merchants that were passing by. They offered twenty pieces of silver in exchange for Joseph and he was led away to Egypt.

3. How did Joseph's brothers deceive their father?

They dipped Joseph's coat in animal blood, returned it to their father, and told him that Joseph had been killed by a wild beast.

CHAPTER 7: JOSEPH IN EGYPT: THE BUTLER AND THE BAKER

Questions for Review

1. Why was Joseph thrown into prison?

Potiphar believed his wife's lie which accused Joseph of a sin.

2. Whose dreams did Joseph interpret while they were in prison?

The baker and the butler.

3. What did Joseph hope for after successfully interpreting their dreams?

To be let out of prison.

Double Puzzle

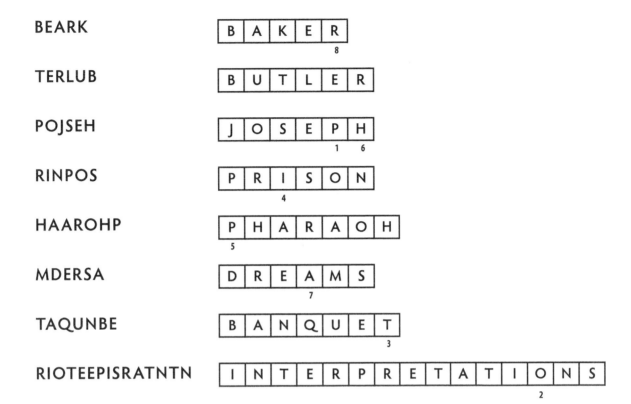

BEARK → B A K E R (8)

TERLUB → B U T L E R

POJSEH → J O S E P H (1, 6)

RINPOS → P R I S O N (4)

HAAROHP → P H A R A O H (5)

MDERSA → D R E A M S (7)

TAQUNBE → B A N Q U E T (3)

RIOTEEPISRATNTN → I N T E R P R E T A T I O N S (2)

Who placed Joseph in charge of his house?

P O T I P H A R
1 2 3 4 5 6 7 8

CHAPTER 8: JOSEPH MEETS HIS BROTHERS AGAIN

Questions for Review

1. How did Joseph first test his brothers?

He accused them of being spies and put them in prison.

2. After the feast, how did Joseph again test his brothers?

He put a silver cup in their sack to make it look like they stole it.

3. What was the fulfillment of one of Joseph's dreams as a boy?

When his brothers fell to their knees and offered themselves as slaves.

Crossword Puzzle: Joseph and His Brothers in Egypt

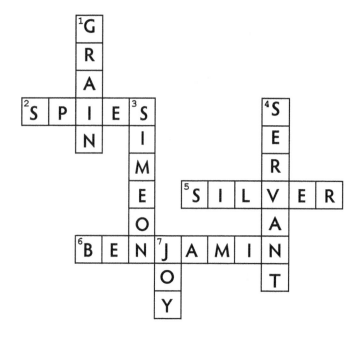

CHAPTER 9: THE ORIGINS OF MOSES: FROM BIRTH TO PRINCE OF EGYPT

Questions for Review

1. Name the terms used to identify God's chosen people.

Israelites, Hebrews, and Jews.

2. Why did Pharaoh enslave the Hebrews?

He was jealous of the strength and wealth of the Hebrews and feared they might have ties with rivals of Egypt.

3. How did Moses's mother protect him when Pharaoh decreed that every Hebrew boy should be killed? Did the plan work?

She placed him in a basket and sent him down the Nile River, praying that God would protect him. Yes, the plan worked. Pharaoh's daughter found and adopted Moses and protected him in the palace.

Maze: Moses Floats Down the River

This maze has multiple different solutions.

CHAPTER 10: THE PLAGUES

Questions for Review

1. What was the first of the ten plagues?

Moses turned the water of the Nile River into blood.

2. Who helped Moses carry out the plagues?

His brother Aaron.

3. Why did Pharaoh change his mind so many times about letting the Hebrews go?

His heart was hardened.

Word Search: The Plagues

```
I  E  F  B  S  M  K  E  N  K  A  N  D  I  S
B  Q  L  L  K  G  J  C  Z  U  X  F  A  Z  J
A  W  I  T  I  N  D  T  X  G  U  O  R  M  U
O  O  E  O  T  B  V  N  L  E  D  Y  K  O  Y
B  Y  S  F  W  A  P  Y  G  U  Z  K  N  S  T
U  Q  W  M  N  L  C  X  W  K  L  N  E  G  Y
I  G  N  Z  A  H  G  Y  Q  W  C  Y  S  O  E
W  P  F  G  N  A  T  S  K  J  V  L  S  R  A
W  R  U  G  B  T  G  D  T  Y  A  X  L  F  A
T  E  H  W  E  S  T  S  U  C  O  L  H  A  Q
S  V  W  U  B  P  B  L  I  U  K  A  C  J  U
I  C  M  K  Y  F  R  L  P  C  I  J  I  I  Z
T  J  Y  G  W  O  D  R  O  L  Z  G  Z  U  B
E  G  A  I  Q  C  W  V  Z  O  S  N  T  A  N
M  A  E  N  Q  L  J  S  Q  T  D  S  E  G  E
```

CHAPTER 11: THE TENTH PLAGUE AND THE PASSOVER

Questions for Review

1. What was the tenth plague?

All the firstborn Egyptian children were to die, as well as the firstborn of the cattle.

2. How were the Hebrews spared the plague?

The Hebrews spread the blood of the Passover lamb on the doorposts and the destroying angel passed over their homes.

3. When was Pharaoh's heart finally softened?

After the firstborn of every Egyptian family lay dead. He summoned Moses and Aaron and told them to lead the people of Israel out of the land of Egypt without delay.

Double Puzzle: The Passover

SARVSEPO

P	A	S	S	O	V	E	R
	10				16		

MLBA

L	A	M	B
15			

SORPOOTSD

D	O	O	R	P	O	S	T	S
9		18				13	3	

TIIMDGNH

M	I	D	N	I	G	H	T
	14	12			1		

NAGLE

A	N	G	E	L
		6		

SYHSOP

H	Y	S	S	O	P
		4			

GALPEU

P	L	A	G	U	E
	8				

HOPHARA

P	H	A	R	A	O	H
					5	

SSMEO

M	O	S	E	S
	7		17	

LIENLT

L	I	N	T	E	L
	2	11			

What did God command the Hebrews to ask of their Egyptian neighbors?

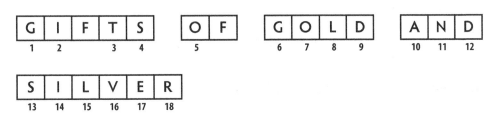

G	I	F	T	S
1	2	3	4	

O	F
5	

G	O	L	D
6	7	8	9

A	N	D
10	11	12

S	I	L	V	E	R
13	14	15	16	17	18

CHAPTER 12: THE EXODUS AND PARTING OF THE RED SEA

Questions for Review

1. To lead the way for them, what did the Lord appear to the Hebrew people as by day? And by night?

He appeared as a pillar of cloud by day and a pillar of fire by night.

2. What did Pharaoh do as soon as he regretted letting the Hebrews leave Egypt?

He prepared his chariot and his entire army. With six hundred chosen chariots and all the captains of the army, he pursued the people of Israel.

3. What happened at the Red Sea that allowed the Hebrews to escape the Egyptian army?

God commanded Moses to lift up his rod so that the sea would part and the Hebrews could cross on dry land. When they crossed, God commanded Moses to again stretch out his had so that the waters would close on the Egyptians.

CHAPTER 13: THE TEN COMMANDMENTS AND THE GOLDEN CALF

Questions for Review

1. Name the Ten Commandments.

"I am the Lord your God, who brought you out of the land of Egypt. You shall have no other gods before me."

"You shall not take the name of the Lord your God in vain."

"Remember the Sabbath day, to keep it holy."

"Honor your father and your mother."

"You shall not kill."

"You shall not commit adultery."

"You shall not steal."

"You shall not bear false witness against your neighbor."

"You shall not covet your neighbor's wife."

"You shall not covet your neighbor's house or anything that is your neighbor's."

2. What did the people hear and see at Mount Sinai when God gave Moses the Ten Commandments?

Thunder, lightning, a trumpet blast, thick smoke.

3. What happened when Moses came down the mountain and saw the Israelites worshipping an idol?

He was furious and shattered the two tablets on which the commandments had been written. He then burned the idol and commanded that those who had led the idol worship should be killed. He asked God's people to stand with him and immediately the sons of Levi did. They drew their swords and slew the guilty.

CHAPTER 14: JOSHUA, COMMANDER OF THE ISRAELITES

Questions for Review

1. After wandering the desert for forty years, what did the Israelites have to do before making Canaan their home?

They had to conquer the land and drive out the inhabitants.

2. How did Joshua find out the strengths of the cities they needed to conquer?

He sent two spies to Jericho and the surrounding neighborhoods.

3. What made the walls of Jericho fall?

Seven trumpets sounded a continuous blast, the people gave a mighty shout, and the walls fell.

Word Search: Joshua, Commander of the Israelites

I E A H Y S S U N B U H D C Q
X N T W E O S G A H E P M B P
M P H I N B P T D U O H A R V
R K P A X D R D R I S F T K D
P S D W B U A C O X S M B J L
R W F N M I R U J K S G I S T
L G X P U S T O H W L G O H Z
M R E P M C W A G S S U P R Y
Z I R Y J A C M N G O W M U E
A P D L E O D C X T I J U N R
A R K E R Z Y R S Z S K G E D
N G N Q I S Z W E N A A N A C
P Y D C C A K W T U I N X F P
Q X H N H T K T L Z V B U M C
M F N F O S B J L S D D R R M

CHAPTER 15: MIGHTY SAMSON

Questions for Review

1. How were the Philistines finally able to capture Samson?

He fell in love with a woman named Delilah, who found out his weakness was in his long hair. So at night while he was asleep, Delilah cut his hair and called in the soldiers to capture him.

2. What began to happen to Samson while he was in the dungeon?

His hair began to grow back.

3. How did Samson conquer his captors? And what happened to him?

Samson was brought out from prison because his captors wanted to amuse the guests and make fun of him. They didn't realize his hair had grown back. He was led to some pillars; then, calling upon the Lord to restore his strength, Samson took both pillars in his hands and shook them. The house fell and many were killed, including several princes of the Philistines. But Samson also perished.

Maze: Help Samson Escape Gaza

CHAPTER 16: THE PROPHET SAMUEL

Questions for Review

1. Why did the Hebrews think they needed to bring the Ark of the Covenant to battle?

They thought if they brought the Ark, they would be victorious.

2. What happened in the battle?

The Hebrews were defeated and the Ark was captured by the Philistines.

3. What did Saul warn the Hebrews about bringing the Ark into battle?

That it was not a good luck charm.

Word Search: The Prophet Samuel

```
E X C K G C J H T P C P O Z Y
F V J J N M K S L H H R N W D
P H I L I S T I N E S O W E Y
A E F C H F I F B T G P Q A M
C N L Y T C H R Y A T H K R Y
G F K T P O E X D S T E C J P
A X V O T W R I X H A T A M T
Z J N Y S A W I U K B K T X D
U T I V F E B G O M B R T X L
A R K P U N U L Y U C F A Y P
G U J A E S V E B E S G V R T
I Z C Z L E U M A S H M Y Y I
V N K U O O Z D I Y W Q V W H
X K C W X N N N F W C I I B W
B O T F E U K O J U A D S R N
```

CHAPTER 17: KING SAUL AND THE SHEPHERD BOY DAVID

Questions for Review

1. How did Samuel know that he had met the man who was to become king?

He was out walking and God revealed that he would meet Saul, the future king, that day.

2. What did Saul do to displease God?

He took from the spoils of war even though God instructed him not to.

3. How did the shepherd boy, David, help Saul?

When Saul started to lose his mind, his servants called for David, who played the harp and soothed Saul.

CHAPTER 18: DAVID AND GOLIATH

1. When David said he could fight Goliath, how did his brothers react?

They laughed at him.

2. How did David defeat Goliath?

He used a slingshot and a stone. The stone struck Goliath between the eyes and David cut his head off with his sword.

3. When the Israelites praised David for his defeat of Goliath, what was Saul's reaction?

He was jealous, but he still insisted that David come live with the royal family in the palace.

Word Search: David

CHAPTER 19: DAVID'S REIGN

Questions for Review

1. How did Jerusalem become the capital city?

David's army captured it from the Canaanites and he made it the capital.

2. What did David bring back into the city?

He brought the Ark of the Covenant.

3. What was David's grave sin?

He fell in love with Bathsheba, who was already married to Uriah. He gave orders for Uriah to be placed in the front line of battle. Then he commanded Uriah's fellow soldiers to fall back and leave him there alone to be killed. His devious plan worked: Uriah was killed, leaving Bathsheba free to marry David.

Maze: Help David Bring the Ark Back to Jerusalem

CHAPTER 20: SOLOMON

Questions for Review

1. When God asked Solomon what he desired, what did he ask for and what did he receive?

He asked for wisdom. God was so pleased that he had not asked for great wealth or a long life, so not only did he grant him the wisdom that he desired, but God also gave him great wealth and a long life as well.

2. How did Solomon decide the case of the two women who claimed the same child?

He tested them by threatening to cut the child in half. However, in his wisdom, he knew that the true mother would cry out and give up her child to the mother who was lying, rather than let him die.

3. In what ways did Solomon turn from God?

He became obsessed with pleasure and riches. He taxed the people to pay for his many expenses and he married gentile women and built temples to their false gods.

Crossword: King Solomon

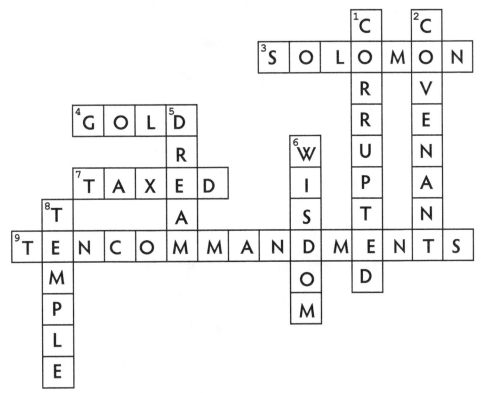

CHAPTER 21: JEROBOAM AND REHOBOAM

Questions for Review

1. What did Rehoboam do to provoke a rebellion against his rule?

He said that he would increase the people's taxes instead of reducing them.

2. Why did Jeroboam's hand wither?

It withered because he spoke out against the prophet and tried to take him captive.

3. How did the prophet Ahijah know that the disguised woman was really the queen? What did he tell her?

He knew she was the queen because God told him. The prophet said her son would die and her husband would be rooted out of the land, and her people would be taken into captivity.

Word Search: Jeroboam and Rehoboam

L	E	A	R	S	I	D	F	S	W	N	J
R	V	Y	S	B	P	E	N	S	C	E	S
R	E	H	O	B	O	A	M	H	I	D	E
B	B	J	L	V	I	Q	A	E	C	L	I
G	J	H	U	R	E	R	Y	C	V	O	X
Z	V	E	Y	D	I	L	G	H	R	G	X
U	O	S	R	O	A	S	P	E	K	W	N
S	S	D	T	O	E	H	M	M	O	E	E
A	G	Q	V	X	B	U	D	J	E	Z	T
C	Z	T	A	Q	E	O	U	O	W	T	R
E	D	T	H	N	O	H	A	Y	D	D	Q
F	A	L	S	E	D	G	Z	M	U	Q	C

Clues:
1. Rehoboam
2. Schechem
3. taxes
4. chariot
5. Jeroboam
6. false
7. Judah
8. Israel
9. Temple
10. golden
11. Assyrians

CHAPTER 22: ELIJAH THE PROPHET

Questions for Review

1. What did the prophet Elijah tell Ahad would happen because of his idolatry?

Elijah said there would be a great drought and no rain would fall for three years.

2. What did Elijah do when the widow's son died?

He prayed to God and asked him to restore the boy to life. God raised the boy from the dead.

3. How did the people come to believe that God was the one true God and not Baal?

The fire of the Lord fell and consumed the offering.

Maze: Elijah Finds the Widow

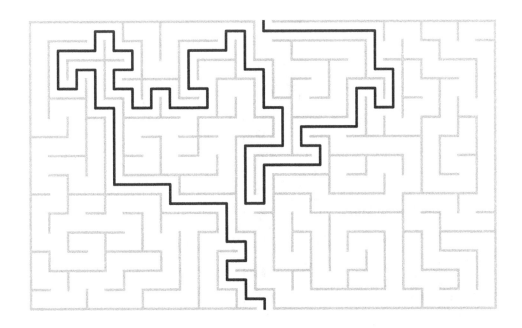

CHAPTER 23: THE STORY OF JOB

Questions for Review

1. What were some of the things that Job lost as part of his trials?

He lost his oxen, sheep, camels, servants, his children, and his health.

2. How did Job please God?

Job pleased God by being patient during his suffering.

3. How did the Lord reward Job?

The Lord restored Job's health, doubled his wealth, and gave him seven more sons and three more daughters.

Crossword: Job

CHAPTER 24: JONAH

Questions for Review

1. Why did God send Jonah to Nineveh? Why did Jonah head the opposite direction?

God sent Jonah to Nineveh because the people there were wicked and God wanted them to repent. He headed the opposite direction because he was afraid of the cruel Assyrians.

2. Why was Jonah thrown from the sea? How was he saved from the sea?

He admitted that he was the cause of the storm and told the crew to throw him overboard. A great fish swallowed Jonah and cast him up on the shore three days later.

3. What did the people of Nineveh do in response to the Jonah's preaching?

They fasted, put on sackcloth, and repented of their wickedness.

CHAPTER 25: TOBIT

Questions for Review

1. Why did Tobit go into hiding?

The king did not like his acts of charity and wanted to kill Tobit.

2. What happened to Tobit's eyes and how did this affect him?

The droppings from birds sitting above him on a wall fell into his eyes and blinded him. As a blind man, he was unable to work as he had before, so he became poor.

3. Who was disguised as the guide that accompanied Tobit's son and what did the guide do?

The angel Raphael was the guide. He told him to cut out the heart, the gall, and the liver of a fish, and to save them for medicine. When Tobias asked his guide what they were good for, Raphael told him that the gall was good for anointing and curing eyes. In the end, the gall cured his father's eyes.

Word Search: Tobit and Tobias

CHAPTER 26: JUDITH

Questions for Review

1. Why did Judith feel the need to speak out to the elders?

After they had been defeated by the Assyrian general, the elders of Bethulia decided to surrender if no help came in five days. Judith was angry that they tested God by putting a time limit on his power.

2. After Judith promised to put an end to the battle herself, what did she do?

She visited the Assyrian general and pretended to help him find the best routes into her city. The general was so pleased, he invited her to a feast, but became drunk. Judith cut off his head with his own sword.

3. How did her own people welcome her home?

They were shocked at her bravery and welcomed her with great joy.

Maze: Help Judith Find Her Way to Attack Holofernes

CHAPTER 27: THE BABYLONIAN CAPTIVITY

Questions for Review

1. What did Jeremiah prophesy about the people of Judah?

Jeremiah prophesied the evils that would come to the people of Judah if they relied on Egypt.

2. What did Jeremiah do as a warning of what was in store for the people of Jerusalem if they continued their wicked lives?

He walked the streets of the city with a yoke around his neck.

3. What did Jeremiah and some Levites do to protect the Ark of the Covenant?

While the Babylonians were plundering the city of Jerusalem, Jeremiah and some Levites secretly removed the Ark of the Covenant and the altar of incense. They carried them across the Jordan and hid them in a cave in Mount Nebo.

Crossword: The Babylonian Captivity

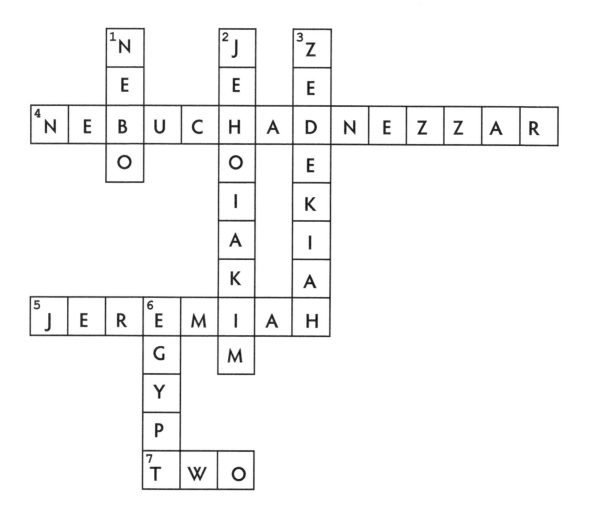

CHAPTER 28: DANIEL IN THE LIONS' DEN

Questions for Review

1. Why was Daniel thrown into the lion's den?

He disobeyed a law that forbade him to pray.

2. How did he keep from being eaten while in the lion's den?

God sent an angel to protect Daniel, and despite the lion's hunger, they did not harm him.

3. Who was Habakkuk and what did he do?

He was a prophet in the land of Judah. He was carried by an angel to take food to Daniel in the lion's den, then carried back home safely.

CHAPTER 29: THE PROPHETS ISAIAH, JEREMIAH, AND EZEKIEL

Questions for Review

1. What is a prophet?

A man of God who spoke of future events, often warnings. His main mission was to draw the Jewish people back to God and encourage them to repent of their sins.

2. How was Isaiah purified of his sins?

An angel of God came down and touched his lips with a burning coal.

3. What did Jeremiah warn the people about?

The Jews were carried off into captivity by the Babylonians. For forty years the prophet Jeremiah had been warning them that this terrible punishment would come upon them unless they repented of their sins and returned to God. But they refused to listen to him.

4. What were the four creatures Ezekiel saw in his vision that became the symbols of the Gospel writers? Did you remember which creature represents each writer?

A man, a lion, an ox, and an eagle. St. Matthew is represented as a man, St. Mark as a lion, St. Luke as an ox, and St. John as an eagle.

CHAPTER 30: SUMMARY OF THE OLD TESTAMENT

Quiz Activity: Old Testament Timeline

Joseph (6)

Noah (2)

Adam and Eve (1)

Abraham (3)

David (9)

Jacob (5)

Solomon (10)

Saul (8)

Moses (7)

Isaac (4)

CHAPTER 31: THE ANNUNCIATION

Questions for Review

1. What did the angel Gabriel say to Mary when he visited her?

He told her she was full of grace, blessed among women, and that she would conceive the Son of the Most High.

2. How did Mary respond to the angel?

She said, "I am the handmaiden of the Lord; let it be done to me according to your word." This showed that she was willing to accept God's will and anything he sent her.

3. What happened when Mary visited her cousin, Elizabeth?

When Mary greeted her cousin, the Holy Spirit revealed to Elizabeth that Mary was the Mother of God and the infant in her womb leapt with joy.

CHAPTER 32: THE NATIVITY

Questions for Review

1. Why did Joseph and Mary leave the city of Nazareth in Galilee and go to Bethlehem in Judea, the City of David?

The Roman emperor Augustus issued a decree ordering that a census be taken, so Mary and Joseph had to travel to Bethlehem, where Jesus would be born.

2. Why did Joseph and Mary have to stay in a stable and have Jesus there?

Because all the inns were full.

3. Who did the angels appear to, asking them to go and adore the Infant?

The shepherds.

Maze: Help the Wise Men Find Jesus

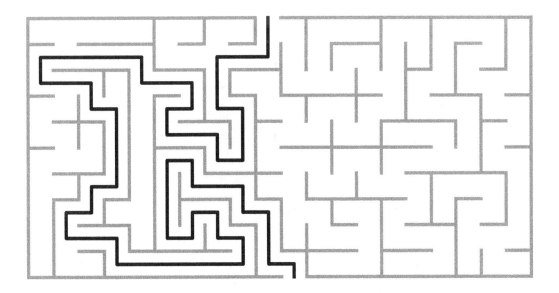

Word Search: The Birth of Jesus

```
K V D M C D H B E S M P F W R
O X B O X I W L K Y A S M I A
I H C F H A B J G S R J V T B
J X P Q Y A Z H V B Y V I U G
F E I N T B C B E D X Q I C Y
L W S S X M V T N A F Y M U D
P E P U A E H Z O K A Z Z X N
V T U G S L S D R E H P E H S
N N I N E Y J J B S O H U A F
C B V H A N J E Y R H P J S K
C Z E Z G M T F S M N E S B G
A M D G J X M J K V C S I D B
C E N S U S K E L U H O I A Z
B E D D J G N Q L O W J U O S
K N I S R Y T R K H J B X F O
```

Clues:
1. Bethlehem
2. Jesus
3. Mary
4. Magi
5. shepherds
6. Joseph
7. stable
8. Emmanuel
9. inn
10. census

CHAPTER 33: JOHN THE BAPTIST

Questions for Review

1. When John questioned Jesus about why he needed to be baptized, what did Jesus say?

Jesus explained that he must be baptized because it was part of God's plan for redeeming the human race. Humbly, John obeyed, and he baptized the Savior of the world.

2. In what form did the Holy Spirit appear after Jesus was baptized? What did God say at this time?

The Holy Spirit appeared as a dove. God said, "This is my beloved Son, in whom I am well pleased. Listen to him!"

3. Who hated John the Baptist and what did she tell her daughter to do?

Herodias, the wife of Herod, hated John. She asked her daughter to request of Herod the head of John the Baptist on a dish.

CHAPTER 34: JESUS CALLS HIS APOSTLES

Questions for Review

1. What does *Rabbi* mean?

Rabbi **means teacher.**

2. What did Jesus call Simon?

Jesus called Simon *Cephas***, which is the Aramaic word for "Peter," which means "a rock."**

3. Which apostle was the tax collector before being called by Jesus?

Matthew.

Word Search: The Apostles of Jesus

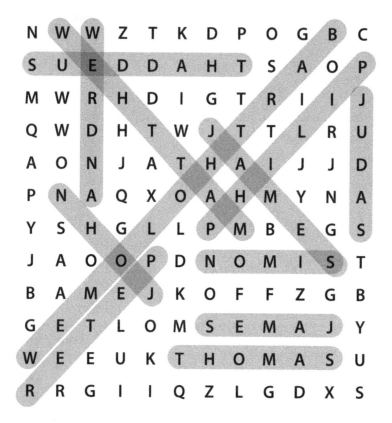

Clues:
1. Matthew
2. James
3. Thomas
4. John
5. Andrew
6. Peter
7. Philip
8. James
9. Judas
10. Simon
11. Bartholomew
12. Thaddeus

CHAPTER 35: THE WEDDING AT CANA

Questions for Review

1. How did the people know Jesus was truly speaking of God?

The miracles Jesus performed were the evidence God provided to show the people that he was his divine Son.

2. Where did Jesus perform his first miracle?

Jesus performed his first miracle in Galilee at a wedding feast in Cana.

3. What prompted Jesus to perform this miracle?

His mother, Mary, prompted him to perform this first miracle because the wine had run out at the wedding. Jesus respected her wishes and changed water into wine, thus performing his first miracle.

CHAPTER 36: JESUS TEACHES: THE PRODIGAL SON

Questions for Review

1. What is a parable?

A story that teaches a moral lesson. Jesus often used them to teach his followers.

2. How did the younger son squander his fortune? How did his father react when he returned?

The son squandered his fortune by living a wild and wicked life. But when he returned home remorseful, his father greeted him with a celebration.

3. What is the main lesson of the story of the Prodigal Son?

That no matter how badly we sin, God will always welcome us home and be merciful, so long as we are truly sorry for what we have done wrong.

Maze: The Wayward Son

CHAPTER 37: JESUS TEACHES: THE GOOD SAMARITAN

Questions for Review

1. Why did Jesus tell the parable of the good Samaritan?

He wanted to show that love must be the most important thing in our lives, not only in the family, but in our relationships with everyone.

2. What was surprising about this parable?

Three people passed the injured man. The first two were a priest and a Levite, and the last a Samaritan. The Jews did not like the Samaritans, so it was surprising that he served as the most loving of the people from the story.

3. How do you think this story teaches us about loving our neighbor?

Jesus could simply tell us to love our neighbor, and he did, but it helps us understand what this means to hear it in a story. As we listen to it, we put ourselves in the place of the injured man, and we know in such a situation we would want someone to help us. We then understand how compassionate the good Samaritan was and we admire him for it and want to be like him. This inspires us to go out and live like we are also good Samaritans, helping our neighbors who are in need.

Double Puzzle: The Good Samaritan

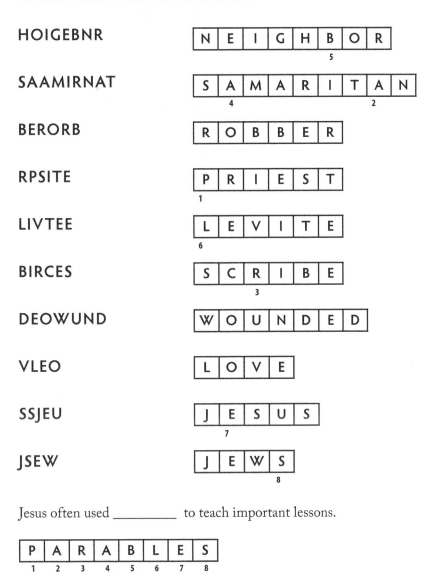

HOIGEBNR — N E I G H B O R (5)

SAAMIRNAT — S A M A R I T A N (4) (2)

BERORB — R O B B E R

RPSITE — P R I E S T (1)

LIVTEE — L E V I T E (6)

BIRCES — S C R I B E (3)

DEOWUND — W O U N D E D

VLEO — L O V E

SSJEU — J E S U S (7)

JSEW — J E W S (8)

Jesus often used _____ to teach important lessons.

P A R A B L E S
1 2 3 4 5 6 7 8

CHAPTER 38: JESUS TEACHES: THE KINGDOM OF HEAVEN

Questions for Review

1. Try to explain the first parable of the wheat and weeds in the field. What did each thing symbolize: The man sowing seeds, the wheat, the weeds and the enemy who sows those, the harvest, the reapers (or workers), the barn, the fire?

This parable gives us a symbol for the world. Jesus is the one who sows the good seed, trying to help us be holy in the world, which is represented by the field. This good seed can turn into healthy wheat, which would be good people living loving and sacrificial lives. But the one who sows the weeds, the bad people, is the devil. At harvest time, at the "end of the world," Jesus will send out his angels, the reapers/workers, and take up the wheat and store it in the barn (heaven), while the weeds will get tossed into the fire (hell).

2. How does Jesus compare the kingdom of God to the mustard seed? What was this comparison trying to show?

The mustard seed starts small but grows into a big tree. Similarly, Jesus's Church would start small, just a few followers at first, but would grow into a Church seen all over the world.

3. Do these images of the world and heaven help you understand them? How so? Why do you think Jesus used stories like this to explain difficult teachings?

Answers will vary.

Word Search: The Kingdom of Heaven Parables

```
M  W  W  L  P  N  N  X  U  T  P  V  Q  O  G
L  E  Z  H  E  E  M  L  R  X  X  I  B  R  L
R  Z  R  V  E  T  G  E  N  S  S  N  P  S  J
Q  U  A  C  L  A  A  O  K  Z  L  E  S  C  R
Q  E  Q  B  H  S  T  G  X  Y  R  D  X  I  W
H  T  Q  X  U  A  A  Y  Q  R  A  R  W  D  A
Y  B  V  R  E  I  N  Y  L  V  E  E  H  J  M
V  W  E  C  F  L  I  T  Q  E  P  S  W  T  J
W  E  E  D  S  F  B  I  K  X  U  S  U  K  M
S  F  S  C  K  P  M  A  K  I  B  E  C  T  K
D  R  A  T  S  U  M  T  R  L  N  R  A  D  I
Q  S  O  A  C  F  S  S  T  A  E  G  C  Z  U
U  I  C  D  S  Z  K  T  S  U  P  U  D  Q  F
Y  O  P  M  W  R  V  N  A  U  Y  V  B  O  B
L  V  E  W  X  B  U  Y  Z  F  N  Q  J  R  M
```

CHAPTER 39: JESUS TEACHES: THE SERMON ON THE MOUNT AND THE BEATITUDES

Questions for Review

1. What did Jesus teach us from his Sermon on the Mount?

Jesus taught us the eight Beatitudes during his Sermon on the Mount.

2. Why is it called the Sermon on the Mount?

It was preached on the side of a small mountain, or hill.

3. What does it mean to be "poor in spirit"?

It means to not be attached to worldly goods, like money and possessions, but rather be focused on the things of heaven. While the poor in spirit forego riches in this life, they are promised heavenly riches in the next life.

CHAPTER 40: JESUS TEACHES: THE RICH YOUNG MAN

Questions for Review

1. Why did the rich young man turn to Jesus?

He wasn't satisfied with himself. His heart was on fire with holy ambitions, and he wanted to make better use of his talents and his wealth. He thought that Jesus could advise him on what to do.

2. Why did the rich young man go away sad from Jesus?

Jesus told him to sell everything he had and give away all his possession. This made him sad because he didn't want to give away everything he had. He was still too attached to his possessions. Although he felt a great desire to follow Jesus, he didn't have the courage to give them up.

3. What do you think Jesus meant when he said: "How hard it is for those who trust in riches to enter the kingdom of heaven!"

People who focus only on material possessions will become dependent on them for their happiness, and these things often lead away from God. Their money and their possessions actually become a stumbling block to holiness. Even if a rich man can purchase for himself all the finest things of this world, he won't be

able to gain the happiness of heaven. If God gives him the grace, however, he may understand the foolishness of his ways before it's too late. If he becomes generous with what he possesses, God will have mercy on him.

Maze: Finding Our Way to Heaven

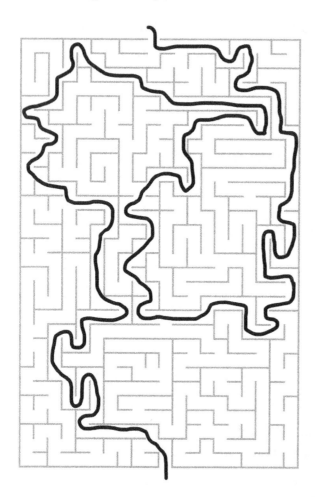

Crossword: The Rich Young Man

CHAPTER 41: MIRACLES: JESUS HEALS

Questions for Review

1. What did Jesus do one evening while staying in Capernaum with his disciples?

He healed many who were afflicted with various diseases, and he cast out many demons.

2. How was the paralyzed man able to get to Jesus?

His friends removed the tiles from the roof of the house Jesus was in and lowered the paralyzed man in front of him.

3. Why were the Pharisees angry that Jesus forgave the sins of the paralyzed man?

They believed Jesus was committing blasphemy by forgiving sins, because only God can forgive sins. They failed to see that Jesus was God in their midst.

CHAPTER 42: MIRACLES: THE LOAVES AND THE FISHES

Questions for Review

1. When the apostles came to Jesus to tell him to send the 5,000 people away so they could go into the villages to buy food for themselves, how did Jesus reply?

He said, "They don't need to go away. Give them something to eat."

2. How many loaves and fishes did the apostles realize they had to give to the crowd of 5,000?

Five loaves and two fishes.

3. What miracle did Jesus perform?

Jesus took the five loaves and the two fishes, and looking up to heaven, he blessed the loaves, broke them, and distributed them to his apostles to give out to the multitude, along with the fish. In this way, he multiplied the loaves and fishes, feeding thousands of people with very little food.

Double Puzzle: The Loaves and the Fishes

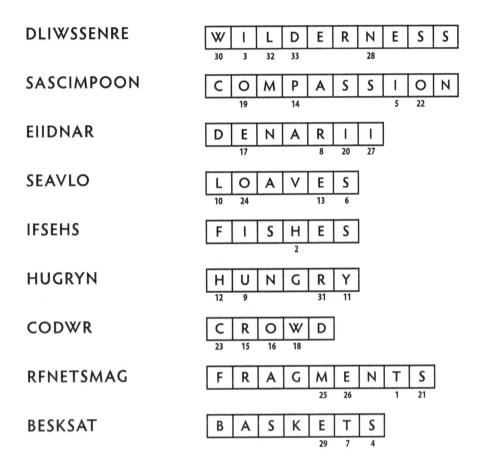

DLIWSSENRE — W I L D E R N E S S
(30, 3, 32, 33, 28)

SASCIMPOON — C O M P A S S I O N
(19, 14, 5, 22)

EIIDNAR — D E N A R I I
(17, 8, 20, 27)

SEAVLO — L O A V E S
(10, 24, 13, 6)

IFSEHS — F I S H E S
(2)

HUGRYN — H U N G R Y
(12, 9, 31, 11)

CODWR — C R O W D
(23, 15, 16, 18)

RFNETSMAG — F R A G M E N T S
(25, 26, 1, 21)

BESKSAT — B A S K E T S
(29, 7, 4)

When the people saw the great miracle that Jesus had performed, what did they say?

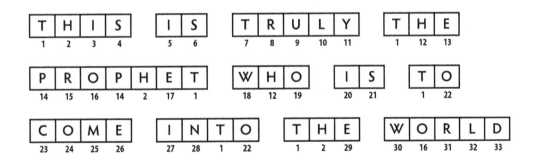

THIS (1 2 3 4) IS (5 6) TRULY (7 8 9 10 11) THE (1 12 13)

PROPHET (14 15 16 14 2 17 1) WHO (18 12 19) IS (20 21) TO (1 22)

COME (23 24 25 26) INTO (27 28 1 22) THE (1 2 29) WORLD (30 16 31 32 33)

CHAPTER 43: MIRACLES: WALKING ON WATER

Questions for Review

1. What did the apostles think was coming toward them on the water?

They thought it was a ghost.

2. What did the figure on the water say to them?

"Take courage! It's Jesus; don't be afraid."

3. Why did our Lord tell Peter he had little faith?

Peter at first was able to walk on the water, but when he saw how strong the winds were blowing, he became afraid and doubted that God would continue to protect him through this miraculous event. He then felt himself sinking, and was only saved by Jesus, who told him he didn't have faith in God enough to continue walking on the water.

Crossword Puzzle: Jesus Walks on Water

¹F		²M			³G	
A	⁴C	O	U	R	A	G E
I		U			L	
T		N			I	
⁵G H O S T					L	
		A		⁶P E T E	R⁷	
		I		E	O	
		N			U	
					G	
					H	

CHAPTER 44: RAISING THE DEAD

Questions for Review

1. What did Jesus do to raise the widow's son back from the dead?

He touched the wooden frame on which the body was being carried, and those who carried it stood still. Jesus said, "Young man, I say to you, get up."

2. What did Jesus say to the people who were standing about weeping for the daughter of Jairus, and what was their reaction to his words?

Jesus said to them, "Don't weep. The girl isn't dead, but only sleeping." The people laughed at him scornfully.

3. How long was Lazarus in the tomb? Describe him as he came out.

Lazarus was in the tomb four days. When he came out, he was still bound hand and foot with bandages, and his face tied up in a cloth.

Word Search: The Widow's Son and Jairus's Daughter

```
V  E  B  M  Z  U  W  K  G  J  M  R  P  R  T
L  Y  S  G  U  I  L  N  P  A  C  E  E  E  U
H  D  Y  I  D  A  I  C  V  I  E  T  F  C  F
F  H  E  O  A  P  N  Z  A  R  W  H  I  T  L
K  J  W  M  E  R  Z  R  U  U  U  G  L  Y  Q
H  T  A  E  D  C  D  B  E  S  Y  U  C  M  L
Y  D  L  Q  J  E  U  A  M  P  H  A  J  R  M
S  S  Y  T  O  E  Q  I  H  T  A  D  C  O  S
F  Q  O  H  E  F  U  X  D  C  D  C  E  U  C
N  C  Y  W  M  A  L  P  I  Z  P  J  O  H  C
X  C  G  Q  B  N  C  T  A  O  E  I  V  S  E
B  E  L  I  E  V  E  H  F  S  S  R  N  Q  P
J  R  Q  H  I  D  T  X  E  W  H  Z  L  B  U
U  K  Y  V  V  D  O  Z  R  R  X  T  D  A  P
R  R  C  P  Z  V  I  U  Y  Q  E  W  F  P  G
```

CHAPTER 45: PETER THE ROCK

Questions for Review

1. Which apostle did Jesus make the rock of his Church? What was his name originally and what did Jesus change it to?

It was Simon and his name was changed to Peter.

2. Why did Jesus call him "the rock"? What did this mean?

Jesus referred to Peter as the rock, meaning Peter would be the foundation on which he would build his Church.

3. What role would he go on to play and what was his authority?

Peter was to become the first pope, telling men what they must do to please God and to be saved. Together with the rest of the apostles, Peter would have the authority from Christ to say what was right and what was wrong, what was true and what was false. God would watch over him and protect him from error, and whatever he commanded would be the law for the Church.

CHAPTER 46: JESUS, THE GOOD SHEPHERD

Questions for Review

1. Why did Jesus tell the story of the Church being like a flock of sheep?

This was a useful comparison because raising sheep was one of the principal occupations of the people in the days of Our Lord.

2. What is a hireling and how is Jesus as the Good Shepherd different?

A hireling is someone who does not own the sheep, but has been hired by someone else to watch them. This meant he did not care for the sheep's wellbeing as much and would leave them at the first sign of danger. Jesus as the Good Shepherd is the opposite, someone who will protect his sheep at all costs, even to the point of laying down his own life.

3. What did Jesus mean when he said, "I have other sheep as well that are not of this sheepfold. I must bring them as well, and they will listen to my voice, and there will be one fold and one shepherd."

The first sheepfold Jesus was referring to were the Jewish people, the Chosen People of God. But here he was teaching that his flock of sheep would include not only the Jewish people but the Gentiles as well (all of humanity). Together, they would make a single flock with one Shepherd, Jesus himself.

Maze: Jesus Finds His Sheep

Double Puzzle: Jesus the Good Shepherd

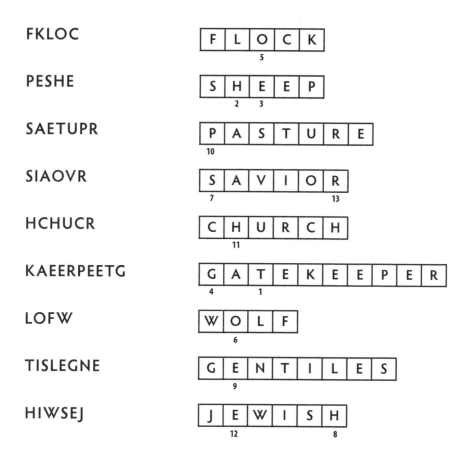

FKLOC — F L O C K
5

PESHE — S H E E P
2 3

SAETUPR — P A S T U R E
10

SIAOVR — S A V I O R
7 13

HCHUCR — C H U R C H
11

KAEERPEETG — G A T E K E E P E R
4 1

LOFW — W O L F
6

TISLEGNE — G E N T I L E S
9

HIWSEJ — J E W I S H
12 8

What title did Jesus give himself?

T H E   G O O D   S H E P H E R D
1 2 3   4 5 6   7 8 9 10 11 12 13

CHAPTER 47: JESUS AS THE BREAD OF LIFE

Questions for Review

1. What lesson can we draw from Jesus multiplying the loaves and the fishes?

That miracle was a sign that Jesus cared about people's basic needs, and wanted his disciples to help others. But it was much more than that. This particular miracle gave Our Lord the opportunity to teach about the Eucharist. Just as he fed them with earthly bread that day, so would he feed them with spiritual or heavenly Bread, his Body, through the Eucharist.

2. What story from the Old Testament does the multiplying of the bread and the Eucharist point to?

It points back to the story of God raining down the manna (like bread) from heaven while Moses and the Israelites wandered in the desert.

3. How did Jesus respond when the people said, "How can this man give us his flesh to eat?"

Jesus said: "Truly, truly, I say to you: Unless you eat the flesh of the Son of Man and drink his blood, you will not have life in you. Whoever eats my flesh and drinks my blood has eternal life, and I will raise him up on the last day."

CHAPTER 48: THE TRANSFIGURATION

Questions for Review

1. Where did Jesus go to pray and who went with him?

He went to Mt. Tabor and took Peter, James, and John with him.

2. What happened while Jesus was at the mountaintop?

He was entirely transfigured; that is, his appearance was transformed. This is why this event is called the Transfiguration.

3. Who else appeared on the mountaintop and what did they do?

Two men appeared and began to talk with Jesus. One was Moses; the other was the prophet Elijah.

Maze: Jesus and His Apostles Heading for the Top of Mt. Tabor

CHAPTER 49: THE TRIUMPHANT ENTRY INTO JERUSALEM

Questions for Review

1. What did Jesus ask two of his disciples to do?

Jesus told them to go into the village. There they would find a donkey tied, and her colt with her. He told them to untie them and bring the animals to him.

2. What feast was being celebrated at this time in Jerusalem? What present day feast do we celebrate to commemorate Jesus coming into Jerusalem (hint: remember they laid down palms before him on the road!)

The Jewish people were celebrating the Feast of the Passover. Today, we celebrate Palm Sunday commemorating this event of Jesus entering Jerusalem.

3. What did the crowd yell out as Jesus was passing by on the donkey?

"Hosanna to the Son of David! Blessed is the One who comes in the name of the Lord! Hosanna in the highest!"

CHAPTER 50: THE LAST SUPPER AND THE GARDEN OF GETHSEMANE

Questions for Review

1. What Jewish feast did Jesus and his apostles celebrate during the Last Supper and what did it commemorate?

It was the Feast of the Passover, which commemorated the Jews deliverance from slavery.

2. When Jesus said, "Do this in remembrance of me," what did he mean? What was he establishing?

By these words, he gave to them and to their successors, the priests of the Catholic Church, the power to change bread and wine into his Body and Blood, and to offer up until the end of time the Holy Sacrifice of the Mass.

3. What did Judas do in the Garden of Gethsemane?

He betrayed Jesus. He came with a band of soldiers so they could arrest Jesus, kissing him on the cheek so they would know which one Jesus was.

Word Search: The Garden of Gethsemane

```
Q  J  B  D  U  R  A  S  E  J  F  X  A  L  G
B  G  H  X  S  E  E  N  R  H  G  N  L  X  N
X  V  A  D  B  L  K  N  M  X  G  I  J  O  I
D  T  C  R  T  M  G  I  A  E  W  P  P  K  P
Q  L  A  S  D  Y  R  B  L  T  X  Q  W  G  E
O  H  O  E  G  E  M  A  T  U  K  Y  F  Y  E
L  P  Q  C  W  Q  N  S  F  J  Y  P  C  F  L
A  J  P  N  Y  S  B  B  V  E  J  T  J  B  S
R  F  A  C  O  O  B  A  C  B  N  X  T  I  P
K  P  R  A  Y  I  N  G  B  E  G  U  I  Y  E
D  O  O  L  B  B  S  Z  X  T  K  A  C  S  S
B  I  T  D  U  M  N  L  I  R  Q  Y  Q  G  A
J  J  T  F  D  O  E  H  U  A  V  S  X  R  D
M  I  N  M  G  Q  B  X  F  Y  F  E  E  U  U
N  D  W  F  W  P  G  Y  P  A  K  N  T  W  J
```

CHAPTER 51: THE PASSION AND CRUCIFIXION OF JESUS

Questions for Review

1. To where was Jesus lead away to be crucified?

To the top of a hill named Golgotha, or Calvary.

2. Who was the Roman governor who sentenced him to be scourged and crucified? Who helped Jesus carry his cross when he was weak? Who else was crucified along with Jesus?

Pontius Pilate. Simon. Two thieves.

3. Who was the only apostle to stay at the foot of the cross, who Jesus gave his mother to?

John.

CHAPTER 52: THE RESURRECTION

Questions for Review

1. Who owned the tomb Jesus was buried in?

Joseph of Arimathea.

2. Why did Pilate send guards to watch over the tomb?

The Pharisees thought the disciples might pretend Jesus had risen from the dead by stealing his body, so they asked Pilate to send guards.

3. What was the apostles' first reaction when the women told them Jesus was not in the tomb?

They did not believe them.

CHAPTER 53: THE ASCENSION

Questions for Review

1. How many days after the Resurrection did the Ascension take place?

Forty days.

2. Who did Jesus promise he would send to the apostles?

He promised to send the Holy Spirit.

3. What did the angels say who stood beside the apostles after Jesus ascended into heaven?

They promised that Jesus would return one day in the same way he had risen into heaven.

Crossword: The Ascension

```
        ¹W
        A
        T      ²S              ³B
    ⁴J  E  R  U  S  A  L  E  M
        R      F              T
    ⁵C         F              H
⁶O  L  I  V  E  S              A
    O         R          ⁷A  N  G  E  L  S
    U                        Y
    D
```

CHAPTER 54: PENTECOST

Questions for Review

1. Where were the apostles gathered when the Holy Spirit descended upon them?

They were in Jerusalem in the Upper Room, the same place they had been for the Last Supper with Jesus.

2. Describe what happened to the apostles in the upper room.

Suddenly there came a sound from heaven like a mighty wind, and it shook the whole house where they were assembled. Tongues of fire appeared to all those in the room and settled on each of them. They were all filled with the Holy Spirit. Then they began to speak in foreign languages that they had never learned, as the Holy Spirit prompted them to speak.

3. What were the twelve apostles doing on the rooftop?

They were preaching in different languages.

CHAPTER 55: PAUL'S ADVENTURES

Questions for Review

1. What was Paul's original name?

Saul.

2. Why was he on his way to Damascus?

He was a ferocious enemy of the Christians and was traveling to hunt them to bring them back to Jerusalem in chains.

3. What happened to Saul on his journey? How did he change after this?

A sudden bright light blinded him and he had a vision of Jesus, who asked why he was persecuting him. He obeyed the Lord's commands after this, had a conversion to Christianity, and became one of the Church's best writers and apologists.

Maze: Paul's Missionary Journey